Thinking in Indian

A John Mohawk Reader

Edited by José Barreiro

FULCRUM
GOLDEN, COLORADO

Library of Congress Cataloging-in-Publication Data
Mohawk, John, 1945-2006.
  Thinking in Indian : a John Mohawk reader / edited by José Barreiro.
    p. cm.
  Includes bibliographical references and index.
  ISBN 978-1-55591-738-8 (pbk.)
  1. Seneca Indians--Social life and customs. 2. Seneca Indians--Economic conditions. 3. Seneca Indians--Politics and government. 4. Seneca Indians--Civil rights. 5. Mohawk, John, 1945-2006--Philosophy. 6. Indian philosophy. 7. Indians of North America--Social life and customs. 8. Indians of North America--Economic conditions. 9. Indians of North America--Politics and government. 10. Indians of North America--Civil rights. I. Barreiro, José. II. Title.
  E99.S3M64 2010
  974.7004'975546--dc22

                        2010019989

Printed in the United States
0 9 8 7 6 5 4 3

Design by Jack Lenzo
Cover photograph © Claus Biegert

Fulcrum Publishing
4690 Table Mountain Dr., Ste. 100
Golden, Colorado 80403
800-992-2908 • 303-277-1623
www.fulcrumbooks.com

Contents

Acknowledgments vii

Foreword: Remembrance of Sotsisowah, August 30, 1945–
December 10, 2006, by Oren Lyons ix

Introduction: John Mohawk's Essential Legacy: "The Sovereignty
Which is Sought Can Be Real" by José Barreiro xiii

Part I: Earth Spirit

The Creator's Way 3

All Children of Mother Earth... 7

Hopi and Haudenosaunee: Sharing Prophetic Traditions 14

Wild and Slow: Nourished by Tradition 20

The Sacred in Nature: Mythology Can Change Our Minds 24

Enduring Seeds 27

Indians and Sugar: Thoughts on Nutrition, Disease 29

Part II: Indigenous Economics

The Darkening Horizons 43

Our Strategy for Survival 53

Present Potential, Future Reality 60

Indian Economic Development: The US Experience
of an Evolving Indian Sovereignty 65

Sovereignty Requires New Institutions, Problem-Solving Skills ... 76

Regaining Control of Our Lives: The Promise
of Appropriate Technology 79

Technology As Enemy: A Short History 91

Small, Indian, and Beautiful: Development
through Appropriate Technology 104

Part III: Nation and Governance

The "Disappearing Indian": Twentieth-Century Reality
Disproves Nineteenth-Century Prediction 111

The Future Is the Family 118

Indian Nations, the United States, and Citizenship 130

Review: The Spirit of Regeneration: Andean Culture
Confronting Western Notions of Development 141

Review: American Indian History: Five Centuries
of Conflict and Coexistence 144

Part IV: Native Rights

The Confusing Spectre of White Backlash 153
The Great Bowhead Controversy:
  "We Are the People of the Whale"..161
The Longest Walk: Vignettes of the Day......................................170
The Iroquois Land Claims 182
Rights of Indigenous Women Are Advancing
  on Several Fronts 188

Part V: Political Philosophy

Traditionalism: The Wave of the Future 195
Traditionalism: An Organizing Tool for Community Survival 203
Marxism: Perspectives from a Native Movement 213
Racism: An American Ideology... 224
Thoughts from an Autochthonous Center:
  Postmodernism and Cultural Studies 232
Thoughts of Peace: The Great Law.. 240
We Are By Nature Social Animals.. 249
Western Peoples, Natural Peoples: Roots of Anxiety 259
Words of Peace—A Six Nations Tradition.................................... 271
Clear Thinking: A Positive Solitary View of Nature......................274

Afterword: A Constellation of Memories
  by Katsi Cook Barreiro 279
Credits.. 281
Index... 283
About the Editor.. 291

Acknowledgments

A special thanks to Dr. Carol Cornelius, Forest Brooks, Charlene Brooks, and Talonwe Mohawk at Oneida, Wisconsin, for your friendship over the many years. Much appreciation is also due Nicholle Dragone, Urszula Piasta, and Gerri Jones for their early assistance in preparing the manuscript.

Foreword

Remembrance of Sotsisowah
August 30, 1945–December 10, 2006

A strategy for survival must include a liberation theology—call it a philosophy or cosmology if you will, but we believe it to be a theology—or humankind will simply continue to seek more efficient ways to exploit that which they have come to respect. If these processes continue unabated and unchanged at the foundation of the colonizers' ideology, our species will never be liberated from the undeniable reality that we live on a planet of limited resources, and sooner or later we will exploit our environment beyond its ability to renew itself.

Sotsisowah—Basic Call to Consciousness: Presented by the Haudenosaunee to the Nongovernmental Organizations of the United Nations at Geneva Switzerland, 1977

These prophetic words encapsulate the old wisdom of the Haudenosaunee and Native peoples at large. We depended on John Mohawk, known as Sotsisowah (Corn Tassel) among his people, to translate that Native wisdom into the languages of the colonizers. He was, in my judgment, the resident intellect of Iroquoia.

Sotsisowah had great analytical skills. These skills, coupled with his writing abilities, steeped in the Haudenosaunee cosmology and ancient understanding of human relationship to the natural world, fueled his passion to sustain the Gayanashagowah, "The Great Law of Peace." His parents, Ernie and Elsie Mohawk, were respected elders of the Newtown Longhouse in Cattaraugus. His father instructed him in the teachings of the longhouse, its history, the great cycle of ceremonies, the songs, dances, speeches, and societies of the longhouse.

Sotsisowah was a farmer because his father was a farmer; he learned by doing, and farming was one of his passions throughout his life. His curiosity was enhanced by his father's teaching about "The Three Sisters," corn, beans, and squash; the old Indian potato and beans; the instructions in the Gai'wiio about sharing the fields of your labor not only with your fellow man, but also with the free animals of the fields and forests.

These instructions energized his curiosity to learn more. His master's project at the University at Buffalo (UB) focused on the old Iroquois agriculture. He wanted to search and find the old Indian potato, smaller and hardier than today's potatoes (the best example turned up at the Farmers' Museum in Cooperstown, New York). His search for the old-style beans was rewarded when he found elderly couples in different Six Nations territories growing beans by their doorways, waiting for someone just like Sotsisowah to come by.

He developed a community garden to study the dynamics of communal energy. The garden was so successful that his group sold produce in several markets. They supplied produce to Six Nations meetings across Iroquoia and took food produce to the Mohawk camp in Ganienkeh. Later, they developed markets for the white corn in New York City and Philadelphia. He was trying to revitalize agriculture in Iroquois country.

Sotsisowah and Barry and Marilyn White recruited me to come to UB in 1971 to create a Native American studies program in the Department of American Studies. Some of our students went to Washington, DC, in 1972 with the Trail of Broken Treaties and continued on to Wounded Knee in 1973. We challenged the local schools in the Buffalo District to upgrade their texts and to get rid of racist texts dating back to 1932.

Sotsisowah never really left the program in spite of his many projects and commitments. He returned as an associate professor in 1993 and continued to advance the program up until his death. During all of this, he continued to write and publish books.

From *Basic Call to Consciousness* to *Exiled in the Land of the Free* to *Utopian Legacies*, he supported the tenets of the Great Law of Peace and traditional governments of the Haudenosaunee. His last book, *Iroquois Creation Story: Myth of the Earth Grasper*, may well be his seminal contribution to the Haudenosaunee future generations. We are losing our story-teaching culture to television and the computer. Our stories are best told to seated groups waiting in anticipation, preferably in low light. He told us our story in a book, but in a style similar to that of our elders and storytellers.

Sotsisowah was a man of the times. He not only thought and wrote, he initiated and participated. His work as editor of *Akwesasne Notes* (1976–1983) created a journey with insight for a public not used to dancing with "live" Indians. He stood solidly with the traditional Iroquois leaders and he paid for it. His life was threatened and his house was burned while at Akwesasne.

He was a leader of his generation. During the tumultuous seventies, he teamed up with Tom Porter and some Mohawk elders and toured universities, colleges, and Indian nations in a bus as part of a group called the White Roots of Peace. They educated the public during very crucial times and gained support for Indian nations in struggles and turmoil.

Sotsisowah was a man of great wit and humor. He enjoyed life, and you could hear his burst of laughter in the most dire circumstances. He appreciated a well-presented meal. From the Pueblos to Moscow, his curiosity was insatiable. He could be observed pulling out his ever-present three-by-five-inch notebook, jotting down some thought of the moment.

He was a very good son, a good father, and a very happy grandfather. Like all of us, he suffered bad luck and setbacks. He lost his wife, Yvonne Dion-Buffalo, to cancer in 2005. He is survived by two sons, Taronwe and Forrest, and two daughters, Charlene Brooks and Lisa Marie Spivak.

Sotsisowah was an international figure, but we, the Haudenosaunee, will miss him most. He was a great example of the Iroquois Man—HO-DIS-KANG-GE' DE'NH, "The men without titles, who carry the bones of our ancestors on their backs." They are the backbones of our nation. He was, to his last, a patriot of our people.

JO AG QUISHO (Oren Lyons)
Wolf Clan Onondaga Nation
On behalf of the Haudenosaunee

Introduction

John Mohawk's Essential Legacy:
"The Sovereignty Which is Sought Can Be Real"

I

In Wakpala, South Dakota, June 1974, at the first International Indian Treaty Council, the chiefs from the Lakota Treaty Council requested that John Mohawk speak. The Wakpala meeting was a seminal moment for the world indigenous movement. With more than two thousand people in attendance from various nations, councils of elders, educators, organizers, and major activists of the American Indian Movement (AIM) decided on an international strategy of Indian rights. They would take the cases of American Indian peoples to the United Nations and the world arena.

At least half a dozen vigorous AIM speakers and other leaders from the host region were ready to talk at the meeting. But when the elders asked John Mohawk (Sotsisowah, Corn Tassel), a Seneca man from the eastern woodlands of the Six Nations Confederacy, to provide his thoughts to the gathering, nobody could object.

John was just twenty-eight years old at Wakpala, but he was already an elder voice in the widespread traditionalist and Native rights movement of which AIM was a militant sector.

Among the Haudenosaunee longhouses, John was a respected lifelong ceremonialist and a superb singer of the ancient song cycles. He had emerged to prominence, naturally and with certainty, as a thinker, philosopher, and strategist who dutifully helped out the longhouse clanmothers and chiefs in land rights and other treaty rights and nation issues. John spoke often at traditionalist gatherings and was a traveler-lecturer-writer on the Iroquois communications group White Roots of Peace, based at the Mohawk Nation with the Native advocacy journal *Akwesasne Notes*.

At Wakpala, John titled his speech, "The Sovereignty Which Is Sought Can Be Real." It was published in *Akwesasne Notes* the following year, 1975.

The Wakpala address—one in a very long run of speeches and writings—came at an important juncture of the American Indian activist movement. Native people were embarking on the difficult task of projecting an international representation of multiple communities and nations. John was at the meeting as a proponent of the international strategy.

By the early seventies, adopting an Indian rights strategy that would go beyond national borders was a serious discussion not only in the international Indian treaty movement. The various Haudenosaunee (Iroquois) traditional governments had called it to the attention of Grand Council meetings at Onondaga Nation, near Syracuse, New York, where Chief Oren Lyons, Tadadaho Leon Shenandoah, and many others,[1] posited the fox guarding the henhouse analogy about domestic Native policies of nation-states not providing adequate guarantee to the survival of Native nations.

Support from many respected chiefs, and John's unique oratory, sealed the strategy and the Haudenosaunee resolutely endorsed the call to encase indigenous rights and perspectives within international law and development policy.

At Wakpala, John also led strong support for a second focus: the right of Indian Country to break free of the overbearing federal bureaucracy. As AIM—with whose leadership he had his contentions over time—was challenging that paternalistic bureaucracy, he offered to support them "in every way I can." Then, as he would do so many times throughout his career, at major forums and at Indian camps, meeting houses and barricades, he proceeded to raise the intellect of the house. Casually, and with great communicative skills, he presented a complex global historical perspective on detribalization and retribalization, laced with a piece of his favorite topic—the origins of the mind-set and social construct called "the white man." This sustained the attention of his Indian audience. But it was all precursor to landing on his main and long-sustained message: the call to rebuild community among Indian peoples as the basis of cultural survival required to manifest political sovereignty.

At Wakpala, and in a rolling argument over his nearly four decades of activism, John Mohawk would signal to Indian audiences that "the Sovereignty which is sought" is no simple inheritance, but that only the people can actually make it real. Sovereignty was not only about taking cases to the international tribunals and commissions again, which he endorsed. Sovereignty, he argued, is about real people, in communities, living and building and rebuilding their own cultures as nations of people. This was the message of his Native elders. Principle one: ensure and recover the land base. Principle two: rebuild the families and strengthen the people from your own cultural base. What are or can be the foundational guiding principles and lessons of our surviving cultures—and how do Native peoples protect and rebuild our nations based on those principles and lessons?

Said John Mohawk to the Indian assembly at Wakpala, "The culture of Native nations was built around the knowledge of how to survive in an environment. To continue that culture meaningfully requires that the people be free to continue to nurture the environment in which we live and grow."

He also said, "Colonization interrupts the pattern of learning to survive and substitutes learning to serve."

> The sovereignty that is sought—an indigenous sovereignty—is real...Peoples throughout the world have developed localized cultures. Cultures are learned means of survival in an environment. Our cultures involve such things as language, education, technology, and social organization, which transmit those learned means of survival from generation to generation.

II

John Mohawk would go on to provide intellectual and cultural leadership after Wakpala to a wide swath of the Native world. John passed away in December 2006, at sixty-one years of age, but over four full decades as longhouse activist, as scholar, as author and professor, as international lecturer, and as conflict-resolution negotiator, John tackled many topics—global history, Western imperialism and colonialism, the origins of racism, the debates of early conquest, Indians at the founding of the American republic, the legacy of treaties, cultural-spiritual dimension in movement, creation epics, the history of technologies, international economics, community development, agriculture, and agricultural ways of life.

Authentically grounded in the natural-ways teachings of his Haudenosaunee elders, as early as 1974, John's main theme on the practical wisdom of those teachings was convergent with a variety of thought currents and movements in the broader world. Sustainable economics, food sovereignty, biodiversity movements, and the threats currently presented by global environmental degradation now consistently point in the directions of John Mohawk's traditional Seneca thinking. In the face of globalization, he would say, "Localization."

It never does to minimize John Mohawk's intellectual curiosity. But as I recently reread John's writings and speeches, I was struck by the consistency of this theme. John always understood clearly that Native societies, accosted and gravitationally moved by the global market trends, would embrace all manner of economic activity, even if under the continuous and common banner of self-determined government and jurisdictional sovereignty. He accepted that land self-sufficiency might not be top priority, particularly in a North America entering the twenty-first century, yet he sustained with certainty to the end of his life that it should have centrality. He argued for the endorsement of the set of land-self-sufficiency skills as the basis of cultural knowledge and as proper long-term survival safety net for Native peoples, particularly on reservation territories.

John would often note that he was fully comfortable only in two places, the longhouse and the university. He brought these two traditions together in a way that lifted his perception beyond the limitations of either perspective. Intensely conversant in the spiritual ceremonial traditions of his people, John the scholar represented the Native traditional school of thought in a way that was as authentic as it was brilliantly modern and universal.

Steeped in global studies, a voracious reader, John's guiding texts were ancient, deeply documented and yet culturally alive foundational messages of Haudenosaunee culture and history: the Creation story of the coming of the Sky World Woman, known also as "The Myth of the Earth Grasper," which he learned at the feet of elders and understood to be the basis of longhouse cosmology and ceremonial life; the story of the coming of the Peacemaker and the Great Law of Peace, constitutional basis of the Confederacy of the Six Nations; and the Good Message of Handsome Lake, the Seneca prophet, which forms the basis of the historical-contemporary longhouses on several New York State and Canadian reservations.

An enrolled member in the Seneca Nation of Indians and born into the Turtle Clan of the Longhouse at Newtown on the Cattaraugus Reservation, John Mohawk was a man deeply rooted by lineage and by intense personal commitment to the perpetuity of Seneca (and by extension Haudenosaunee) culture. In the trajectory of his career, he dedicated his prodigious intellect to the range of historical, cultural, legal, and political issues that face Indian people and humanity. But his own world was Iroquois—grounded in the ancient league of the Haudenosaunee, Iroquois, or Six Nations Confederacy of Mohawk, Oneida, Onondaga, Cayuga, Seneca, and, after 1720, Tuscarora.

The people of the Iroquois nations still hold six sizeable reservations in New York State and half a dozen more in the Canadian provinces of Ontario and Quebec. As a young man, John Mohawk came of age in the culture of the Longhouse at Newtown, on the Cattaraugus Reservation of Western New York. His father, Ernie Mohawk, an electrician, was a respected speaker of the longhouse and his mother was a culture-bearing elder. They kept large gardens and lived in the context of a society of longhouse families that were largely self-sufficient, making skillful primary use of their homesteads to produce foods, medicines, and other useful items and crafts. Haudenosaunee traditional longhouse culture is very much alive throughout Iroquoia, and the Seneca people retained copious ceremonial knowledge that encompasses hundreds of cycles of songs, many speeches, and formal religious and civic ceremonies throughout the year. A wide range of knowledgeable Haudenosaunee elders populated John's formative years. The Seneca language was strong and the depth of cultural knowledge, including "thinking in the Indian logic," as John would say, was palpable. Throughout his life, John would enthusiastically love, respect, examine, and utilize their teachings and perceptions on the tried-and-true workings of an Indian society that was reasonably healthy, diligent, and self-supporting, as well as invested with an ancient narrative of human existence and a precontact, centuries-old, and quite brilliant structure for governance.

o o o

The young John showed himself a bright child. His mother, Elsie, told me on an afternoon in 1983, with John out of earshot: "The old longhouse people loved John. Even as a little boy he could sing long ceremonial songs. And he remembered everything!" Friends from elementary school in Gowanda, New York, just off Cattaraugus Reservation, remember him in second grade, arriving at school with briefcase in hand, a fitting image for those of us who rejoice at the thought of the incipient intellectual, young boy/old spirit, destined to lead his generation to a fuller understanding of the world.

A graduate of Gowanda High School, John went on to Hartwick College for his bachelor's degree in 1968. He started at the University at Buffalo's (UB) graduate program in 1970, but taking long periods, often years, to join activities of the Indian movement, organizing, lecturing, and writing on the activist trail. He would not receive his master's degree and doctorate until later, but he nevertheless conceptualized UB's American studies program's indigenous studies program and went on to direct it. Mohawk received a master's degree in American studies in 1989 and doctorate in 1994, both at UB. Hartwick College awarded him an honorary doctor of humane letters degree in 1992.

From 1976 to 1983, he was the executive editor of the international Native journal *Akwesasne Notes*. Later, he was professor of American studies and director of the Center for the Americas at UB. He authored, edited, and coedited several important books, including: *Basic Call to Consciousness*, *Exiled in the Land of the Free*, *Utopian Legacies: A History of Conquest and Oppression in the Western World*, and *The Iroquois Creation Story*. He published over one hundred articles, most blending the line between scholarship and journalism. Mohawk was also founding editor of *Daybreak*, another national Native magazine, which from 1987 to 1995 led much of the coverage on Native American and indigenous topics. He was a roaming editor for Cornell University's *Native Americas Journal* (also for ten years, 1995–2005), always on the leading edge of Native themes in the thinking media. From 2002 until his death, in 2006, he contributed numerous opinion columns to *Indian Country Today*. John framed a good piece of the discussion by Native leadership on the crisis of environmental assault and degradation. He spoke out early and often on the dangers of the globalization juggernaut and warned against homogenization of indigenous cultures, postulating that Native "political sovereignty is predicated on cultural distinctiveness."

He was founding board member of several important Indian organizations, including Seventh Generation Fund and the Indian

Law Resource Center, and he was principal strategist in the Iroquois land-claims cases and committees, including the Seneca Nation's Salamanca Lease Committee, where he served as a main negotiator of the 1988 Salamanca Settlement Act. He was a most trusted advisor and runner to the Haudenosaunee Confederacy Grand Council, for which he fought many campaigns.

The activist-scholar was an accomplished negotiator in several tense situations of community versus police standoffs. He did not hesitate to enter dangerous situations if serious traditional people were themselves in danger. In 1980, he was pivotal in holding off impending violence at the Mohawk Nation's explosive Racquette Point crisis in northern New York/southern Quebec, and ten years later, in 1990, he was also a Grand Council delegate at the crisis on the Canadian Mohawk community of Oka. During the years I worked in daily activity with him at *Akwesasne Notes* and for another stint on *Daybreak*, his life was in a mode of constant response to the needs and concerns of Native people. John spoke everywhere, thousands of times, it seems, in literally hundreds of reservations and urban Native communities and at as many colleges and universities. For his efforts, his house was once burned down by vigilantes, and he patiently bore many other abuses. Haudenosaunee elder chief Tom Porter said at John's funeral, "He was always there. Whenever the clanmothers called, when they needed something done, if it was land claims or teaching the young people, any time, anywhere, he always came. He always came. For this, the chiefs and clanmothers will always remember him with love, gratitude, and respect." In 1986–87, John was a peace facilitator in the Haudenosaunee initiative to help end the war between Miskito Indians and the Sandinista government of Nicaragua. In that role, he appeared in *National Geographic* magazine in the fall of 1987.

III

There are many stories of John Mohawk and more and more they will be told. I think on a 1976 gathering on the territories of Haudenosaunee, at Loon Lake, in the Adirondacks, two years after Wakpala, where John Mohawk led a think tank of chiefs, clanmothers, and activists from all walks of life and several Iroquois communities. Across the Haudenosaunee longhouses that year, an increased sense of activism was leading groups of people to many projects. Since the fifties, principally in the Northeast, the traditionalist activists and elders had moved about Native country in "Unity Caravans" that traveled and visited other traditionalist circles on reservations, exchanging deep cultural stories, comparing ancient prophesies, and discussing Indian rights. It was during those years, John would tell, when after intense discussions with Hopi spokespeople, Haudenosaunee elders hung a feather from the ceiling of the Onondaga longhouse to signify a treaty between the two Native nations to work to defend the Mother Earth from industrial degradation. The heightened discussion among Six Nations communities during that time led to increased activism. The international newspaper *Akwesasne Notes*, founded in 1969 by the Mohawk Nation's Chiefs Council, had become an important communications vehicle for the traditionalist movement.

At Loon Lake, after the elders had made their call for discussion and chiefs and clanmothers had spoken, John, as was becoming customary, was asked to wrap up the discussion. The encompassing discourse that time oriented the activists and their cultural leaders to strive for sovereignty—not only to assume it, but to study it and make it the goal in every major area of social life. He outlined five areas of sovereignty that a people must control and exercise in order to achieve sovereignty. Beyond the important area of self-governance and conflict resolution, he cited land and economics, health and reproduction, education and socialization of children, and the realm of the mind and spirit or the psychospiritual. In each of these five main areas, he instructed the group of activists, "all our personnel, our teachers in the schools, our nurses in the clinics, our counselors, our businessmen, and economic planners, all need to strive to have a sovereign-minded strategy for the rebuilding of their community and nation." His prescription for a Native tribal sovereignty was thus more than just about government, but intended to involve everyone working in these five major areas of endeavor to think and act sovereign in their assertion of being "a people."

More than John Mohawk, this was Sotsisowah, as he was named in the longhouse, speaking to his people and the "talk at Loon Lake" remains an important contribution, even potential primer, emerging from traditional-culture thinking. It might seem simple to some scholars, but proposing a social organization that would braid movement across the spectrum of crucial societal activity was classic Sotsisowah. It was consistent with how a deeply cultural activist would always carry forward ancient traditional principle into contemporary quests for direction. As the Peacemaker braided clan and nation to unite the Haudenosaunee people, so John braided profession and nation in the rebuilding of community. A number of compelling projects were inspired by John's thinking at that time. The Akwesasne Freedom School, a Mohawk-language-immersion educational institution, several corn-growing gardening projects, Native self-sufficiency centers, women's health and midwifery projects, several other self-sufficiency and educational efforts, even a national foundation. As he had at Wakpala, John went beyond those who simply assert a locked-in, historically justifiable, legalistic description of sovereignty in Indian Country. John did not present sovereignty as fait accompli but rather as a dynamic process in need of constant regeneration and recovery.

Throughout the eighties, John immersed himself in Indian community economic development strategies, issues, and projects. One major discussion was about how "economic life was organized prior to contact and colonization." The geographic and social experience of the reservation, John reasoned, was "an experience to stop Indians from thinking like Indians and to make them think like missionaries and bureaucrats." But it wasn't always so. He would cite the records about Seneca corn production kept by Marquis de Denonville in 1687. The French military expedition recorded finding large silos filled with from one to three million bushels of corn and hundreds of planted acres.

Such a large production of corn, a social safety net and feed for the combined armies of the confederacy, John challenged, represents a serious organizational capacity, raising questions about methods and principles. Of particular interest to John was how as long as three hundred years ago the Seneca people accomplished so much agricultural production and economic coordination without "means of coercion to enforce decisions." He focused the theme in 1989 in his lecture "Economic Motivations—An Iroquoian Perspective," and again in 1992, in his essay "Indian Economic Development: The US Experience of an Evolving Indian Sovereignty."

Characteristically, he would constantly query elders on how work parties and mutual aid societies had operated within

xxii Thinking in Indian

longhouse culture, comparing, discerning, and conflating evidence from ancient, historical, and contemporary times. In community projects that he advised, he would work to reintroduce the customary norms around organizing work parties. He always also emphasized these two main points: "Indians exist as distinct groups and have existed as such from time immemorial." And, "Alone among [ethnic identities of] of English-speaking North America, the Indians were not valued for their labor but for their land." His consistent goal: to move Indian communities from "powerlessness to self-sufficiency."

John's dynamic method is well-illustrated in the work of preparation by Haudenosaunee leaders for the 1977 United Nations (UN) conference on indigenous human rights, in Geneva, Switzerland. The United Nations had requested three substantial position papers from the specific nations attending the first major international indigenous gathering following Wakpala. The Six Nations Grand Council asked John to write their papers. He did so and twice traveled to Onondaga to read his drafts to the chiefs and clanmothers, who would critique it, ask questions, and suggest new ideas. Sometimes the group of chiefs and clanmothers traveled to our camp in the mountains. Again, John would read his latest draft and they would critique. I remember an elder chief who asked: "We know about ourselves. But we want to know, why does the 'white man' think the way he does? Why does he hate the woods [nature] so much?" The question became a central theme of John's research effort.

The method evidenced his depth of comfort—in the longhouse and in the potentials of community-guided scholarship. In the traditional world, as Sotsisowah, he learned to imbibe the Native attachment and connectivity with the living world, a thinking formed in the current of a living community that in his childhood was the actual continuum of culture from the ancient Haudenosaunee, through its impressive historical agency to the long and culturally resistant trajectory of the nineteenth- and twentieth-century reservation era. While in the scholarly world he appreciated the rigor of the search for documented factuality, he recognized Indian logic as the thinking inherent in the cultural and cosmological precepts (truth) of his traditional culture. That work for the 1977 UN conference turned into the seminal book *Basic Call to Consciousness*, perhaps the first and only analysis of the Western world culled and elaborated from the thinking of an ancient indigenous political body. As John joked with the elders, "it is, in a way, the modern world seen through Pleistocene eyes."

The essays here complement that book. Separated—arbitrarily—into five sections, these pieces necessarily layer in overlap and reconfigure each other. We are lucky to have them. They represent work over thirty years, yet they read well today, and a touch of the prophetic is always discernable. These essays were written mostly on the hoof, on long car rides of constant activity, in motel rooms and borrowed spaces, and readers can be assured, completely: you are reading in the logic of John Mohawk's genuine and authentic indigenous thinking. More than a writer, John was an orator. There was a guttural depth to his perspective, his Native intellect, and those fortunate to have heard it, in the ether of the longhouses, in makeshift tipis, urban Indian centers, college campuses, and even in numerous prisons, will all remember the power of his charac-ter, his compelling personality, his wry and consistent humor, his keen and penetrating intellect.

IV

By 1992, the Indian world in the United States was undergoing a second wave of movement around sovereignty. The era of sovereignty as protector of high-stakes Indian gaming was quickly maturing, and it promised financial and economic independence for tribes, albeit at the risk of embracing intense materialistic values. Through the nineties, too, educational gains of the new Native generations propelled a substantial new wave of Native professionals into a wide variety of fields.

The advent of tribal casinos was perhaps the most unexpected fork in the road for the traditionalist scholar-activist. That the hard-fought, spiritually-based movement poised to reaffirm the foundational Native values would so forcefully evolve into high-stakes gaming and huge profit margins for dozens of tribal nations deeply unnerved him. The ensuing economic explosion propelled many tribes to positions of substantial political power and greater economic stability, in their home regions and even nationally, while also exacerbating serious problems of injustice in tribal political and social life.

John adapted an initial sense of despair and betrayal into one of pragmatic wonderment. Yet, his consistent analysis of the world pointed to the likely dangers of economic and environmental depression, even collapse in the national society, and he posited that the duty of Indian leadership must include thinking seriously about the skills required for community self-sufficiency. Over time he would derive some satisfaction in the surge of political economic clout of Indian nations. He would decry, occasionally, the lack of cohesive Indian strategies, even in high-stakes economics. But he came to accept the new leadership's call for his advice. He also noted the growing pride in culture among young Indian people. Although, about that he knew much, so he would sometimes comment: "The longhouses are full at ceremonies. Still, our religion is dying."

John was a stalwart and true to his formation. Even as he advised tribal councils on how to base their sovereignty on cases that undergird the gaming and tax-protected economies, he continued to signal that great economic clout among many tribes still did not change his main message: the teachings of the traditional culture remain completely valid and merit attention. When John said that "though the longhouses are full [meaning at ceremonies and the growing sense of identity], still, our religion is dying," he was indicating that the religion was not the ceremony, but the way of life that the ceremony celebrated. And that way of life was the mutually assistive, nonmaterialist (spiritualist) sharing of labor and goods seen in the agricultural longhouse Indian community. This "way of life," this ability of the young Indians to know how to live from the land and in community, he complained—even as he himself consistently planted the old corn, year in and year out— "is in danger of dying out."

In his 1978 sequel to "The Sovereignty Which Is Sought Can Be Real," called, "The Only Possible Future," he had written,

> We must bring to their minds the possibility of developing real economies which meet the people's needs. We must find ways of instilling in our people a love of our cultures, and of taking pride in our Indian ways. We must look to some new ways of doing ancient things, and by that I mean that we must look to some innovative technologies that perform the duties of ancient technologies where contemporary conditions make ancient technologies

impossible. The buffalo may be gone, for this time, but that does not mean that we cannot develop ways to produce food.

A part of that process is going to require that we encourage our own people to lower their expectations and values concerning the level of materialism that they think is appropriate to their needs. It is not fashionable, in many parts of the country, for people to raise their own food, to make their own clothes, to build their own house. But that is what self-sufficiency is all about, and that has to become part of our politics, a part of our culture once again.[2]

Nearly thirty years later, I heard John speak in public in Washington, DC, at the "Hear Our Stories" media conference in March of 2006, a few months before his death. I am happy to have the memory of that day. Again, to appreciate John's intellectual power one had to experience his oratory. He was a scholar activist; I would repeat: he left much of his scholarship in the ether of the longhouses, in the ether of thousands of meetings across Indian Country, often reporting on substantial—not to be published—projects of research for the Indian leadership. Thus his impact was direct, and it was essential. This is, of course, as Tom Porter asserted at his funeral, the strongest piece of the legacy.

In 2006 in Washington, he talked about memory, about how easily our society forgets. His lesson involved an indigenous folk in isles off India who survived the 2004 tsunami by remembering an oral tradition about moving to high ground if the ocean suddenly receded. Elsewhere, elephants had also scampered for high ground ahead of the appearance of the massive wave.

It reminded John of the many stories learned in his childhood describing how the Seneca people survived the Great Depression of 1929–1933. It is crucial to remember those times, he said, chiding that "human beings must have a gene that they recover from disasters in such a way that they mostly can't remember the disaster." He recalled how the lifestyle of Indian homesteads, more or less adapted to some wage income but mostly self-sufficient from the land, had been a crucial factor for Indians on the reservation. "When the Great Depression happened, Indian Country was insulated against it. Times were tough, but survivable. People knew how to live from the land. Many urban Indians moved back to the reservations during the Great Depression and found that people on the reservation have a culture of helping one another."

John was characteristically prescient in the spring of 2006. The national strategy of "borrowing Chinese money to buy Chinese goods" will soon bring "an adjustment" that will bring "a contraction of the US dollar." Hard times are coming, he warned, asking again: are we ready? Are we at all ready for the hardest times? Which are, he asked, "our best options for survival?"

He did not prescribe a subsistence economy locked into some vision of the past, he reminded folks, but one that adapted new, improved methods and sciences. It does not need to be the only aim of a tribal economy, he emphasized, but let a subsistence capability be "the cushion" that the people regain the means of actual survival, so that "the bare minimum is the worst it ever gets." "Without subsistence," he warned, "you keep going until you hit rock bottom, and rock bottom is not good."

Inspired by ancient wisdom and informed by purposeful scholarship, Sotsisowah's words ring true: "In times of crisis, in times of economic distress, our lands, our skills, our heritage, and our cultures have served to help us survive. It's just a reality."

—José Barreiro
Crows Hill, New York

Notes

1. The Haudenosaunee Grand Council gathered discussion from many prominent clanmothers and council and pine tree chiefs in the seventies, from all of the six nations.
2. John Mohawk, "The Only Possible Future," *Akwesasne Notes*, Late Spring 1978, 5–8).

Part I
Earth Spirit

The Creator's Way

One looks into the eyes of another to find oneself. Each of us finds an identity through the reflections of ourselves that we see in others. When we know what others think of us, we must either agree or disagree with that which they see. They will judge us by the standards by which they judge themselves. If they are not humble, they may consider humility a weakness. Such are the ways by which human beings place values upon themselves and upon others.

It is the Creator's way that all are taught to direct their energies toward the well-being of the unborn generations. This is a part of the natural way that all are encouraged to follow. The unborn generations' faces come toward us from our Mother Earth, still part of her flesh and spirit. They are the community of human beings whose welfare our actions today affects, and it is they who will judge the life that we who are living now leave to them.

And so, when we judge the life that we lead on this earth, we always try to do so through the eyes of the unborn generations. We cannot pass judgment upon the coming generations, unlike people whom we can see, however, and so we may never justify our treatment of them through arrogance or self-righteousness.

The Creator's law is the real natural order. Just as the Father Spirit combines with Mother Earth to form life, and as all living things in the natural order tend to form groups of families, so do extended families form nations. The nations, as seen by traditional peoples, are groups of families whose dedication is to the betterment of life for the future generations. We are taught that we must be real in our ways of thinking and behaving so that the nations may be real in the ways of the natural order. In that way, life on this earth as we know it will continue.

It is our awareness of the spirit of a common dedication to the provision of a good life for our children and our children's children that makes the nations real. Real nations provide for peace within the local community and also within the community of human beings because they exist in the hearts of the people, and peace, the unity of spirit and reason, is the natural condition of society.

Each individual is born into a family. Just as a living deer is the combination of a deer's body and spirit, so is a living family a combination of a group of related people and love. The spirit of family life is love.

A living family is a real family in the same sense that a living nation is a real nation. The young respect the old because the old provide love and wisdom and make family life real, and the old respect the young, for they too provide love and they represent the future.

An individual must view his or her existence in this world in relation to the things upon which he or she places value. Each human being at one time belonged to the unborn generations whose faces come toward us from the earth. A human body is composed of matter that was once part of soil, rocks, ocean, plants, and other animals, and all of those beings have spirit. A human being also has spirit, for a body without spirit is a corpse. A human being must be aware that his or her existence results from a combination of flesh and spirit in order that he or she develops an awareness of spirit. With such awareness, one may then come to understand the elementary truth of existence—that the human being has a spiritual relationship to the entire universe: to the sun, to Mother Earth, to serpents, and to other forms of life. But the knowledge of a spiritual relationship to all these things is merely the flesh of the Creator's way of life.

Awareness of something is not that thing's reality. Because one is aware of the existence of love does not indicate that one has loved. The human being creates an awareness of families and nations, but these things only become real when humans become real, when humans fulfill their individual obligation to attend to the spirit of the nation and the spirit of the family.

Individual human spirits combine to create the spirits of nations and families—but man does not create his own spirit or the spirits of birds or water or stars, for these are the works of the Creator. All things in the universe combine to make life as we know it, and just as one must act in a certain way to make a family real or a nation real, so must one live the Creator's way to realize a real life.

Awareness of spiritual relationships (the flesh of spiritual existence) combines with spirit (undefined but manifested by active individual and collective dedication to the laws of the Great Spirit) to produce human life.

Real people (among Haudenosaunee or Iroquois, *onkwehonwe*) have more than an awareness of the relationship of spirit to matter, for they strive to live the Creator's way and that experience of living leads them to a spiritual life.

We see manifestations of the Creator's way all around us in the wind, the rocks, the mountains, the rain, and our spirits are often lifted by the incredible beauty of these things. The spirit of the human being also produces beauty in the things that he or she creates, in the family, in the nation, or in carved stone or wood.

It is the Creator's way that mountains rise and fall, rivers change their course, islands appear, disappear, and reappear in a new form—but always there is maintained a spiritual consistence throughout the universe. That way is not theory—it is living and all the universe experiences that life.

Experience—not words—defines life in the real world to real people. Experience verifies again and again the laws of the Creation. One learns from water as one learns from hawks or deer. The actual experiences of learning the ways of the Creation come when one learns from a real hawk, and not from the image of a hawk. From a man-made image of a hawk one learns about the creator of the image, and from a real hawk one learns of the plan of the real Creator. One knows that a hawk is a spiritual being enacting a role in the Great Plan of Life, that it is spiritually one with deer and man, and only from the hawk may a human being learn of the nature of that relationship.

That is why it is not possible for a person to find a spiritual life through written or spoken words. To discover one's relationship to wind, one must experience wind, and to know the spirit of the sun, one must experience the sun. To discover a spiritual life, one must experience spirit, and that means one must live a spiritual way, both personally and in the human community.

North American people were once given a spiritual way of life, handed down from generation to generation orally, so that the People changed, the way of life did not. Then as people began to move away from their personal spiritual commitment to the Creator's way of life, concern for the future generations faded, the spiritual strength of the nations faded, and even love within families began to disappear until grandparents no longer lived with their children and brothers no longer cared to help each other.

That is why, in so many of our communities, the ceremonies seem to have become meaningless and have lost their reality. These ceremonies were handed down through the visions of a people who lived the Creator's Way, and the spirit of those ceremonies can only be regained through the visions of a people who again live a spiritual life, one that goes beyond the power of words, a life that is real.

It is the Creator's Way.

All Children of Mother Earth...

All things that are, are of the Creation.

The Creation is the earth and the sky, the grasses and the trees, the birds and the animals. All things of the Creation carry on in their own way, and the way of the beings of the Creation is the way of the Creation itself.

The Earth carries on in the Earth-way in the Creation. When the Sun rises in the eastern sky, he brings light and warmth to the body of the Earth. And when this happens, the Earth breathes, as a living being breathes, giving forth a breath of life to the other living things on the Earth. The Earth is a living being, and from her body come many other living beings. That is her way in the Creation—the way of the Earth Spirit.

It is because the Earth Spirit carries on in this way that Life as we know it exists here. The Earth is Mother to the Life that exists on the Earth. In the Natural Way, the Creation's Way, to all the life on the Earth she is Mother Earth. Mother Earth carries on in the way of the Creation, and therefore there is Life.

The Mother Earth is a Spirit. She is an energy force that shows itself to us in matter, and we call this matter Earth.

That is the way of the Creation—many energy forces in this Creation manifest themselves to the People in matter and are, therefore, real. This is the way of the Spirit, for they are often manifested in matter. Thus, are the spirits often real. In this way, the Mother Earth is real, for she is a real being, and because she is a real being, she is also Mother to real beings. Because she is a spiritual being, she is also Mother to spiritual beings.

Thus are the grasses and the trees that exist upon the Mother Earth both real and spiritual beings. They exist, and they exist in a way that follows the ways of the Creation. They also make life as we know it, in this place. If the grasses ceased to follow the way of Creation, if they ceased to grow and to provide food for the other things of this place, Life as we know it may cease.

The grasses, too, are real beings. They carry on in certain ways, grass ways, and their ways are life supportive. Each blade of grass is real, and each is a manifestation of the Grass Spirit, the energy force that exists upon the earth and that is shown to us through the existence of that species of grass. Thus there is upon the earth real grass and an energy force manifested to the Creation that we call the Grass Spirit. It is an energy force that has great power, for within the grasses there is a power to heal and a power to bring beauty. The grasses hold the Earth together, and they are beings to which the animal life is tied. It is their way of being that they are spiritual participants in the process that is Life in the Creation.

Thus, Life as we know it depends upon the Spirit of the Grasses, that their spirits be kept strong and powerful and that they be able to maintain balance on the Earth.

And as we look about us on the Earth, we see that there are many, many other spirits, and that they too are participants upon the Earth. We can see that there are trees and that they are manifestations of the Tree Spirits that exist on this place. The oak tree is a manifestation of the Oak Tree Spirit. That power alone can come to be an oak tree. And as we look about us, we can see that the Oak Tree is not a spirit unto itself, for the Oak requires the Mother Earth upon which to plant its feet. But the Oak Tree is a powerful Spirit, and as with all things in the Creation, it so operates with the other spirits to create Life on this planet, including its own life. The Oak Tree has a way of being in the Creation—it is a part of the Creation. It too participates in the process that creates and sustains life in this place. And those ways are manifested to the rest of the Creation in real ways, for the individual oak is real. Its body is real and its leaves are real and its way of being in the Creation is real. This is the way of Nature—that its beings are real beings and that the ways of those beings are real ways.

The Spirit of the Oak has a power to participate in the Life-producing processes of the Universe. We can only say that the source of that power is a Great Mystery and that the power is manifest through the Spirits of this Universe. That is why we say that the Sun is a spiritual being, that it is real, and that it manifests the Power of the Universe. We know of that Power because we are able to observe the many ways in which it is revealed to us through the Spirits of the Universe. In this way, the Sun is also a messenger whom we sometimes call Father and sometimes we call Elder Brother.

The Elder Brother Sun is also a messenger of the Great Mystery, and through the Sun's ways, we come to know of a way of the Great Mystery. And this is also true of the Spirit of the Grasses and the Spirit of the Oak Tree. We speak of the source of Power of the

Universe as the Great Mystery. All that is manifested to us by that Power is named by us "the Creation." That which is the source of the Creation we call the Creator; when we say Creator, we mean the Spirit of the Creation. The Spirit of Creation is manifest to all things in that which created Life.

The Human Beings who walk upon the Earth are beings of the Creation. They are spirits also, a part of the processes that support Life. If we look about us at the Natural World, we can see that many people call themselves the Natural or Real People. The People who call themselves by these names know that they are a part of the Creation—they know that they are real in the way that the Oak Tree is real.

In the same way, there is seen to be a Spirit of Human Beings that is recognized by the Real or Natural People. The Spirit of the Natural People is said to be of the Mother Earth, and the Real People know that all the People who walk upon the earth are brothers and sisters, for they share the same Spirit of the species and they are all the children of the Mother Earth.

All the beings upon the Earth follow the Natural or Real ways— the ways of the Creation. And all of those beings are related in that they belong to the family of Creation. They support one another. The Oak Tree gives of its oxygen that the Rabbit may breathe, and the Rabbit gives of its flesh that the Fox may live. And the Fox, in death, returns to the Earth from which the Grasses feed, and the Grass gives of it flesh that the Rabbit may live. All things, in their real ways, support life. It is only when beings leave their real ways that they cease to support Life—that they break away from the Life Cycle. It is the way of the Creation that all things exist in real ways, and in the world of human beings, it is necessary that all things maintain real ways for all life to continue as we know it.

The Natural People have a great reverence for Life, a great respect for all living things, for they are a part of those living things. They know that the flesh of the grass is the flesh of their ancestors, and they see their own lives in the lives of the trees.

This respect for the Natural World is a manifestation of great wisdom, for it is based on the knowledge that from the flesh of the Earth will come their own flesh and that of their future generations. And they know that they must be respectful of the living things on the earth, for they (as the Oak Tree) all represent a power to sustain Life. And if that power is destroyed (as when the Oak Tree is destroyed) the processes of life on this planet must be weakened, and if the spirits of enough things that produce Life are destroyed, all Life as we know it must cease.

And the Natural People know also that they are both observers of the Creation and actors in the Creation.

Throughout the Natural World, the beings are responsible actors. They do not strive to respect the Natural World only in their minds and hearts (although they do this), but, rather, they try to make their lives a celebration of life.

Thus, do the Natural People see beauty in the things and processes that support and produce life. They call their ceremonies of the seasons "celebrations," and they ritualize their version of the Real World by showing greeting and thanksgiving to the things of the world. Truly, the Creation has provided all things real humans should want or need. Does it not provide flowers and songbirds to delight the human spirit? Is there not food and sweet air and beautiful water? Are not the rivers and the trees and the eagles of incomparable beauty?

Are not these things beings of the Creation, supporters of Life? And do they not lift the human spirit? The people of the Natural World are the spiritual proprietors of the Universe, not because they possess the things of Creation, but because they celebrate them. That celebration is an active one. The rituals of Life-Celebration are not the actual celebration, but a reflection of reality. Just as the grasses have a way of being in the world, so do the Natural People. The way of being of the Natural People is the active participation in the daily celebration of the Life-supportive processes. That is why they do not call theirs a religion, but a Way of Life.

The Natural People know that the Human Beings who walk upon the Earth are also spiritual beings and that each individual is a manifestation of the Human Being Spirit. And they attempt to enact with that spirit, as they do with other spirits, in a Life-supportive way. The Natural People know that to respect other human beings means to participate in the Life process with them. Thus, to them, love is not distinct or separate from respect, and respect means participation. To the Natural People, respect means love and participation in the process of Life. And the processes of Life are not limited to human life—rather they extend to all Life, to all the living things on the Earth. It would be contrary to the ways of the Natural People to participate in ways that deny people an access to the celebration of all life or that are destructive to another life species.

The Real People of the Earth are those who seek to strengthen the Human Spirit through participation in all processes of Life and who seek that participation for their children and for generations to come. That is why they will seek to participate in the lives of their children and their elders, as well to experience and participate in the process of the Universe that creates the Birds and the Grasses. They are the people of wisdom and vision, of love and truth, of beauty and happiness, for theirs is the way of the Creation. They are the true sons and daughters of the Earth and the Power that they call the Great Mystery. The Real People, the *Naturales*, the Natural People, are the true manifestation of the Spirit of the Human Species. They are the manifestations of the real spirit of the Human Species, brothers and sisters of all the living things of the Earth because they follow and participate in the real ways of the Creation.

And we, who would be Real People, are those who must now struggle to regain those real ways, not in words or ceremonies, but in reality, for the Real Ways are not ways of words or even of rituals. Thus are we brothers and sisters, Natural People who seek to participate in the ways of the Creation. We are now the People who seek to know the wisdom and power of the Creation through our actions in participation in the Natural World.

It is said among Natural Peoples that the real beings of this place are not permanent on the Earth.

And it is said that, just as the spirits of this place prepared the Earth so that it could sustain Life, and just as the beings of this place are now sustainers of Life, so must those who are living in this place conduct themselves in a way that will support Life of the future generations. As we look about us, we see that things of this place have a balance. When that balance is broken, when a being fails for some reason to carry on in the Natural Way, it is said that things within the Creation begin to change. Of all the beings of this Universe, Humans have the ability to choose or to fail to choose to participate in the Life-Supportive Ways. Thus it is possible for humans to fail to have a reverence for Life, for them to turn their eyes and their hearts away from the Life Supporters, the spiritual beings of this place, and to cease to be a spiritual people.

Everything in the world needs to know that it is appreciated. It is true that plant beings are nourished by soil and air, but it is known too that their health and well-being is encouraged by our words. Thus, do the Natural People speak to the plants, encouraging them to carry on in their plant ways, and for this reason, our grandparents walked among the Corn Sisters and talked to them, encouraging them to grow. It is a way that our spirits encourage the spirits of other beings of this World. Everything in the world is encouraged in this way.

The Natural World People say that this is the first duty of the People, that they show an appreciation and a high regard for one another. We can see that it is the natural way, just as the first thing people do upon meeting is to greet one another with a wish of good health. This is the way of a Natural People, in the greeting of other human beings, and it is their way to extend these greetings to the other beings of this world also.

The Real People come together to express an appreciation for the beings of the Universe, such as the feathered beings and the grass beings, and in this way they are participating in one aspect of the Life-Supportive process. And it is said that there are those who do not participate in this process, who do not have an appreciation of the other spirit beings of the world, who are not Natural People.

The Natural People are those who participate in the natural processes and the natural processes are nurturing ones. It is the way of a Natural People to nurture the Life-Supportive Processes of the World through the process of appreciation and greetings and thanksgiving.

It is true that the individual human beings who walk upon the Earth are not permanent here, but it is also true that in the Life-Supportive Process of the Natural Way, men and women can come together to produce new Life. We say, when this happens, that they are a family, and that is the duty of the Natural People to nurture the young that they may survive. And it is said that it is the duty of the People to provide for their survival, that the People can remain in balance.

It is the duty of each People to care for and take care of one another and to seek to resolve conflicts among the people that the process of Life will not be interrupted. And it is the way of Natural People to help one another to obtain the things people need to survive, and in that way to participate in the Ways of the Creation. And it is their duty also to teach the people of the Natural Ways, that all will be aware of their duties to participate in the Life-Supportive Processes and to encourage all the people to continue in that way. And it is the Natural Way too that an appreciation and a good feeling be shown to the people, that the Life-Supportive Ways can continue.

And that has been the way of Human Beings for most of the time they have existed upon the Earth. The Creation nurtured the People, provided them with food and clothing, with beautiful things and good medicines, and the People took part in the process of the Natural World. They gave a greeting and a thanksgiving to the things that produced their lives, and they gave a greeting to one another for the same reasons.

And the people who lived in this way celebrated Life because they were happy. And the people who live in this way celebrate Life because they are happy.

Hopi and Haudenosaunee:
Sharing Prophetic Traditions

Harry Watt, Longhouse leader from the Allegany Indian Reservation in western New York, told a story about a visit from a carload of Hopi in 1948. The Hopi said they had prophecies of working with some Indian people in the East, but that they had been told all the Indians east of the Mississippi had been killed. Then, during World War II, some of their young men encountered Indians from New York State.

The Hopi produced a piece of paper with a drawing depicting five men holding hands and said these were the people they were looking for. They were directed to Onondaga, capital of the Haudenosaunee Confederacy, because the symbol was one of the images that appear on a wampum belt depicting the unity of the five founding nations of the Six Nations Iroquois Confederacy.

Today, hanging from the ceiling of the Onondaga longhouse is a small feather. It is evidence, to those who know the story, of the visits paid by the Hopi and of the treaty of friendship the Hopi and Haudenosaunee entered into during the 1970s. The Hopi came with a request and introduced one of their people, Thomas Banyacya, as their spokesman to the outside world. They were on a mission, they explained, to warn the world about an impending danger, and they wanted assistance because their prophecy foretold of a house of mica on the East Coast and that the representatives of the people of the world gathered in this place. The Hopi wanted to deliver their message to this house, and the confederacy agreed to help.

Banyacya was a tireless messenger. He traveled all over the world, addressing large groups and small, always with the same message.

He carried with him a fabric banner with a facsimile of a pictograph he said was on an ancient rock not far from Oraybi, Arizona. Oraybi is said to be the oldest continuously inhabited town in the lower forty-eight states. Of great general interest for more than a hundred years, Hopi mythology and prophecy have been the subject of numerous books, articles, and documentaries. For the most part, people have been curious and respectful of the Hopi prophecies, but little serious attention was paid to Banyacya or the Hopi message. The general public tends toward things deemed entertaining or inspirational, and the Hopi ancient wisdom was lengthy, complex, and out of step with the industrial world's religion of progress.

The Oraybi rock pictograph comprised two symbols, which appear on ancient Hopi pottery—a circle representing the sun and a reversed swastika, which is said to represent the winds. Beneath these were drawings of two parallel lines connected at right angles by two shorter lines. The bottom line was straight and had representations of people and corn; the top line curved downward in a zigzag pattern and appeared to go nowhere.

Banyacya used these illustrations to tell his story. This was an ancient prophecy, he said, and the two lines represent the way of life of distinct peoples. On the bottom line is the way of life of those who live in harmony with nature. They are seen as living a permanent existence. On the top line are people who do not live in harmony with nature—such as industrial civilizations.

In ancient times, he said, there existed previous worlds. In each of these, the people were not satisfied with their lives. They wanted more and more material goods, and they came up with all kinds of inventions that allowed them to do marvelous things, like fly.

But in order to do these things, they gave up their relationship with nature and the sacred. In time, the spirits of nature were revolted by this behavior, and they caused a great purification—fire, floods—and swept all away. Survivors went on to build again, and another thing happened. Greed and materialism prevailed, the spirits of nature became angry, and again the world was destroyed. And again there was purification. Three times this happened, three times the world was destroyed, and today, we exist in this, the Fourth World.

The pictograph illustrates peoples on two roads, and the lines connecting them represent two times the Earth would shake, and the second time the two symbols would appear and things would go on for another generation or two. (The two symbols are thought to represent the rising sun of Japan and the Nazi swastika, and the second event, of course, is World War II.) Then the upper road, the path with the zigzag lines, would no longer be sustainable and those people are destined to suffer greatly and their way of life will end. But the people on the bottom line, those who maintain the way of life in harmony with the creation, will go on as before, and they will not feel the destruction.

It will be difficult for the Hopi voice to be heard in 1999 because there are a number of prophets of doom competing for attention. There have been stories similar to this in other cultures; the most famous among them is the story of the floods and Noah's Ark. The Hopi have explained that they have been trying to warn the world since the end of World War II. The sincerity of their message is clear to anyone who has heard their story and is, in these times, reinforced by the fact they did not establish an 800 number or tell people where they can send money to avert disaster. The most cynical among us cannot point to a profit motive but might think this is simply an indigenous superstition or revitalization movement; that the events described either never happened or, in the case of two world wars, were either invented after the fact or were simply coincidences.

What if the Hopi prophecy is none of these things? What if this story is what remains, in the form it had to take, of a philosophy of history? What does this story say if we view it from this perspective?

There have not been very many philosophies of history, even in Western culture. One of the most famous and long-lived appears in the writings of Augustine of Hippo (a.k.a. Saint Augustine), who taught that history was the unfolding of God's plan for humankind on the road to the establishment of the Kingdom of God and the Second Coming and Judgment Day. This was a way of viewing the world as progressing (and progressive) toward a day when all the believers were to become immortal and the world would be perfected. It is, upon reflection, profoundly anthropocentric and without much consciousness about nature.

Niccolò Machiavelli, the author of *The Prince*, thought that politics was at the center of the historical process and that people ambitious for power would endlessly compete with one another for dominance. Immanuel Kant had an interesting view of history because he thought it was both moral and progressive and that it moved toward the idea of humanity, in which humankind progresses toward freedom from the "shackles" of an ultimately mysterious and unknowable nature. But he was unable to reconcile the idea of progress because it came at a cost. The happiness of one generation ultimately comes at the sacrifice of the happiness of previous generations, and this price was immoral.

Francis Fukuyama thought history was the story of conflicts among opposing principles and that the collapse of the Soviet Union, and its system of Communist rule, signaled the end of these conflicts and the triumph of capitalism and liberal democracy. He designated this moment of a perceived absence of opposing principles "the end of history," an idea that some think sounds absurd but also follows the general discourse that is the philosophy of history in the West.

The Hopi prophecy truly comes from a different world than these thinkers. The popular Western versions of the philosophy of history are anthropocentric. The Hopi may find human beings as the critical players, but humankind is far from the only player. The Indians of the Americas represent hundreds of different cultures, stretching from the mountains and forests of South America to the woodlands of North America, and a number of these are agricultural. Some of these peoples developed agriculture in the most difficult environments, including high deserts, mountains, lowlands, rainforests, and so forth. The record of civilization in the Americas is one of triumph of human ingenuity. Some of the irrigation projects abandoned by Indians hundreds of years ago in places like Colombia and Bolivia are today being revitalized because, essentially, no one can improve upon the original designs.

Ultimately, the most important thing to know about these cultures is that they were extremely successful. American Indian farmers developed an extraordinarily diverse list of edible crops, ranging from potatoes and tomatoes to grains and tubers that most people in North America know nothing about. The result of all this effort was unique. The history of Western civilization is littered with accounts of famines and plagues and long periods of time when food supplies, while not at famine levels, were in short supply. When the Spanish arrived in Mexico, they found a culture in which people had enough food to eat.

Despite this, the archaeology of the Americas provides plenty of evidence of civilizations that rose, flourished, and then disappeared, or at least dramatically declined. Such cultures can be found on the Pacific coasts in South America, Mexico, and Central America and in the American Southwest. Some of these cultures declined for reasons unknown. Some may have declined because of internecine violence, and some appear to have declined because of climate change. The Anasazi culture, antecedent to the modern Pueblo, including the Hopi, may have declined because of climate change. According to the Hopi story, it happened more than once.

Western civilization had similar experiences in the ancient world. Ancient civilizations destroyed their forests, which speeded soil erosion, and they suffered from salinized and exhausted soils and sometimes became unable to feed their populations. Many explanations have been put forward to explain the fall of the most powerful of the civilizations of the ancient Mediterranean—Rome. Among these, several are interesting: greed (the owners of the great estates learned to escape taxes, which eroded the ability of Rome to defend herself), declining soils, the disappearance of firewood, and an economic crisis initiated by a Roman version of globalization, which worked to Rome's disadvantage.

Western versions of the philosophy of history usually project that things are moving forward to some kind of utopian future where all the experiments have been tried and the best selected. This is the point Fukuyama has made about the triumph of representative liberal democracy. The Hopi version proposes that civilizations are not permanent and that a primary reason for their decline is the tendency of people to prefer a material prosperity of the present over responsibility to ecological imperatives and the future. The people of the Hopi First, Second, and Third Worlds did not heed warnings about the consequences of their excesses.

The parallel is compelling. Contemporary industrial society has produced quantities of greenhouse gases, and the subsequent global warming is producing weather patterns never seen before in some parts of the world. We experience more intense storms, unprecedented hurricanes, longer droughts, and the prospect of melting ice caps producing rising ocean levels that are already threatening some islands with destruction. Scientists can be offered monetary rewards to report that the evidence of global warming is questionable—evidence of the power of greed mentioned in the Hopi story—and politicians are aware that the steps needed to reverse the trend are going to be unpopular and that the public is not clamoring for such measures.

Could it be that similar kinds of things happened to civilizations of the Southwest long ago? When the first frosts came in June, or when the drought went into its third year, did people go about business as usual? Did a small number of them take steps to prepare? What kinds of steps did they take? What did the elder Hopi mean when they urged people to become more in tune with creation? Most curiously, why did they try to warn a mostly uncaring world about impending disaster?

From everything we know about the history of agriculture in the Southwest, although various cultures declined, the people of those cultures persevered. In some stories they are said to have retreated into the Earth until the disaster passed, but in every case they reemerged. The Indians of this area adapted agriculture to the desert and developed a culture that enabled them to live in what is, by any account, a hostile environment. Modern desert cities are colonial outposts that depend on the outside world for many of the things that support life. Unless there are dramatic changes in lifestyle, modern desert cities will disappear if the wider system of support declines. Civilization is always in danger of extinction, even civilizations that have lasted thousands of years.

This seems to be one of the messages of the Hopi philosophy of history. Modern civilization is no exception. The idea of purification may be archaic, but it has its basis. If global warming continues, the Arctic and Antarctic ice will melt, ocean levels will rise, and the waters will inundate the cities that dot the coasts on every continent except Antarctica. That sounds like purification.

For more than forty years, Thomas Banyacya and other Hopi elders sought to address the United Nations at New York City in the "House of Mica." For about twenty years, they were joined by delegations from the Six Nations Confederacy. In 1992, a decade of indigenous peoples was declared and, on a December afternoon, Banyacya was, at last, invited to address the United Nations. He told a version of the story that is recounted here. As he spoke, one of the worst storms in memory swirled out of the Atlantic and battered New York, causing flooding in the streets and high winds in a demonstration of nature's fury. The storm may have been a coincidence. Global warming may be a coincidence. The Hopi philosophy of history, as presented here, counters the Western notion that changes occur over time in desirable, and therefore, progressive ways, and urges that nature reacts in unpredictable ways and that humans have a moral obligation to pay attention. The patterns of the Hopi message that bring us to this kind of conclusion may also be a coincidence. But, then again, maybe not.

Wild and Slow: Nourished by Tradition

It has been apparent for well over a decade that when indigenous peoples shift from their traditional diet to a modern, highly refined, carbohydrate diet, they become exposed to a range of degenerative diseases. The most pervasive is diabetes mellitus.

This disease is epidemic among all indigenous peoples in North America (and many other parts of the world) and seems especially destructive among desert populations. A population that is introduced to a radical food—a food that either does not appear in nature or is probably not intended for human consumption—can require long periods of exposure before becoming physically adapted to it. No one knows for certain how long this might take, but it is clear from the current health profiles of Native populations that not enough time has passed to render these foods safe for indigenous consumption.

In Mexico, some 3.8 million people suffer from the direct and related effects of diabetes.* This is also true throughout indigenous America, where a range of groups, such as Native Seeds/SEARCH's Desert Foods for Diabetes (www.nativeseeds.org) and Tohono O'odham Community Action (www.tocaonline.org) in Arizona, has been mobilized to promote a new message of nutrition education among Native peoples.

The "cure" for the malady, it turns out, has been with them all along. It lies in their own indigenous foods, which include, for desert people, such traditional favorites as cacti and prickly pear and an impressive list of foods gathered from the desert.

Diabetes is so prevalent in some communities that up to 65 percent of the adult population has been diagnosed with it. Given that a pathway to health is known, as represented by a return to traditional, nutrient-dense foods, one might expect it would be easy to make changes that could reverse the unhealthy trend. But the problem can be daunting. One of the most powerful traditional garden foods, the tepary bean, is known to provide dramatic positive results. People who add such high-fiber beans to their diets have been known to reverse their disease symptoms. But knowing what to do isn't the same as being able to do it. Not too many

*In 2010, this figure is 10 million.—Ed.

people are growing tepary beans. Young people raised on diets offered by fast-food restaurants complain they don't like tepary (or any other) beans.

This situation is at the crux of behavioral science. What causes people to change their food habits? No one knows, but one thing is certain: attitudes and behaviors toward food are formed early in life, and it's not easy to change people's eating patterns once they are formed. The list of health issues related to diabetes is daunting: circulatory ailments, stroke, kidney failure, obesity, and so forth. The preferred lifestyle changes that would help reverse the trends are predictable: traditional foods, increased exercise, and avoidance of harmful foods and habits.

Traditional foods have qualities that are somewhat rare in a contemporary grocery store. All foods that are gathered from the natural world, such as cacti and wild berries, are what have been designated "slow foods." They are wild foods that have not been cultivated. Cultivated foods rely on human activity to protect them from enemies such as weeds and even drought. They reward the agriculturalist with high yields, but they differ nutritionally and otherwise from their wild relatives.

One way in which cultivated foods are different is that they are generally easier to digest and to cook. As a rule, the more a plant is hybridized, and the more its fruit is refined by machinery or chemistry, the more rapidly its carbohydrates are likely to be absorbed in the bloodstream. For people who are in a hurry, foods that speed up the digestive process seem to be a good thing. But for Native and indigenous peoples and others who are sensitive to rapidly absorbed carbohydrates, these foods produce a higher level of blood sugar than do the wild foods, leading to increased risk for diet-related diseases.

Some indigenous peoples have survived on the wild foods growing in their homelands for centuries. Those foods once saved them from hunger. Today, they can help save them from degenerative diseases.

I once heard that culture is what one does without thinking about it. This was mentioned in regard to the foods people eat, as well as the customs they follow. There was a time when Indian people didn't need to think about what they needed to do. It was a given that people would get enough exercise because there wasn't much choice.

There were no cars and, in most cases, few horses, so unless one was going to just lie around, one had to walk. And since food stamps or hunger relief programs were unknown, people who wanted to eat had to do something: hunt, fish, garden—all good exercise.

A healthy diet was fairly easy to come by as well. Indeed, there were few alternatives to healthy foods. If you wanted to eat junk food, you were out of luck.

In the contemporary world, doing things without thinking about them is not working out. This is true for all people, because the same issues are impacting all populations worldwide. We are seeing an unprecedented growth of the same kinds of diet-related diseases, even among affluent suburban populations. The antidote may require some organizing.

The first step is nutrition education, but simply telling people about the problem is not enough. Something like a mini cultural revolution needs to happen in order to change behaviors. People who are motivated to change are going to need to find alternatives to unhealthy diets and lifestyles. They will need to support one another and share ideas and, in this case, recipes.

They need to share experiences about which available foods are slow foods or influence metabolism as slow foods do. Many of these highly nutritious foods are found in the fresh fruits and vegetables section, but people can't live on fruits and vegetables alone. They want and need variety—treats and comfort foods—with all the dangers that modern, cultivated foods represent.

It helps if people organize themselves into support groups to help each other. This is consistent with the societies created by indigenous cultures of people who were committed to helping one another. In this case, the help might come in the form of shared recipes and information about how some foods are beneficial and others are dangerous. Regular meetings can offer information about the traditional culture and provide information about sourcing traditional slow foods. There are ways to share foods, recipes, and success stories.

Such a movement should appeal to, be open to, and focused on children and young adults, as well as the general public. Every day in public schools, a new message could be served along with new meals made from highly nutritious slow foods. The message is that exercise is important, food is important; self-esteem and a long list of other healthy things are important; and sharing a path toward healing is the most important of all. The ancient Indians knew that, and contemporary Indians need to learn it and practice it. This can be a way to cultural as well as physical health.

The Sacred in Nature:
Mythology Can Change Our Minds

Some scientists are among the most awestruck witnesses to the glories of the unfolding universe and among its most eloquent guides. They are aware of the immense distances, the enormous powers of gravity, and the depths of the unknown. Scientists can testify that the miracle of life on earth can and should inspire awe and have expressed their own humility in countless ways. They are also engaged in a discussion about the possible and probable limits of what can be known in pure science: "One of the questions the science of science is considering is whether humanity, in its quest to build consistent logical explanations of the universe, is stuck on the Gödelian treadmill, confronting a universe inevitably more complex than our brains."[1]

The issue is not, however, whether the universe is more complex than our brains. The universe, in a metaphorical sense, is our brain, and vice versa. The human species is not apart from it; it is a part of it. As the universe expands into ever-evolving complexities, we are witnesses to its grandeurs, and therefore, the universe is witness to itself at the same time. Our consciousness is not separate from, but a product of, the universe. We are not superior to nature, but rather its fellow traveler, its coconspirator, its self-conscious manifestation of itself.

Our most powerful contradiction as a species is our ability to imagine that human society is a god, superior to the universe that has created our bodies, our air, our food, our history, our future. Conversely, we also possess the ability to conceive ourselves as harmonious members of a natural world community, and in this the philosopher-scientists can be powerful allies to the expression of Indian thinking. However, even when we know all about the majesties of the universe in the giant trees of the forests, the myriad forms of life under the microscope, the comets and the life cycles of the salamanders, we know less than we think we do.

Václav Havel has observed that modern science appears to "have exhausted its potential," that it no longer fulfills a need to find meaning in the world: "We may know immeasurably more about the universe than our ancestors did, and yet it increasingly seems they knew something more essential about it than we do, something that escapes us."[2]

This view reflects an emergence from a former time, when the world was viewed as a mechanism. For the mechanistic view to hold, however, it would be logical, as modern nihilists have argued, that life is meaningless. Human beings are generally unwilling to accept this conclusion. In a former age there existed an assumption that the universe was rational in all its details, but contemporary science has backed away from this as well. A former age thought that human beings possessed the potential to think and act absolutely rationally, but contemporary psychology suggests that not only is there little evidence for this potential, it may not even be desirable.

Ancient peoples may not have known the speed of light or even the configuration of the solar system, but they were aware that the universe was much greater than what they could see or feel. They accepted the concept that there were things that were unknowable about the universe and the acknowledgment of this limitation rendered invisible beings sacred. Because the universe is such a mysterious entity, it is difficult to talk about it in a meaningful way. How does one describe the human relationship to a mystery? The answer is that cultures throughout the ages have devised mythic narratives that describe in metaphorical terms a memory of how the universe appears to work. These mythic narratives often contain elements that invoke a visual image and are proposed to have power over affairs important to humans. Humans have historically invested these ideas, images, and narratives with both attention and power. Are mythic narratives real? They are as real as the power the people have invested in them. People who come together around cultural themes and who act them out exercise a kind of collective power.

The issue of humanity's relationship to external others—the environment, the animal world, the plant kingdom, other cultures, and nature in general—is emerging as an important issue for the first time in more than three millennia. For most of history, the threats to civilization came from drought or barbarians, pestilence or invaders from afar. Today, modern civilizations may be creating conditions that could destroy the interlocking web of life upon which they are founded. Finding ways to bring cultural thinking toward profound respect for the works of nature is becoming a priority. It is easy to see that one way of accomplishing that objective is by learning about cultures that locate the sacred in the manifestations of nature and that have also developed traditions of celebrating that sacredness.

Notes

1. "In 1931, the Austrian mathematician Kurt Gödel captured this dilemma in one of his famous incompleteness theorems. Once a logical system becomes as complete as arithmetic, he showed, it cannot prove its own consistency. Doing so requires a more complex system. But then to prove the consistency of that system one needs a yet more powerful system, and so on ad infinitum" (George Johnson).
2. "Scaling Lofty Towers of Belief, Science Checks Its Foundation," *The New York Times*, July 10, 1994, Section 4: 1, 6. Václav Havel, "Searching for Something of Value," *The Buffalo News*, July 10, 1994: F8.

Enduring Seeds

While reading Gary Nabhan's new book, *Enduring Seeds*, one has the dreadful feeling it is something of an obituary. Let us hope it is not. Let us hope, rather, that it is a text that will inspire people to a new understanding of the world we inherit and one we will leave behind for future generations. *Enduring Seeds* is one of those books that should set off alarms. One suspects it actually will set off alarms in a small number of people, but that might be enough to start along the road that lies ahead.

Nabhan's book is about wildness and the relationships of cultivators to their ancestors. Cultivators are those plants (and with some stretch of the use of the word, animals) humans cultivate for food and fibers. Every one of these had an ancestor that existed without human intervention in the wild, but human manipulation and selection has invariably induced changes, with the end result being dependency on humans for reproduction.

This has been the case in the Americas, especially with corn, beans, squash, and turkey; each of these has an ancestor that was different in important ways from the varieties we have today. Nabham's book is a series of stories about looking for these ancestors, but behind these stories is a serious concern. The gene pool of commercially produced food crops is growing narrower and narrower, and the traditional diversity of such food crops is disappearing as peasant farmers throughout the Americas continue to disappear. As the native farmers disappear, so too do the environments that have supported the wild ancestors of these crops and the wide diversity coaxed from the parent crops over centuries. There has been plenty of discussion about indigenous knowledge in recent years, and the relationship of human beings to the life forms that occupy the same bioregions over innumerable centuries is the kind of indigenous knowledge that should be treasured and practiced.

Most contemporary people have been socialized to applaud modernity without ever becoming aware of some of its costs. Investigate the roots of the epidemic degenerative diseases that plague the twentieth century and you will find that these are outgrowths of the Industrial Revolution. The foods of the agricultural revolution behave differently in the body than did their wild ancestors. Among some Indian tribes where obesity, circulatory disorders, and adult-onset diabetes is epidemic, those individuals who return to their ancestors' diets experience a reversal of the disease or at least improvement in health. Indigenous wisdom can be lifesaving.

Large-scale market-oriented agriculture has had an enormous impact on cultivated plant diversity, all of it negative. A truly large modern grocery store may have a million items for sale, but fewer truly distinct beans than did a sixteenth-century Iroquois village. It carries fresh fruit in the middle of winter, but the only masa flour is in the processed-food aisles and it is an unrecognizable product to traditional Hopi and Mexican cooks. We have more of what industry can provide and less of what human societies and nature provided in a colloquial setting. What we have has survived because Native farmers carefully preserved it over the millennia, but the Native farmers are disappearing and the legacy of the relationship of human beings to the wild is disappearing with them. Also disappearing are many of the varieties of corn, beans, squash, and other food products from Native gardens. *Enduring Seeds* is a stirring report about lost and almost-lost plants and one that Indians and non-Indians alike would be wise to heed.

The general trend of agriculture since the Industrial Revolution, a trend certain to accelerate during the age of biotechnology, has been to remove plant and animal biology from the uncertainties of nature. This has produced profits in agribusiness, but has weakened the biology of plants and people.

Indians and Sugar: Thoughts on Nutrition, Disease

It was very early that morning when I got up and went outside. The little cabin we were living in couldn't have been much larger than ten feet by fourteen feet, and even the main house, perhaps forty yards away, was a small, three- or four-room, one-story affair. I went down to the gully past the main house and sat for a while observing the stream below and enjoying the sunrise. Dawn on the northern Great Plains. Before and below where I sat, the grasslands stretched forth for miles, a sea of green and blue and brown that rose in the purple distance to some buttes and hills.

Far below, a small herd of cattle gathered beneath a tree, and beyond that I could hear some crows busy in a field just out of sight.

People had begun to stir, and the day's activities were under way. As I approached the house, I passed a small chicken coop with a fenced-in yard not more than ten feet on an edge. Beyond that was an arbor and not far from that, on the side toward the creek, the skeleton of a sweat lodge.

Within moments, one of the children came over to where I was standing and announced that breakfast was ready. I went inside.

The people of this community are very hospitable. Guests are treated with utmost respect and warmth, and even though the families on this Indian territory are visibly poor, and although there is no running water or central heating or paved roads to this remote community, there is a sense of human decency that can often be found to be missing in many communities in the United States.

Inside, we washed at the washbasin in the kitchen and then proceeded to the dining table, which was in the living room. There had not been much conversation this morning. It seemed to be one of those quiet mornings when people took a little time before they began truly talking to one another. Breakfast was on the table very quickly, and soon everyone who was up was sitting around the table.

Breakfast was a real education, and one that I wasn't entirely prepared for. There are many things I like and admire about the people of the northern plains and their various cultures. They are (especially the rural, traditional peoples) often generous to a fault. Many of them exhibit a sincerity about their relationships to other people that is becoming rarer and rarer. Their communities have some of the sense of belonging to a place, a people.

And here, in this particular community, there are strong ties to the past. Only a hundred years ago, the ancestors of these people were still free, still hunters, still close to the beginnings. And then the soldiers came, and the missionaries, and the schools, and the alcohol, and the diseases. It has been a difficult century.

But the people have survived it all, up to this point, amazingly well. They still speak their own language in the rural communities, and they still carry on their culture, especially the ceremonial aspect of it. But many of the people have adopted many of the ways of the West. Alcohol is one of these ways.

The long table was a study in twentieth-century food politics. First, there were drinks made from powders mixed with water and sugar—powders that consisted mainly of artificial flavorings. And there was white bread and store-bought cookies. There were three different breakfast cereals offered, two of them the kind that are generally thought to be aimed at a children's audience. And jam. And donuts, the kind with a powdery coating outside and an artificial fruit syrup filling inside. It wasn't lost on me that people here sometimes put three teaspoons of sugar in their coffee and a like amount on their prepared cereals.

It was especially interesting too because the night before, we had been sitting outside under the arbor, and the people had explained that one member of the family was a serious diabetic (he was an older man) and that others were having problems ranging from arthritis (even among relatively young people) to gallbladder ailments. It wasn't necessary for people to mention that obesity was becoming a problem in that community.

Of the things that are certain in this narrative, the first is that most of the diseases that we now consider to be common to Indian communities were practically unheard of fifty years ago in the same communities. The second is that the single most impressive characteristic of the breakfast that I described above was that it represented an enormous intake of refined white sugar. It is said that the average American consumes some thirty-two teaspoons of sugar every day. But the way I added up the items on this particular morning, one could easily have eaten half that amount in the first meal of the day.

Sugar. Sucrose. It is the subject of one of the hottest debates of our time. The experts clearly disagree, some of them saying that sugar may be the cause of many, if not most, of modern man's diseases, ranging from coronary disease and cancer to tooth decay and poor eyesight. Those who condemn sucrose do so with a passion, while its defenders are equally passionate (and its professional defenders are probably fairly well-compensated to boot).

For the purposes of this discussion, it should be stated from the outset that the term *sugar* is intended to refer exclusively to refined white sugar or sucrose and is not meant to include the other kinds of sugars that are listed under that generic name.

Sugarcane, the plant, probably originated in the vicinity of New Guinea. It is possible that crude methods of refining cane into granular sugar were developed sometime in the first millennia BCE, and it is said that officers of Alexander the Great's army reported finding something that sounds a lot like sugarcane growing along the Indus River in 325 BCE. Because of its climatic origin, sugar was for a long time one of the most expensive luxury condiments in the Western world. It was used at various times as a medicine, a potion, and as a sweetener for foods of the very wealthy. Columbus is credited with importing sugarcane cuttings to the Americas on his second voyage, in 1493.

From these humble beginnings, refined white sugar has emerged as the single most popular ingredient in the American diet today. In fact, about 20 percent by weight of all the food eaten in the United States is white sugar, although most of that is hidden sugar. And refined-sugar consumption has actually increased in recent years and appears to be increasing.

In 1815, Americans were eating an estimated fifteen pounds of sugar per year. Today, Americans eat in the neighborhood of about 120 pounds annually per person,* more than two pounds of sugar per person per week—every man, woman, and child. One of the points about sugar that is not in dispute is that sugar consumption has increased enormously over a very short period of time and that never before in the history of the human race has so much sugar in so concentrated a form been consumed. The people who have been attacking sugar have done so from a number of angles, and some of their arguments are pretty imposing. The sugar defenders, on the other hand, have been saying that there is no scientific

*In 2010, this amount is 156 pounds.—Ed.

proof that connects sugar (sucrose) consumption to any diseases except perhaps tooth decay. Also, perhaps indirectly, because of the increase in calories that sugar introduces, as a concentrated carbohydrate, it can be argued that it causes obesity. Other than those two things, they say, there is no provable connection—sugar is safe, or at least relatively so, is the message.

First, let it be pointed out that the arguments against sugar are not to the effect that sugar per se is any kind of poison. The arguments against sugar are that sugar consumption in the quantities common today produces a drastic increase in sucrose in the human body and that there is no reason to believe that the human body has had time to physiologically adjust and adapt to this fairly drastic chemical change. Second, sugar is said to be a pure carbohydrate, a condiment that has no vitamins or minerals, no protein or fiber, and, in fact, no food value whatsoever except calories. Third, there are those who argue that sugar consumption actually replaces in people's diets foods that do have necessary nutrients, thus adding to health problems by what it does not do as opposed to what it does. There are also those who argue fairly complex scientific theories to the effect that sugar causes reactions in the human body that lead to such ailments as hypoglycemia, adult-onset diabetes, and gallbladder disease.

Native peoples in North America and other areas of the world provide interesting, perhaps ultimately critical information about health problems and the relationship of those problems to, among other things, diet. When Western man first enters any non-Western country, he usually encounters peoples who are rarely afflicted by the degenerative diseases associated with civilization. For example, Native peoples in Africa and the Americas prior to contact (and even long after contact but who remain on their traditional diet or some non-Western diet) have a remarkably low incidence of degenerative diseases.

There is almost no adult-onset diabetes among the rural Native peoples of Africa, for example. Nor do they generally suffer from diseases such as coronary thrombosis, gallbladder ailments, schizophrenia, hypoglycemia, peptic ulcers, cancer, or diverticulosis. Those diseases were also either very rare or unheard of among the Native populations of North America prior to contact, especially among the precivilized peoples. Indeed, those diseases have generally appeared in Native communities only recently. They are accompanied by other conditions that were unheard of or very rare in the precontact days, especially obesity.

Even the pro-sugar lobby will admit that many degenerative diseases, especially adult-onset diabetes and gallbladder disease, are almost wholly absent in non-Western societies. They say that this is because people in the United States and the industrial world live a lot longer than people in other countries, and they argue that longevity is a factor adding to the increase in adult-onset diabetes.

Notwithstanding whatever scientific or chemical expertise lies behind such theories, they simply do not hold up against careful examination. First, if non-Western peoples have a lower or shorter life expectancy, it is usually because of conditions of environment imposed since the colonization of their country by Western peoples. Any place in the world that has high infant mortality and problems with nutrition (and these two conditions generally go hand in hand) also has colonial interests occupying their most productive farmlands, where they grow everything from tea and coffee to bananas and, of course, sugarcane and sugar beets. That land was at one time used to grow food for the people who live there, not for the production of an export cash crop.

Second, if it is true that there is greater longevity in the United States than exists in the average "developing nation," it is also true that the communities that boast some of the longest-lived peoples in the world are peasant communities of Indians in Mexico, peasants in the Soviet Union, and peasants in Northern India who are eating essentially the same diet their forefathers were eating at the time Julius Caesar crossed the Rubicon. These people live in societies that evidence remarkably low incidences of degenerative diseases such as heart trouble, sugar diabetes, and gallbladder disease. They also live in cultures that require vigorous activity and exhibit very little obesity. Those people eat very little refined white sugar.

The next argument is that some of these diseases, especially adult-onset diabetes, are closely associated with obesity (although thin folks sometimes get it too) and hereditary factors. If you eat too much sugar, you may become obese, and thus more likely to contract adult-onset diabetes.

But if sugar contributes to obesity simply because it is a carbohydrate, then we must wonder how this correlates to the experience of Natural World Peoples. First, a good number of pre-civilized societies subsist on very-high-carbohydrate diets. Also, as stated earlier, they do not exhibit much obesity. One likely reason: they do not eat the highly refined carbohydrates, specifically sugar (and white flour). It is the refined nature of this particular form of carbohydrates that appears to substantially contribute to the increased intake, in many instances, of calories.

None of this proves to the scientific community that sucrose (refined white sugar) is a causative factor in adult-onset diabetes. The facts are simply that obese people are far more likely to contract adult-onset diabetes than are thin people. Sucrose, even the sugar advocates admit, contributes to obesity. Obesity contributes to adult-onset diabetes. All of this does seem to suggest to the deductive mind that people who do not consume great amounts of refined carbohydrates will probably not become obese, and if they don't become obese, they will stand much less of a chance of contracting adult-onset diabetes.

There could be, and almost certainly are, other factors in addition to the consumption of sucrose in huge amounts that contribute to the modern epidemic of degenerative diseases. The first of these that comes to mind is the fact that people in industrial societies generally exercise much less than do people in hunting and gathering cultures. And exercise is proving to be as critical as nutrition to the maintenance of good health. Until very recently, industrial societies took pride in the fact that they were required to do very little walking or running, and that attitude has only begun to change because heart specialists have begun to tell people that a sedentary human is a prime target for death from a circulatory or heart ailment. Nutrition and exercise, for people who don't know, are integral parts of a people's culture. Of the two factors, it can probably safely be said that there is hardly anybody out trying to convince people that exercise per se is bad for people. But every day, in advertisements across the newspaper pages and on the television screen, Western people are barraged by messages urging the consumption of a vast array of commercial products. These products, such as soda pop, cakes, cookies, canned fruits, and a multitude of processed foods, contain alarming amounts of sugar. They are urged upon the public as either good tasting or good for you.

There are a good number of Native societies to test the theories against, and it might be worthwhile mentioning a few of the more interesting of them. The Canadian Inuit, for example, have been introduced to the white man's diet only in recent years. Before that, they lived on a hunter's and fisherman's diet of meat, fat, and fish. In fact, according to many modern nutritionists, the traditional Eskimo never did enjoy a balanced diet by US government standards. In fact, the Inuit people have been among the most vigorous peoples on earth, able to survive the rigors of a climate beyond comprehension for most of us. But in recent years, the Canadian government has been trying to get the Inuit people to change their way of life, to come in off the ice into villages, and to end the hunt. One of the results of that policy, a result made possible with increased transportation capabilities in the Far North, has been the introduction into Inuit society to twentieth-century foods, including sucrose. The introduction has been very rapid. Although the program to deculturize the Inuit in terms of food began a mere twenty years ago in some communities, already some of these Inuit communities consume well over a hundred pounds of sugar per person per year. Now there has appeared a very high, indeed alarming, incidence of dental caries, appendicitis, adult-onset diabetes, and gallbladder disease. All these diseases have appeared within a decade of the introduction of Western foods—in communities where these diseases were practically unknown before the alteration in diet. Obesity and premature aging has begun to appear among those communities also.

The pro-sugar lobby will say that it all means nothing, that the Inuit people are getting heavier because of a "better" diet from the South, and that the obesity is the major contributing factor in the onset of degenerative disease. The evidence would suggest, however, that the Inuit may be becoming obese while their diet now contains fewer calories than it did under their traditional hunting culture. The calories are in a new and more dangerous form. Refined, concentrated carbohydrates could contribute to obesity while blubber (whale fat) apparently does not.

Degenerative diseases have reached epidemic proportions in the civilized populations. In fact, heart and circulatory ailments are the major killers of the civilized world, with cancer running second place. It is interesting to note that those diseases are all but unknown in most Natural World cultures.

Obesity is an especially interesting manifestation of the general set of problems in modern health. In the Natural World, animals do not appear to overeat—at least, animals in the wild do not appear to get fat. An abundant food supply does not lead to obese individuals, but to an increased population. This appears to have been true until fairly modern times among the human species also. Using historical evidence as a guide, it could be said that refined carbohydrates could very well be the sole source of obesity in the human species. It may be possible that there are other causes or causative factors, such as sedentary lifestyles, but that is not entirely clear. People have developed relatively sedentary lifestyles and have not experienced obesity. The consumption of refined carbohydrates must be one of the main, and very possibly is the main, cause of obesity in the West.

Refined white sugar has been compared to a drug. Nutritionists state that refined white sugar is addictive (as is refined white flour). The ingestion of huge amounts of sugar causes a certain amount of stress on the human digestive and blood systems. The body then becomes accustomed to the stress. When sugar is removed from the diet, there is a withdrawal period, just like with a drug withdrawal. The individual feels uncomfortable without it, is relieved when he gets it, and there are increasing tolerance levels. In just about every way, sugar acts like a drug.

The Cherokee people have been among the most acculturated of the Native nations in North America. And obesity is a very common problem among contemporary Cherokees. The ancient diet of maize, meat, berries, fish, and other natural foods has been largely replaced by a steady diet of processed foods—white sugar and white flour—and the process has resulted in the Cherokee people being a very unhealthy group statistically.

The Cherokees show among the highest incidences of diabetes of any people in the world. In a sample of five hundred individuals over the age of thirty, 26 percent, based on an arbitrary blood-sugar criteria, showed symptoms of the disease. (In India, on the other hand, where sugar consumption is much less per capita, the diabetes rate for the adult population averages out to about 1 percent.) It bears repeating: today's Cherokee diet is, as are most diets in Indian Country, based on white flour and white sugar.

The Cherokee are not alone in this problem area. Gallstones, along with obesity and diabetes, have shown startling increases, as has been mentioned, among the Canadian Inuit. American Indian communities have the highest incidence of gallbladder disease in the world. The evidence, at least the historical evidence, is that this is not simply the result of people's mass overeating—it is also a function of what people eat. What the Native communities of North America are eating increasingly comes in the form of refined carbohydrates—white sugar and white flour.

A good number of people who read this are going to sit back and say that all this is very interesting, but that they themselves are not guilty on this count. "Why, I don't even use sugar in my coffee" is a common response. But most sugar is not to be found in the sugar bowl on your dinner table. Imagine, the average person consumes more than a quarter pound of sugar every single day. Thirty-two teaspoons every twenty-four hours. And most of it is in the form of hidden sugar.

An average-size chocolate bar has seven teaspoons of sugar in it, a half cup of sherbet also has seven teaspoons, and a piece of cherry pie has about fourteen teaspoons of sugar. A bottle of soda pop has more than five teaspoons. Sugar is everywhere.

In North America, before Native people began eating huge quantities of refined carbohydrates, they did not suffer very much from obesity either. Since the appearance of refined carbohydrates (which in some Indian communities dates back to early last century), all those diseases have been steadily rising. Today they are epidemic in proportion. The old people don't live as long as they once did. The number of crippled and blind older people, victims of diabetes, is truly alarming in many Native communities.

The antidote to these ailments would appear to be either a return to the traditional diet (which is practical in some areas, but impractical in others), or a conscious effort in some Native communities to popularize a low-carbohydrate, high-protein diet to meet community needs.

The ingestion of huge amounts of sucrose appears to age people well before their time. And although it might be argued that heart disease and circulatory ailments are more the result of a lack of exercise than diet, it is also true that overall body metabolism is related to factors of both diet and exercise. So, in addition to looking older than is necessary, there seems to be good evidence to indicate that people who eat too much sugar are likely to be too fat, to have bad teeth, and to be generally more susceptible to the killer diseases of the heart and circulatory system.

The alternative to a sugar-rich diet could involve an entire alteration of lifestyle. In the climates where that is possible, it could mean that people might look to their gardens as a source of foods once again. I wouldn't be a bit surprised if, in time, researchers found that the only practical diets in North America parallel Native diets of peoples in this hemisphere and possibly Native peoples in similar climates in other parts of the world. Traditional diets in North America are amazingly healthful. For the most part, they are high-fiber, reasonably high-protein, and low-to-medium complex-carbohydrate diets. Depending on which Native culture we are talking about, many are almost health food regimens in themselves.

The evidence is that sugar and the refined carbohydrates cannot be proven in a chemistry lab to cause diabetes or any other disease except dental caries and perhaps obesity. But historical evidence is that those and many other diseases start appearing in populations sometime after they begin ingesting great amounts of the refined carbohydrates. Intelligent people will make a serious effort to reduce their sucrose intake based on the information we now have about the relationship between the appearance of degenerative diseases and consumption of refined carbohydrates. Those who do reduce that intake will predictably look and feel a whole lot better because of it.

Part II
Indigenous Economics

The Darkening Horizons

People who are supposed to know say that the Western world will demand more energy than can be produced at some point between 1985 and 2025. Between now and then, and probably for some time after that, there will be a worldwide scramble for the world's remaining fossil-fuel energy resources and also for the technologies for replacement energy production, and that activity will result in exploration and development in the remote corners of the world. Meanwhile, experts in other fields predict a world food-production crisis within ten years, widespread changes in the weather patterns, and possible disasters resulting from industrial pollution. Nearly all indicators point to a future of lowered material affluence, imminent problems in wide areas of production, and a changing way of life for the industrialized nations.

The prediction of shortages of oil and natural gas has probably created the greatest amount of both concern and controversy. The so-called Arab oil boycott of 1974 brought wide consciousness of the consequences of American lifestyles a real shortage of oil or gas would bring. There has been widespread controversy concerning the long-range availability of these resources. President Carter himself has predicted oil shortages by 1985.

Many others disagree. A conference convened by the United States reported that world oil supplies should continue to meet demand until the year 2020 at least. Critics of the large oil companies say that the "energy shortage" is a manufactured shortage based on responses to profit motivations and that there is plenty of oil to go around for many years to come.

There is probably some truth to both positions. There is an estimated thirty-five years of oil that exists in provable reserves. That doesn't mean that in thirty-five years the world will run out of oil, but it does mean there are only that many years of absolutely provable reserves. Undoubtedly, more oil will be discovered and developed. The problem is that it will be harder to reach and not be, in any practical sense, *cheap* oil.

Supplies of both oil and natural gas have declined by 5 percent during 1976. Figures such as this are misleading, however, to the point of being meaningless. The oil industry manipulates fossil-fuel reserve estimates to serve its own purposes. Two things about the fossil-fuel energy resources question appear to be certain. Fossil fuels are a finite resource. There is only so much oil and natural gas in the world, and no more. And the costs of those fuels will rise as sources near exhaustion.

Oil has been amazingly cheap. The availability of large quantities of cheap fossil fuel has been one of the major factors affecting the course of history this century.

Abundant cheap energy has enabled the rise of automated production, which has, in the industrialized West, largely replaced human labor. This has meant that in manufacturing, machines have increasingly replaced people and that money for investment in machinery has placed labor in a decidedly disadvantageous position in the Western economy. It is virtually impossible to overstate the impact of the changes that the period of abundant and cheap oil supplies has brought to the world.

Since World War II there have been a great number of technological innovations resulting from the availability of inexpensive oil. Oil became so cheap that oil products have largely replaced natural products in some areas of the economy. Profitable technologies have been developed that made possible the production of synthetic materials through chemistry.

It is always wise to look carefully at a society's technologies to determine, in a physical sense, exactly the processes at work. Synthetic-fiber production requires the use of large quantities of chlorine, and chlorine is produced by subjecting salt (sodium chloride) solutions to electrolysis. For technical reasons, because it is best adapted to this purpose, the electrode generally used is made of mercury. Mercuric electrodes mixed with enormous amounts of water in the production of chlorine inevitably result in the gradual loss of mercury to wastewater. That process, as much as any, has resulted in an increasingly dangerous mercury pollution of the environment.

Synthetics manufacturing has simply boomed over the past forty years. Synthetic detergents, herbicides, pesticides, and fertilizers are all relatives of the plastics industry. We live in the age of the throwaway container, and many of these are made of plastic. But plastics do not return to the natural cycles of the earth, even though plastic artifacts seem to decay.

Plastic fibers end up in the water systems, where they collect. Chlorine is a necessary agent in the production of plastics.

And so, cheap oil combined with new technologies have created mercury-polluted waters that also contain suspended particles of synthetic fibers.

The oil industry and the modern technologies that grew out of the availability of cheap oil and natural gas have done far more, however, than simply create mercury-polluted waters. Agriculture has become a major consumer of oil products. Oil drives the machinery that plants and harvests crops. Oil provides the fertilizer and herbicides and pesticides that make modern agriculture possible. Oil and gas products transport the food, process the food, package the food, provide much of the packaging material for the food, and oil and gas often cook the food in the kitchens of the civilized world. In short, the potatoes on your table are made of oil and gas, as is an astounding percentage of the food found in supermarkets.

The garbage from those products—the runoff fertilizers and pesticides and herbicides, and the detergents and the 1,001 products are increasing in volume and are slowly but definitely affecting the ability of the surface waters of North America to support the water life. As the amount of these wastes increases, the amount of oxygen available to purify the waters decreases. *It has been estimated that by the year 2000, North America's waters will be generally too oxygen deficient to purify themselves.* That could have grave implications. Biologists theorize that such waters could provide breeding grounds for new (and old) microbes that have been insignificant because they were unable to reproduce in sufficient numbers to be dangerous to man. If this theory of disease generation is correct, we could begin to experience new forms of diseases. There is some evidence that this process may have already begun, that new microbes have been causing disease in man.

Civilizations (cities) breed diseases. In the past, cities of Europe were devastated by epidemics of diseases. These were largely spawned as by-products of concentrations of populations that supported disease-carrying rodents and insects. Waterborne diseases were also the products of these population concentrations that polluted the drinking waters and the food. That European era was the period of gestation for most of the diseases that were carried to the Native populations around the world, populations that had no resistance to these viruses and microbes because in the hundreds of thousands of years of human habitation of the planet, those diseases were not a threat to man. Those diseases caused the extinction of many Native groups and were a major factor in weakening Native cultures during the onslaught of conquest.

Water pollution is not the only such by-product of the age of oil. The air, as well, has suffered significant chemical changes as the result of burning fossil fuels. In the recent past, smokestacks regularly spewed clouds of smoke into the air, covering the area with unsightly soot. But since the ecology-action days, there has been an effort to force the use of air-pollution devices that catch the smoke particles, thus removing the *visible* aspect of air pollution. However, absent the smoke particles, nitrogen oxide and sulfuric oxide gasses now freely combine with water in the atmosphere. This causes the formation of nitrous and sulfuric acids, which return to earth in the form of rain. Thus today we have the production of acid rains, which fall many hundreds of miles from their source, killing many forms of bird and fish life and altering the chemical composition of the soil in ways that notably upset the ecologies of fragile areas. In the long run, the acid rains could prove a greater threat than even groundwater pollution.

Fossil fuel has made possible, even necessary, a number of processes that have had side effects detrimental to the ecology of the planet. The fact that the world has likely only several decades of oil remaining seems to mean that there will be an intense effort to develop replacement sources of energy. It also means that there is going to be an intensive effort to use every last bit of the earth's remaining fossil fuel because industry and private consumers presently have the equipment to use it (and will never have that equipment again). The industrial world will use *all* of the world's fossil energy "in the search for alternatives" in a kind of exchange, as they see it—oil for time for the development of new technologies.

And the world's projected energy needs are truly astounding. It has been estimated that, present trends continuing, South Asia alone will need five times as much energy by 2025 as was used by western Europe in 1970.

For a number of reasons, especially in the United States and Europe, energy development has leaned toward nuclear reactor development and this has caused a great deal of controversy. Opponents of nuclear energy argue that nuclear reactors are extremely dangerous, an argument that appears to carry some weight. For example, they say that should the cooling process break down (and, despite exceedingly stringent precautions, this has nearly happened several times), the reactors could superheat, causing an "incident" known as meltdown.

Nuclear reactors utilize extremely poisonous substances to generate heat that turns water to steam. The steam, under pressure, turns turbines to generate electricity. A meltdown would happen if the reactor went out of control. The reactor core would get so hot that it would melt the reactor. Then, the ball of molten radioactive material would melt through the floor of the reactor plant and would begin sinking into the earth. No one knows how far it would sink, but it has been speculated that it could sink several hundred feet beneath the surface.

Some say radioactive gasses would then be emitted into the atmosphere—others claim the hot ball of radioactive material might react with subsurface waters, causing a steam explosion that would scatter radioactive wastes over a wide area, killing tens of thousands of people and poisoning an area the size of Pennsylvania for thousands of years.

That is the nightmare scenario of the nuclear power opponents. However, even if meltdown precautions become foolproof, there are other problems. Nuclear reactors use and transfer heat to surface waters, killing water life. Radioactive substances are poisonous for thousands of years, and there is as yet no technology appropriate for the disposal of those wastes. Uranium-enrichment plants use enormous amounts of electricity. And the reactors require the mining, milling, and transportation of materials that could be used in the construction of nuclear weapons.

Projected energy needs are so great, it has been estimated that ultimately, in the United States, thousands of nuclear parks with tens of thousands of reactors would be required. There are persuasive arguments, also, that such plants are uneconomical.

The politics of nuclear reactors in the United States tell us something about the age we are living in. Government has made nuclear power a very lucrative business, offering special tax loopholes to utilities. And, since the rates that utilities may charge customers are based on a formula of return on investment (which in New York State, for example, is a whopping 17 percent!), it becomes *more profitable to build the more expensive plant.* Nuclear plants cost up to twice as much as coal-fired plants.

The incentives to build nuclear plants do not seem to take into account the dangers in creating radioactive materials. An article in *Briar Patch* stated:

> When radiation particles hit cells in the body, they can cause leu-kemia, birth defects, and can cause cells to malfunction as can-cer or other radiation sickness. No one can guarantee, during the many years of the releases of radiation that the many pipes, con-tainers, and waste-disposal systems will never rot, crack and leak. Radioactive materials can be carried by rain, water and wind for long distances, and through the 'food-chain' can concentrate in small organisms on up into produce and into animal and human flesh, reaching levels hundreds of times higher than at the time of its release. Many ill effects may take a while to show up, but we, and especially our children, will suffer from these effects later.
>
> One billion cubic feet of radioactive waste (enough to fill a swimming pool larger than two football fields and one mile deep) will be produced in the USA alone by the year 2000 AD. Eldorado Nuclear has allowed its wastes to enter Lake Ontario. 40,000 tons of radioactive waste has been dumped into the Atlantic Ocean and is now entering the food chain. Nuclear wastes of today will accumulate and remain poisonous for 100 times longer than all of recorded human history.

Meanwhile, the questions surrounding the security required during the production and transportation of nuclear materials capable of poisoning huge populations or being used in construc-tion of nuclear weapons point to the evolution in North America and the Northern Hemisphere of truly repressive police states. Samuel Holden Lovejoy, in an address given in February 1977, reported on the kind of thinking that some nuclear proponents have been applying to the problem:

> A fellow by the name of John Barton, University of Stanford Law School, was contracted by the Regulatory Commission to assess the impact of plutonium on civil liberties. I never thought that I would read a federal government document, printed publicly, anyway, that would say such things.

The first part of the study is: Is there a problem with the plutonium recycling to civil liberties? And the answer is a very bold-faced YES. It only takes 10 pounds to make a nuclear bomb. That's one of the problems. Another of the problems is that it's one of the most potent poisons that have ever been discovered. It can be air-borne easily. It definitely causes lung cancer if it's inhaled. It's what is called the hot particle theory of inducing cancer and leukemia and such biodegradation, if you want to call it that.

The second part of the thing says, "What are you going to do about the problem?" Well, what we're going to do about the problem, according to Mr. Barton, is that we're going to have to keep an eye on, surveil, and then they use the broad quote, "All government dissidents," they don't just say, "military radical activists." They don't just say, "anti-nuclear activists." They say: "All government dissidents." Okay, how do you know that? Well, you have informers. You have agents. You have disrupters. You have wire-tappers. You do everything you possibly can do to keep track of these groups that they say they are identifying.

Then it goes into the third section of the report which is: "Let's postulate the nuclear incident." How are we going to respond to it? Well what we are going to do is we're gong to have to extract information out of them. And that's the line I never thought I would ever read in public, or ever come out of any Fed's mouth in public. And that was, we're going to have to torture, and they used the word *torture*, these government dissidents. And then it comes up with a euphemism for torture...Well, the euphemism for torture, which then torture drops out of the report and they just use the euphemism from then on, the euphemism for torture is "third-degree interrogation techniques."

Then Barton raises the legal question: he says, "Is it legal to torture?"...the reassuring line is that he read all the laws that he could find in American case law, and he said that he could not find one case that said it was legal to torture. Now, that's a reassuring thought. Then he says since it's illegal, what are you going to do about it? And he says that is not a problem. The reason that it's not a problem is because even if there is one, the torture's all done. And, if you solve the incident itself, obviously the American people could care less about a judge's decision that it was a no-no. And as a matter of fact, the American people and the vast majority would support torture in the case of a nuclear incident.

And that's the final conclusion of the report. The American people will support torture in the case of a nuclear incident. So when you talk about running out of uranium, you talk about blackmailing yourself into using plutonium, which is black-mailing yourself slowly into a police state. "When you have this waste running around on your roads, highways, and byways, pretty soon you're going to see armored personnel carriers and you're going to see automatic weapons and fatigues and helmets and trucks. It's going to take quite a military operation to pro-tect these waste shipments." Political questions surrounding nuclear development are far from answered.

Nuclear power opponents argue that there are other, safer ways of utilizing energy, which is certainly true. They point to alternative technologies using the heat of the earth's core (geo-thermal energy), solar (sun) collectors, wind generators, and the harnessing of tidal power. Solar energy, at first glance, is the most attractive. But massive solar energy, enough to begin to approach the present levels of energy consumption, would require collectors that cover literally millions of acres of land. Present estimates of that kind of development project investments ranging from twenty trillion to fifty trillion dollars, and the technology is not yet per-fected. The other forms of energy production have their limita-tions also, in terms of massive energy production.

Industrial society has experienced the most incredible period of growth in human history. Each American today uses the equiva-lent of four hundred human working year's energy per year, a sta-tistic never equaled before. Past civilizations extracted their wealth and power from the labor of slaves and the sun's energy, which grew crops. Modern civilizations use fossil fuels to generate energy to produce food and other commodities. That process has created two crises: the wastes could seriously diminish the quality of life, and decreasing fossil fuel supplies will, by definition, change the way of life of societies deriving their power from these sources.

Societies that are powered by fossil fuel are different from solar energy–powered societies of the past. The Roman Empire, for example, conquered other people utilizing a superior military technology and actively exploited those people through forms of taxation and slavery. Modern industrial society doesn't work that way. It penetrates an area seeking the local deposits of oil or uranium or coal or water, which contain much more energy potential than human labor. It does not need to press people into service. All it requires is that people stand quietly aside while the resources are taken. It is only incidental that the ecology, the life-supportive network of the area is destroyed and that the indigenous people are destroyed also. That destruction is merely a by-product of the technology of that extraction.

Discussions of this process generally tend to obscure the essential questions of our time: will industrial society survive? Will the human species survive? What kinds of responses to the available information are most appropriate?

All projections indicate that the world's ability to produce food should be less than the increasing populations' demand for food sometime between the 1980s and 2020 AD. Many factors will influence this ratio. Food production is projected to increase but world population is expected, in some estimates, to increase even more rapidly. Given the availability of all the needed land and fertilizer (and these are not expected to be available) and the best of weather, the laws of physics lead us to think that famine in the world can be delayed, at best, another forty years.

The most important factor in the area of food production in coming decades involves an area that is not thought of as affected by human activity—the weather. It is true that human activity has and probably will increasingly affect weather in unpredictable ways. It is said that the rain forests of the world are being cleared at a rate of fourteen acres per minute,* and rain forests affect the world's weather. Many elders will tell us that weather patterns seem to be changing. Some scientists say that an oil spill under the ice of the Beaufort Sea or industrial pollution of the air could change the weather. A few have argued that sunspot activity will have this effect.

Will the human species survive all this? Barring a nuclear accident or war, the answer to that, happily, is yes. Will civilization survive? Certainly those of us who live another forty years

*Circa 2010, this figure is 150 acres lost every minute.—Ed.

will see a lot of changes. The conclusion is inescapable that there will be a lot of suffering in the world, although North America will probably escape the famines predicted for the next four decades. The essential underlying question is whether technologies can be developed that will maintain some semblance of the industrial way of life as we know it, or in some altered form.

Almost no one who writes about that subject wants to come to the conclusion that those technologies cannot and will not be developed in time. The fact of the matter is, in this summer of 1977, there is no good evidence to indicate that the technologies of energy development will provide a real answer to the crisis. That is an unpleasant conclusion to a world that is seeking some ray of hope in this developing crisis.

Our Strategy for Survival

The invasion of the Western Hemisphere by European powers was preceded by centuries of social development in Europe that had resulted in societies in which the interests of the few had effectively become national policies, and the interests of the many were without a voice in national affairs. In order that we might formulate a strategy for survival in the modern world, it has been necessary that we look at the forces and processes that threaten survival and begin to understand the real motivations behind these forces. With such an analysis in mind, we may then begin to create viable alternatives and strategies that will enable us to survive in a predictable future.

When history has been presented to us by colonizers, the focal elements have always been political histories. Alexander the Great's armies conquered most of the known ancient world, and when ancient history is studied, Alexander is studied. But are political histories really the correct focus? Does it make any difference in the long run whether Alexander the Great, Nebuchadnezzar, Akhnaton, or any other figure in political history ever lived? Other than the effect that Julius Caesar's rise to power had on some individuals in the Roman aristocracy, would history have been any different if some other general had ever dared to cross the Rubicon? Are political histories the correct focus of history in search for what has affected the lives of billions of the Earth's population?

The really crucial developments in world history have largely been ignored by historians. The most profound changes that have taken place have been in the areas of technological change. Social history has largely been the recounting of the fortunes of the interest groups, which were committed for one reason or another to some form of technological and/or cultural movement. When we are seeking the real cultural revolutions of history, do we not find that the rise of agriculture, animal husbandry, or irrigation technology was a thousand times more significant in the history of humankind than were the adventures and political fortunes of the aristocracy and rulers of European countries?

It is important that we, who are seeking ways of survival in the twentieth century, begin by establishing new definitions and new fields of vision as we try to better understand the past. We need to look to history primarily because the past offers us a laboratory in which we can search to find that inherent process of Western civilization that paralyzes whole societies and makes them unable to resist the process of colonization. We need to identify the process that so often leads people who are honestly seeking to resist and destroy colonization to unconsciously re-create the elements of their own oppression. And, lastly, we need to understand that within colonization are the exact elements of social organization that are leading the world today to a crisis that promises a foreseeable future of mass starvation, deprivation, and untold hopelessness.

The current crisis that the world is facing is not difficult for people to understand. In the Western Hemisphere, the United States, with 5 percent of the world's population, uses 25 percent of the world's energy resources. The world's supply of fossil fuels is finite, and it is estimated that within thirty years, at the present rate of consumption, the peoples of the world will begin to run out of some of those sources of energy, especially petroleum and natural gas. As the planet begins to run short of cheap energy, it is predictable that the world market economy will suffer, and the people of the world who are dependent on that economy will suffer likewise. When the reality of the world's population growth is placed beside the reality of the current relationship of energy resources and food production, it becomes obvious that worldwide famine is a real possibility.

The specter of regional famine, or even worldwide famines, cannot be interpreted as the simple product of a world of scarce resources overwhelmed by the needs of expanding human populations. In the United States, for example, a program of energy conservation—insulation of dwellings, offices, and industrial buildings—would cut back energy consumption by more than 25 percent in ten years. Even given growth predictions in terms of populations and economy, the United States would conceivably enjoy the current standard of living.

The fact is that it is highly unlikely the United States will adopt a program of energy conservation that would drastically cut back consumption. The present US political system is controlled by energy interests who are concerned with profit growths, not conservation, and energy lobbyists are not interested in conservation. In fact, there is no sector of the US economy that will move toward energy conservation as a national energy policy, even though such a policy might conceivably conserve wasted energy that could go toward food production. The problems that we are facing today, as a species that inhabits a planet of limited resources, arise not simply out of physical limitations but from political realities. It is a hard fact that the misery of the world is manipulated in the interests of profit. Politics and economics are intricately linked in the West, and social considerations command inferior priorities in the world's capitals. Energy conservation is not likely to become a policy in the Western countries. The acceptable alternative in the eyes of the multinational energy corporations is the plan to create much more energy through the production of nuclear power plants, especially fast breeder reactors. The predictable misery caused by increases in energy prices that push up food prices (and thus drive the poor from the food marketplace) will also provide the grist for the promotional drives of multinationals. Nuclear reactors will be made to sound more necessary.

Technologies have political cousins. The same people who own the oil interests have enough clout in many governments to discourage serious and broad-based efforts at energy conservation. They have the ability to command governments to support energy development schemes that will leave them in control of the world's usable energy sources and also in control of the world's marketplace. The same people constitute a class of interest in the Western world that seeks to control every aspect of the economic life of all peoples. Practically every people in the West will be dependent on their technologies for energy and food production, and all who enter the marketplace that they control will be colonized.

The roots of a future world that promises misery, poverty, starvation, and chaos lie in the processes that control and destroy the locally specific cultures of the peoples of the world. To the extent that peoples and areas of the world are dependent on the giant multinational corporations that control production, distribution, and consumption patterns, and to that extent only, is the future a dark and ominous one. For this reason, the definition of colonialism needs to be expanded in the consciousness of the peoples of the planet Earth. Colonialism is a process by which indigenous cultures are subverted and ultimately destroyed in the interests of the worldwide market economy. The interests of the worldwide market economy, quite contrary to all of the teachings of the colonists, are exactly the interests that promise to create a crisis for humanity in the decades to come.

The dialectical opposite of that process would be the rekindling, on a planetary basis, of locally based culture. Prior to the advent of colonialism, culture was defined as the way of life by which people survived within their own environment, and their own environment was defined as the area in which they lived. Thus the process of survival involved the use of locally developed technologies that met the specific needs of the area. It was mentioned earlier that technologies have political cousins, and locally developed technologies have cousins too. Decentralized technologies that meet the needs of the people those technologies serve will necessarily give life to a different kind of political structure, and it is safe to predict that the political structure that results will be anticolonial in nature.

Colonialism is at the heart of the impending world crisis. The development of liberation technologies, many of which already exist but have been largely ignored by the political movements (even the anticolonial political movements), are a necessary part of the decolonization process. Liberation technologies are those technologies that can be implemented by a specific people in a specific locality and that free those people from dependency upon multinational corporations and the governments that they control. Liberation technologies are those that meet people's needs within the parameters defined by the cultures that they themselves created (or create) and that have no dependency upon the world marketplace. Windmills can be a form of liberation technology, as can waterwheels, solar collectors, biomass plants, woodlots, underground home construction—the list is very long.

Colonialism, as we know it, was the product of centuries of social, economic, and political development in the West. For hundreds of years, what have been euphemistically called "folk cultures" have been under pressure from a variety of sources, including warlords, kings, popes, and large land owners, who found it in their interest to exploit the labor and lands of the poor and the dispossessed. That process is still taking place today, although it has been refined to the point where the exploitation is in the hands of huge multinational corporations that continue to reap profits at the expense of the world's poor.

It is possible to make a strong argument that food shortages are almost entirely the product of colonial interests. Areas of land in the third world, usually the most productive farming areas, today produce exclusively export crops, while the indigenous peoples, and even the descendants of the colonizers, go hungry, laboring in the coffee, banana, and other plantations of the multinationals. Political movements that have sought to correct those wrongs generally have attempted to overthrow the state, because they correctly saw the state as the tool of oppression and the repository of excess wealth for the interests of the exploiters.

Most of the past "liberation movements" have not been successful in correcting the most horrendous wrongs of colonialism, however, because they assumed that the problem lies solely in the fact that private interests controlled the state for their own benefit. The error of most such movements lies in the fact that they sought to liberate the country from living human beings, much as history assumes that Julius Caesar was somehow significant to the history of the West. They failed to understand that it did not matter whether Del Monte grew sugarcane or a liberated government grew sugarcane; the problem was that export crops do not meet the needs of indigenous peoples. Most liberation efforts, therefore, re-create, in some form, the dependency that they sought to replace. They do not attempt to develop even the concept of liberation technologies, and they do not understand the need to become independent of the world market economy, because the world market economy is ultimately controlled by interests that seek power or profit and do not respond to the needs of the world's peoples.

Given the impending world crisis in the areas of food and energy, a comprehensive strategy for survival will include a concept of liberation technologies that free peoples from dependency on economies that are controlled by external interests. Liberation technologies have political cousins, just as colonizing technologies have, and those political cousins need careful consideration. Liberation technologies are accompanied by liberation political structures and liberation theologies. Of these two entities, colonized peoples in the West would be well advised to place considerable energy into the creation of true liberation theologies as a very high priority.

Liberation theologies are belief systems that challenge the assumption, widely held in the West, that the Earth is simply a commodity that can be exploited thoughtlessly by humans for the purpose of material acquisition within an ever-expanding economic framework. A liberation theology will develop in people a consciousness that all life on the Earth is sacred and that the sacredness of life is the key to human freedom and survival. It will be obvious to many non-Western peoples that it is the renewable quality of Earth's ecosystems that makes life possible for human beings on this planet, and that if anything is sacred, if anything determines both quality and future possibility of life for our species on this planet, it is that renewable quality of life.

The renewable quality—the sacredness of every living thing that connects human beings to the place they inhabit—is the single most liberating aspect of our environment. Life is renewable and all the things that support life are renewable, and they are renewed by a force greater than any government's, greater than any living or historical thing. A consciousness of the web that holds all things together, the spiritual element that connects us to reality and the manifestation of that power to renew, which is present in the existence of an eagle or a mountain snowfall, that consciousness was the first thing that was destroyed by the colonizers.

A strategy for survival must include a liberation theology—call it a philosophy or cosmology if you will, but we believe it to be a theology—or humankind will simply continue to view the Earth as a commodity and will continue to seek more efficient ways to exploit that which they have not come to respect. If these processes continue unabated and unchanged at the foundation of the colonizer's ideology, our species will never be liberated from the undeniable reality that we live on a planet of limited resources, and sooner or later we will exploit our environment beyond its ability to renew itself.

Our strategy for survival is to create and implement liberation technologies that are consistent with and complementary to a liberation theology that arises out of our culture and is the product of the Natural World. It happens that we, the Haudenosaunee, have fallen heir to a liberation political structure that may be the oldest continuously operating governmental system in the world. We know that our traditional worldview and our political structure were largely products of the technological and worldview elements of our society.

The Haudenosaunee presented three papers to the nongovernmental organizations of the United Nations at Geneva, Switzerland, in 1977. Those papers were intended to introduce the people of the Western world to our understanding of the history of the West and the prospects for the future. We have taken many steps since the presentation of those papers to begin the process by which we may provide for the future of our people. Many of our communities are struggling against colonialism in all of its forms. We have established food co-ops, survival schools, alternative technology projects, adult education programs, agricultural projects, and crafts programs, and serious efforts at cultural revitalization are under way.

Present Potential, Future Reality

The United States is in the grip of the worst economic times since the end of the Great Depression. Unemployment on some Indian reservations is far above the national average, and on some of the Indian lands in the West it is reportedly greater than 90 percent. There are already reports of hunger in some places and increasing health problems. For many people, the facts of inflation and unemployment (or underemployment) combine to make a difficult life situation increasingly unbearable. Despite these realities, the idea that people should look at making a living by raising their own food, building energy-efficient homes that use wood and/or solar heat, and developing economies in which people's needs are produced in their own communities has not been widely accepted, especially in tribal government circles. Those ideas, however, are looking better and better to more and more people these days.

The only fair way to judge the viability of those ideas is to ask yourself some questions. How much is your weekly grocery bill, your annual heating bill, your annual payment in rent? Would you be better off, economically, in your present situation, or would your conditions be improved if you owned an energy-efficient house, however rustic, and you raised all (or nearly all) your own food, and if you did not have an electric bill? How much do you have left from your paycheck after you have paid for your car (which you bought so you could go to work), gas for your car, your insurance, and so forth and so on. The amount you have left after you have paid all your expenses—that's how much income you really have. The next question is—what happens during times like these if you lose your job? How long can you afford to eat, to buy gas for your car, to buy all the things that in your new lifestyle are necessities, and that were, to your grandparents, luxuries?

On many Indian reservations, land exists that could be used to grow food for the people, materials exist that could be used for housing, and there are idle people, many with skills, whose families will experience cold and hunger this coming winter. Over the past twenty years, many Native communities have been lured into a dependency situation, and the current economic conditions have left them stranded on islands of economic despair. Federal dollars poured onto Indian lands during the era of the Great Society, the

War on Poverty, and the War on Hunger. Native people, following US government guidelines, created really huge bureaucracies that were intended to provide a wide range of services ranging from keeping the grass cut in the graveyards to housing programs that emphasized the use of electric heat. The whole idea was an effort to acculturate the Native people into roles in the market economy. It is true that many individuals approached this work as a way to relieve the chronic poverty and health problems in the Native communities and that those individuals possessed good motives. But few Native people understood the plans of the people in power and the nature of the dependency that was being created. Now the Great Society days appear to be over, the days of the giant Comprehensive Employment and Training Act programs and the welfare state, which supported a bloated Indian bureaucracy, all but ended.

During that period, attention of Indian people was effectively removed from any focus on the reality of their lives. Indian Country is a resource colony of the US economy. It is in many ways a third world economy in which natural resources are exploited and the benefits of those natural resources exported to distant areas of the country. In some places this reality provides stark contrasts, especially when Indian tribal members are seen paying eighty dollars a ton for coal while their tribe is selling the same coal for seventeen cents a ton.

Economic development does not have to take that course. Native people really can take the power to control their own lives, but to do so they must reassess their values. It is possible for Native people to raise their own food and build their own homes. It is probably possible for people to do a lot more than develop subsistence economies in the classic sense of the term.

The first thing that people need to do is to stop looking at dollar revenues as real income. Real income is the amount of goods and services that a people benefit from. It is not directly tied to the dollar income. Dollar revenue is a relative value. Consider for a moment the following very hypothetical equation. Suppose that in 1970 your tribe sold coal on a contract for eighteen dollars a ton (remember this is hypothetical!). Let us say that during that year a certain tractor sold for eighteen thousand dollars. It took one thousand tons of coal to buy the tractor. But in 1982, while the tribe continues to get eighteen dollars a ton, the tractor now costs forty thousand dollars or more than twenty-two thousand tons of coal. In 1992, that tractor can easily cost sixty thousand dollars, while the tribe is still getting eighteen dollars a ton. The point is that dollars are not a good indicator of real income. Tons of coal and numbers of tractors are real income.

Most of us have been getting poorer and poorer over the past two decades, and the future promises to get a lot worse. The number of minutes of work that once purchased a pound of beans now buys few beans, and the same is true for most consumer items.

The future doesn't need to be absolutely bleak. There are now many fairly new technologies that can enable people to raise the food they need without the use of expensive machinery. There exist technologies that enable people to have a warm house without enormous oil or natural gas or electricity bills. It is possible for communities to begin to take into their own hands the tools and the skills that will provide not only survival but, to a considerable degree, comfort.

Imagine for a moment an Indian community that operated on a basis of enlightened self-interest. It would not be a community that operated on socialist models, in which all farmland is "nationalized" or communalized, but rather one in which the "small is beautiful" ideology resulted in small holdings adequate to people's needs. There would be a strong effort to limit the size and power of the local bureaucracies and an emphasis on the growth and strength of cooperatives.

This would be a community that made every effort to be productive of its own needs through the effective use of all of the usable small-scale, people-oriented technologies available to them. It would have production units that grow vegetables using organic methods and French bio-intensive growing techniques, solar greenhouses, permaculture, and greater recycling techniques. Every effort would be made to produce energy locally, from windmills, silicon solar panels, electrically produced hydrogen, biogas, and so forth. Every effort would be made to conserve energy, including heavily insulated houses, sustained-yield management of woodlot resources, hot water boilers fired by wood scraps and garbage.

Such a community would develop its own community baking facilities for the production of bread. There would be solar drying units for the preservation of food, as well as community canneries. There would be education programs in such areas as nutrition and health, birthing and birth control, chemical abuse, and many, many others. There would be an effort to stamp out the ignorance that has actually been promoted among the American public in all of these areas. There would be schools and communications organizations and midwives and emergency medical service organizations, and all of these would be operated by volunteers and/ or self-generated revenues, and none of it would be dependent on federal dollars for its survival. There would be an emphasis on the development of a local economy that is really local.

Does all this sound like a dream? It is. But it's not an impossible dream. All the technologies are available. The current condition of economic despair is not a situation that is created by some kind of divine inspired necessity. It is a situation created entirely from social priorities, the same social priorities that create "national energy sacrifice areas," and the answer to those conditions, the only viable answer, is for people to create their own social and economic priorities. Individuals and groups of people need to devise plans to raise food, not primarily for the market, but for people.

The economies of this kind of development are subjects people really ought to think about in these times. Consider maize (or masa) for example. In the Northeast, even using conventional growing techniques, one can expect twenty-four bushels of maize from one acre of land. It is true that you can raise three or four times that amount of yellow field corn (an animal feed), but the maize will provide much more food for people than the yellow corn can. Our corn can provide bread, tortillas, and a wide variety of foods not familiar to the average American. Used regularly, it can cut up your food bills to a fraction of their present cost while improving the quality of your diet. As an additional bonus, it tastes good. Rabbits, raised at home, provide a source of almost free meat, as do hogs, goats, and geese. Soybeans can be used to make everything from tofu and a kind of lasagna to ice cream. A single healthy milk cow produces enough cheese, milk, butter, whey, and other product to supply several families.

Instead of looking exclusively for ways to sell natural resources and labor in exchange for money, the enlightened self-interested community will look for ways to produce these and thousands of other goods and to save money as a way of earning it. (You remember the saying "a penny saved is a penny earned.")

At Akwesasne this kind of thinking is beginning to take hold. The community is not generally developed in self-sufficiency, as it has been until relatively recent times, but projects, such as the Akwesasne Freedom School and the First Environment program, as well as a community-generated emergency medical initiative, are under way and hold great promise. At every season, something new is added; a bit more of the foundation is laid. It will be some time before anybody here achieves food self-sufficiency, but as people become more familiar with the paths that lean in that direction, the goal becomes increasingly possible. The same idea is taking form in other Indian places. At Pine Ridge, South Dakota, Oglala families are organizing again under agricultural associations to bring back family gardens. What we are seeing is clearly not a vision of the past, but a blueprint for the future. If you find yourselves in the hall of Washington looking for dollars to support services that lead people to a dependency based on an unrealistic and unreachable lifestyle, think of us once in a while.

Indian Economic Development: The US Experience of an Evolving Indian Sovereignty

The destruction of American Indian economies was one of the most significant impacts visited upon Indian tribes during the invasion of America by western Europeans...The creation of the reservation system by itself would have been devastating enough...but [t]he practice adopted by the young nation in Indian affairs established federal domination over every aspect of Indian life.

—Donald R. Wharton, statement to Senate Select Committee, October 25, 1989

Around 1968, American Indians across the United States began protesting what they termed unfair domination by the US government through its administrative bureaucracies—the Bureau of Indian Affairs (BIA), the Bureau of Land Management (BLM), and a host of smaller, less well-known agencies that had regulated Indian land, water, and lives for well over a century.[1] Federal (and in some cases state) domination over Indian communities was so complete that Indians had practically no power of ownership over their assets and no authority or ability to mobilize capital and labor—the primary ingredients that make development possible.

The contemporary history of Indian development begins, therefore, with the Indian movement for political and economic rights that included the occupation of Alcatraz Island, the struggle for Indian fishing rights on the Columbia River, the Pit River Indians' struggle for land rights, the Trail of Broken Treaties, the occupation of Wounded Knee in 1973, and a number of other events. The result of these incidents was a widespread consensus in Indian Country that power over policy decisions involving Indian resources and development directions must be wrested away from the non-Indian bureaucracies and relocated among the Indian peoples and communities.[2]

United States court decisions involving Indian rights to make decisions over their own lives necessarily involves a discussion around the nature and extent of the sovereignty of Indian nations. In the United States, as in a number of other countries, the Indians began their argument for recognition of rights to economic assets from practically point zero. In an early case involving logs cut by Indians on an Indian reservation and sold to a non-Indian, a US court ruled that the logs belonged not to the Indians but to the US government, that the right of occupancy did not extend to an ownership of assets (*US v. Cook*, 86 US [19 Wall.] 591). The early Supreme Court decisions that outlined the US federal position on Indian sovereignty were written by Chief Justice John Marshall. In *Cherokee Nation v. Georgia* (30 US [5 Pet.] 1, 1831) and again in *Worcester v. Georgia* (31 U.S. [6 Pet.] 515), Marshall defined Indian sovereignty in the context of the powers of the federal government in relation to the evolving rights of state governments around issues involving jurisdiction but ultimately speaking to the real concern of all parties at the time: land.

Eventually the federal courts found that the US Congress possessed *plenary* (virtually absolute) power in Indian affairs[3] and that the US government *owned* the Indian reservations and at one point that it even had the power to eliminate Indian tribes and nations (the policy at the time was called termination).[4] In the course of this period (roughly 1789 to 1968), a huge federal bureaucracy—the BIA—was designated to oversee Indian affairs. The power the BIA assumed over Indian lives cannot be overestimated.

> The Bureau, unique among federal agencies, is the federal, state, and local government of the Indians, and supplants or dominates the private sector as well. It is realtor, banker, teacher, social worker; it runs the employment service, vocational and job training program, contract office, chamber of commerce, highway authority, housing agency, police department, conservation service, water works, power company, telephone company, planning office; it is land developer, patron of the arts, ambassador from and to the outside world, and guardian, protector and spokesman.[5]

There could be no Indian economic development during this period because, by definition, Indians had no power to make decisions about the political organization of their communities or about the priorities involving allocation of resources. All decision-making power resided with the US federal agencies, which, as surrogates for the Indians, had no interest in either Indian political rights or economic growth. American Indians in the United States possessed no recognized or recognizable ownership of their reservations (which the courts claimed belonged to the United States), and in most cases they had no access to any resources, local or external, human or material, from which to build economic growth. In 1969, Edgar Cahn and David Hearne reported: "in sum, the Indian cannot use what is his—money, land, or treaty rights—without first securing approval. Individual Indians constantly report they cannot even find out what land is theirs, or what money is in their own private accounts."[6]

The result of this long period of enforced social stagnation is that Indian communities are among the poorest in the United States, suffering abnormally high unemployment rates and the social ills associated with third world underdevelopment.[7] The foundation for this state of affairs can be traced to nineteenth-century theories of scientific racism, which proposed that American Indians were racially inferior and in effect minors in the sense that they were not competent to make decisions for themselves. This theory coincided rather conveniently with the ambitions of the time to transfer the wealth of the Indians into the hands of others. The idea of Indian incompetence evolved to a practice that required that decisions must be made for Indians, and the institutions that evolved to this task were the various agencies of the War Department and the BIA. It is not accidental that these institutions were not seriously challenged until the 1960s, when theories of racial superiority and inferiority were generally in decline during the US civil rights movement. This theory of Indians as mentally and socially incompetent because of their biological and cultural traits continues to be practiced in a number of nation states in the Western Hemisphere, notably Brazil.

Some people interpret the passage of the 1934 Indian Reorganization Act (IRA) as an early US effort to reverse the policy of total domination imposed on Indians. Nevertheless, by 1968 Indian communities remained the poorest communities in the United States. Subsequent changes in the level of poverty have largely occurred since 1968 and have been little influenced by the IRA. Indian activism, not enlightened and progressive initiatives on the part of judges, bureaucrats, or legislators, has been the primary force for change.

There is today, however, something of a revolution in Indian Country:

> The essential thrust of this revolution is the effective transfer of de facto control and ownership of American Indian reservations from the Federal Government and the Bureau of Indian Affairs (BIA) to the tribes themselves. The economic consequence of the transfer is the deregulation of broad classes of economic activity on Indian reservations. This change, largely the result of Indians' own aggressive assertion of their rights to self-determination and self-government, has significantly unraveled the historic (not to mention demeaning) status of Indians as official dependents of the Federal Government.[8]

The American Indian Movement of the sixties and seventies established a militancy among a younger generation of Indians who refused to continue to be addressed as wards of the BIA and refused to agree that the reservation assets of their grandfathers were somehow transferred to the hands of the United States. The seventies and eighties became decades of political development in Indian Country that saw some communities seize control of their own resources and develop those resources with their own goals and objectives and their own control of both the nature of development and the designated beneficiaries:

> Since 1975 reservation economic development has moved increasingly into Indian hands...For the first time, Indian tribes are making their own strategic development decisions.[9]

A number of conditions preclude successful economic development on Indian reservations and require at least a short, historic evaluation. Indian nations and communities differ from other Americans primarily in the group nature of the communities. Most immigrants and their descendants exist largely as individuals in American society. The Indians exist as distinct *groups* and have existed as such since time immemorial. The United States and most modern industrialized states have a tradition of rights of individuals but little tradition of group rights, and even today Indian rights are poorly defined and poorly understood in otherwise "enlightened" countries.

Immigrants and settlers were largely defined by their value to society as laborers. African and African American slaves were likewise brought to the United States (and Britain's former American colonies) as laborers. Alone among English-speaking North America's ethnic identities, the Indians were not valued for their labor but for their land.

> At the heart of Indian-white relations...was land...Indians were removed *as groups* from lands desired by non-Indians to less desirable lands. On these lands, called reservations, and despite assimilationist policies, both the collective identity and significant aspects of indigenous institutions and culture survived.[10]

After the land was seized, the Indians were supposed to vanish. Banished to (often remote) reservations, Indians presumably languished out of the mainstream's sight and out of mind under the tutelage of federal bureaucracies. When, during the 1960s, other ethnic groups generated demands, those demands focused on redistribution of access to rights within American society. Among Indians, however,

> as one looks back over the increasingly activist Indian politics of the post-War years, what is striking is the persistent salience of goals which have little to do directly with the common American vision of success. Again and again three intimately related concerns emerge: tribal sovereignty, treaty rights, land. All have to do fundamentally with the maintenance and protection of peoplehood, of community...It has been a politics of national survival.[11]

Economic development is a social process that involves the ability to organize to reach for goals and the power to take action to achieve these goals. Indian economic development may be more about creating the conditions for political power in the context of socially responsible choices than for the continued existence and cohesion of the group, i.e., the Indian nation:

> Economic development is not only economic. Regardless of the extent to which decision makers take non-economic issues into account, their decisions have non-economic consequences.

Tribes...are political sovereigns making substantive decisions regarding the future configuration of their societies...Economic development, then, is inherently strategic.[12]

Economic development in Indian Country has been a by-product of an Indian movement toward sovereignty, and sovereignty has meant being able to do what the Indian government decides to do, thus rendering the decisions of the US federal courts, which had largely ignored the idea of Indian sovereignty as providing the Indians with any real political power, as close to irrelevant in the real world as possible.

Several case studies of successful Indian political power evolving into economic power that in turn enhances political power are now available. The Mescalero Apache, the Cochiti Pueblo, and the White Mountain Apache are Indian nations that have dramatically wrested power over their land and resources from the federal bureaucracy and moved diligently to generate employment and tribal wealth from their resources. A list of other examples, with varying degrees of solvency, includes the following.[13]

- The Cherokee of Oklahoma own and operate an electronics manufacturing plant.
- The Quinault, Lummi, Swinomish, and several other tribes in the Northwest and Alaska own and operate fish canneries.
- The Blackfeet of Montana are a major player in the market for writing instruments.
- The Oneidas of Wisconsin, the Gilas of Arizona, and several other tribes own and operate office and industrial parks serving major metropolitan areas.
- The Warm Springs reservation in Oregon owns and operates a major sawmill and a large tourist resort.
- More than one hundred tribes operate bingo casinos, with seating capacities often in the thousands and jackpots approaching the millions.
- The Choctaw of Mississippi own and operate a factory specializing in electrical wire harnesses for the auto industry, as well as a greeting card company.

It was long an article of faith of American policy makers that the reason for the failure of the Indian to be successful in modern society was that Indian cultures were backward. Policies, therefore, sought to acculturate Indians, to bring them to Christianity and modernity, thereupon to fruitful economic life. All manner of acculturation was tried, from captivities such as the Bosque Redondo to sending Christian missionaries to Indian reservations as Indian agents. At one point, many Indian reservations were dramatically reduced in size and the land distributed to settlers. At mid-twentieth century, the US Bureau of Indian Affairs was relocating as many Indians as possible to urban areas in an effort to solve the Indian "problem."[14] The new movement toward self-determination has illustrated that one of the ingredients of poverty on Indian reservations is the culture of enforced powerlessness that has historically characterized US Indian policy.

Since 1968, it has become increasingly clear that culture has less to do with economic success than it does access to political power.[15] Cochiti Pueblo, one of the successful Indian development stories, maintains its traditional Indian form of government. The probability of economic success for an Indian community is greatly enhanced in an environment of fairness and access to opportunity. Fairness, in this context, refers to both the internal decision-making and dispute-resolution processes adopted by the Indians and their ability to gain equal treatment at the marketplace in terms of credit and an environment of fair competition.

Traditional forms of government operated by very conservative (i.e., traditionalist) Indian policies have been successful, as have tribal business councils. This is a significant observation because for two centuries apologists for the failure of US Indian policy have asserted that the primary cause of Indian poverty is the culture of the Indians. The proposal that Indian culture causes poverty completely ignores the fact that the essential ingredients to economic growth—access to means and opportunity—have been forcefully absent in Indian life.

Indians are discovering that the several requirements of effective political organization can be woven into the fabric of their culture. The first requirement for successful development strategies is that the leadership refrain from the activity of "rent seeking" or other opportunistic behavior.[16] In the jargon of Indian economic development, rent seeking occurs when a public official uses the powers of his or her office for personal gain, either directly or indirectly. But opportunistic behavior need not be limited to individual rent seekers. Tribal councils sometimes seek to change the rules after investors have assets in place. Opportunistic behavior

> can give a party a bad reputation and raise the cost of attracting future investment dollars. Opportunistic expropriation through conscious action or unintended instability, if anticipated, can cause investors either to refuse to commit capital to reservations or to stiffen the conditions and charges under which capital is committed.[17]

The same kind of behavior can go a long way toward discouraging Indians from investing their resources in their own businesses and has historically discouraged people from supporting the Indian governments in the United States.

A second requirement, closely related to and perhaps indistinguishable from the first, is that there must be an independent judiciary designed and empowered to render impartial judgments in cases involving conflict between the tribal government and others, including tribal members. The idea that tribal councils must create independent judiciaries and subject themselves to their judgments sounds countersovereign (to coin a phrase), but since most people (including tribal members) won't invest their time or money in ventures in which they fear they will be treated unfairly in the event of a conflict, independent judiciaries are emerging as a necessary cornerstone of the evolution of effective Indian development.

Another requirement is that Indians must create institutions that can act effectively. It is a crucial step from having a dream to having a plan to acting on the plan in an organized and efficient manner. As we have seen, before such institutions can be successful in Indian Country, the necessary environments must be created in the form of Indian governments conducive to proactive institutions and empowered to take action. In some parts of Indian Country the prospect of sharing responsibility, creating a separate and independent judiciary, and restraining rent seeking among some Indian leaders will be extremely challenging.[18]

There must also be planning that allows for some economic pluralism. The number of options for growth are fairly limited: federal (BIA does the planning and implementation), tribal (the tribe does it), entrepreneurial (individuals or small investment groups from within the community do it), and external (when investment and management are provided by external private capital). The first and last choices have become increasingly unpopular among US Indian nations, partly because these are not sovereignty enhancing, and partly because Indian nationalism leans strongly against these choices in many places.

There is one other possible choice: to do nothing. Doing nothing, increasingly, is not a choice at all and may be a choice toward cultural extinction. Most of the development on Indian reservations, predictably, will be that owned and operated by the Indian nations and entrepreneurial ventures of Indian members. The job of the Indian governments will be twofold. First, they will need to be able to operate with business skills, choosing how much to invest in what and when, just as other business leaders must do. In addition, they will need to make decisions about overall economic development consistent with the goals and ambitions of their people. When economic and political environments permit, successful Indian governments will create environments that sustain and support the kinds of entrepreneurial initiatives consistent with the goals of the group.

Indian sovereignty is being redefined according to what an Indian nation can actually do. It is no longer limited to discussions about state or provincial jurisdiction versus Indian jurisdiction, but rather it includes material issues and strategies designated by the Indian population and carried out by increasingly able Indian legal entities. The social implications are enormous. If Indian peoples have the power to make decisions about their future, they can choose educational paths that allow their languages, history, arts, and culture to survive, and therefore, they can perpetuate the very elements that define them as distinct peoples.

Notes

1. Author Vine Deloria Jr. traces the origins of the Indian movement to the Poor Peoples' March, organized by Martin Luther King Jr. in 1968. The march

preceded a bridge blockade at Cornwall Island (near Massena, New York) by Mohawks, the founding of *Akwesasne Notes*, and the founding of the American Indian Movement in Minneapolis the same year. See Vine Deloria Jr., *Behind the Trail of Broken Treaties* (New York: Delta Press, 1974), 33–41.

2. These are major elements, though by no means the only elements, that Indians have argued, demonstrated, and fought for in the years since 1968. For several views of the problems of Indian management of resources, please see: Anthropology Resource Center's *Native Americans and Energy Resource Development II* and also John Mohawk, "BIA Senate Hearing: Witch Hunt for A Straw Man," *Daybreak* magazine, Spring 1989: 26, 27.

3. Established in *US v. Kagama* (1886), 118 US 375, 6 S.Ct. 1109, 30 L.Ed. 228. Also *US v. Sandoval* (1913), 231 US 28, 34 S.Ct 1, 58 L.Ed. 107. See, generally, Newton, *Federal Power Over Indians: Its Sources, Scope, and Limitations* 132 U. Pa. L.Rev. 195, 199 (1984).

4. See "The Termination Era," in David H. Getches and Charles F. Wilkinson, *Federal Indian Law: Cases and Materials* (Saint Paul, MN: West Publishing, 1986), 130–150.

5. Edgar S. Cahn and David W. Hearne, eds., *Our Brother's Keeper: The Indian in White America* (New York: New Community Press, 1969), 7.

6. Cahn and Hearne, 117.

7. See Michael McNally, "Economic Welfare in Indian Country. A Consideration of History 1868–1968" (Cambridge, MA: The Harvard Project on American Indian Economic Development, May 1989): 30.

8. Joseph P. Kalt, "The Redefinition of Property Rights in American Indian Reservations: A Comparative Analysis of Native American Economic Development," unpublished ms., Energy and Environmental Policy Center, Harvard University, Cambridge, MA, May 1987, "Executive Summary," para. 1.

9. Stephen Cornell, "American Indians, American Dreams, and the Meaning of Success" (Cambridge, MA: The Harvard Project on American Indian Economic Development, May 1987): 6.

10. Stephen Cornell and Joseph Kalt, "Assessing the Causes and Consequences of Economic Development on American Indian Reservations: An Introduction to the Harvard Project on American Indian Economic Development" (Cambridge, MA: The Harvard Project on American Indian Economic Development, March 1988): 4.

11. Cornell and Kalt, 2.

12. Cornell, "American Indians," 13.

13. Cornell, "American Indians," 3–4. The list in the text included a cement factory owned by the Passamoquoddy Tribe of Maine, which has since been sold, and the Mescalero Apache, which were already mentioned.

14. Some interesting general readings on this subject include: Philip Weeks, *The American Indian Experience, a Profile: 1524 to the Present* (Arlington Heights, IL: Forum Press, 1988) and Angie Debo, *A History of the Indians of the United States* (Norman: Univ. of Oklahoma Press, 1970).

15. This is not to argue that culture has no influence on economic success, but rather that its influence has been historically overwhelmed by policies that

denied Indians any opportunity to make decisions over their own lives. Indeed, a Stephen Cornell paper contained this interesting hypothesis: *Hypothesis 26*: "Those tribes in which Indigenous groups of intellectuals— guardians of the deeper meanings of group membership, whose task in part is to think about and exemplify what it means, culturally, to be a member of the group—have survived and continue to play a major role in tribal affairs, will have the potential for more powerful community mobilization and, therefore, for more effective development than those where such groups no longer significantly function." Stephen Cornell, "Indian Reservation Economic Development: Some Preliminary Hypotheses" (Cambridge, MA: The Harvard Project on American Indian Economic Development, October 1987): 21.

16. "From Latin America to an excessively litigious US society, rent-seeking can destroy or divert resources from productive use. The key to shutting down rent-seeking lies in the creation of definitive rules of law—definitive property rights to action and resources...Rules of law are fundamentally a problem of enforcement, and enforcement is a relationship between leaders and their constituents." Kalt, "Property Rights," 49–50.

17. Kalt, "Property Rights," 25.

18. The literature on the quality of Indian political life is scanty, at best. An interesting book that charges election irregularities and corruption on the Rosebud Reservation in South Dakota, written at the beginning of the American Indian self-determination period, is Robert Bernette, *The Tortured Americans* (Englewood Cliffs, NJ: Prentice Hall, 1971).

Sovereignty Requires New Institutions,
Problem-Solving Skills

Energy resources have figured strongly in Indian/government relations for nearly half a century. Indian tribes control about 53 million acres of land in the lower forty-eight states, containing huge amounts of undeveloped coal, uranium, oil, and natural gas. The Grant mineral belt, the United States' center of uranium production, is situated in the Navajo Nation.

During the energy rush of the early 1970s, multinational corporations invaded Indian reservations—often at the behest of the Indian leadership—seeking to exploit the abundant energy resources of Indian lands. The recent world market collapse of oil prices has eased some of the pressure on Indian Country, but fundamental inequities have yet to be resolved.

The history of multinational development of Indian lands has generally been devastating. When the interest of development and the interest of the Indian are at odds, the interest of the Indian rarely prevails. Under pressure from energy corporations like Gulf Oil Company and Peabody Coal Company, as well as the federal government, Indians have often sold or leased the right to develop energy resources at prices that were blatantly unfair. In some instances, development has actually lowered per capita income for Indians in the impact area.

Less than twenty years ago, the Navajo Nation entered into an agreement with Peabody Coal that left Peabody in possession of the tribe's coal for about eighteen cents a ton when the going market price was rising above eighty-five dollars per ton.

Gulf Oil stole millions of dollars in royalties from the Northern Cheyenne reservation in Montana by underreporting the amount of oil that they took from the land.

When Indian people sit down at the negotiating table with a multinational corporation, they arrive with a set of goals and objectives almost completely opposite from the goals and objectives of the company. Corporations are organizations that represent the interests of investors. Their job is to protect those investors and to maximize profits by getting the product into the marketplace at the lowest possible price.

The Indians generally arrive at the table on behalf of a rural population that has a low—often below poverty level—income per household. The number of children per household on most reservations is often higher than the national average. Unemployment on the reservations is high, in some places hovering above 85 percent.

Indian people enter into negotiations with multinationals acutely aware that the recent past has been desperate, the present seems hopeless, and the future looks bleak. Like the rest of rural America, Indian people feel disadvantaged in the job market, unable to cope with the needs of the marketplace, and increasingly isolated. They are, in short, ripe for the kinds of promises and high-stakes talk that developers are prepared to offer.

The multinational corporations offer jobs to people who are unemployed—and who have come to believe they are unemployable. Multinational corporations offer the possibility of economic development. They talk about payments to the tribe. They promise restoration of land, well drilling, the development of roads—they promise the moon. These promises find fertile ground in the minds of men and women who have given up all hope of controlling their own futures. But the promise of jobs is often unfulfilled or underfulfilled.

Energy development rarely pays off. Uranium mining tends to produce costly, long-term ecological damage. Coal development, which requires vast amounts of water, could prove disastrous in the arid Southwest, where water is a precious resource to the Indians.

To achieve real development, we need to offer a vision of rural America in which people are in control of their own futures. To do this, we need to borrow some pages from the handbooks of the people whom we have traditionally considered our opponents.

Problem-solving skills should not be the sole property of the business class. Structured problem solving can be taught to people of any background. Negotiating skills should not be the sole province of labor representatives, lawyers, and international diplomats. These skills can be taught to all people to represent their own interests in a more vigorous fashion.

Rural communities already know what they need to know in order to solve their own problems. They know, for example, what assets exist in their community and what their social and cultural needs are. They know what can be done in the marketing environment in which they live. What rural people generally don't know how to do is to organize their thinking and their efforts in ways that create institutions to meet their already well-defined needs.

In the next decade, indigenous people must create and refine the institutions that will allow them to band together and collectively launch new initiatives to solve old problems.

Regaining Control of Our Lives:
The Promise of Appropriate Technology

It was during the era of "the sixties," as they call it these days—complete with antiwar rallies, university riots, and back-to-the-land people dressed in coveralls. A few of us were at a large university, trying to find out what would constitute a Native studies program, holding on to the somewhat dim hope that, were we ever to discover a way to incorporate the university into some kind of real social process, there would be the support in terms of money and political effort to create an actual program.

We focused our attention on the Native communities. What kinds of things did peoples there want to see happen? What were their needs? I remember the theme of one of the orientation programs for incoming freshmen—directed right at Native students: "You can come home again." It was not an inappropriate theme. One of the major problems that people related was that "educated" Indian peoples rarely seemed to return to their communities. Once they attained the skills they sought, they found the high-paying jobs in the cities sometimes thousands of miles from their homes.

We talked to people about the needs. Clearly, Native peoples need some kind of local economy. But there were other considerations that were expressed also. What about the Native culture? How will that be affected? Some kinds of economic development involve technologies that are not only dangerous to the existence of Native cultures, but that would undoubtedly affect the physical quality of life on the reservation.

There were a lot of problems that people rarely mention. On the university campus, if you spoke about social change and the need to organize people to move toward that change (which is what a local economic development would require), somebody said that you were being "brainwashed" by some non-Native person or another. If you came home and began to talk about social change, one group said you were "preaching to the tipi," while another group argued that you were some kind of Communist.

If you argued that economy wasn't a simple matter of control of the means of production, the Marxists denounced you as some kind of reactionary minority, and any suggestion that traditional Native values and culture could serve as a model drew the comment that the strategy was simply a diversion from the real need to organize the working class. If you argued that social development could find positive example in the traditional economies, people shouted that the day of the buffalo had ended and that such thoughts belong in some romanticist's archives. Progressive change was not easily promoted. Mixed into that scenario were the complexities of two hundred or more years of already existing social change on the Indian territories.

There was arising in the Native communities a new kind of Indian person who was, in a way, confusing issues even more. The antiwar protests and the civil rights movement brought to light a basic need among Native peoples to develop some kind of positive identity.

"Born-again" Indians came out of the woodwork to announce to the world that Native peoples are nothing short of saintly and that anything short of ideological perfection was "not Indian," or at least not Indian enough. The practical day-to-day questions of how to put food on the table or a roof over your head never occupied much of their time. "Being Indian is a feeling," they said. It was a popular theme.

I remember hearing that the "Indian Way" was the thing that needed to be taught to the young people. There were seminars and more seminars, conferences and discussion groups. The Indian Way was proposed primarily by the urban and professional Indians and involved a discussion about the suddenly discovered strong points of the "true" Indian personality.

We were asked to believe that all the Native peoples were somehow possessed of characteristics of love and familial devotion and that the Indian Way involved trust and an attention to religion that few priests ever achieve. The Indian Way proved to be tremendously effective in countering any efforts at change. It was possible to denounce virtually anything as not being the Indian Way. Some of the most promising Native peoples who were working toward real change were roundly denounced as being "not Indian enough."

There is a kind of defense mechanism within Western culture that makes it extremely conservative and resistant to change. It is ready, willing, and able to verbalize anything. So much information is available and so many divergent views that people are made impotent simply by the weight of opinions open to them. One is tempted to argue, at times, that an excess of information turns the most articulately expressed and purposefully directed strategies into just as much rhetoric.

What comes to mind is that maybe people were asking the wrong questions. The real issues became clouded, and few people were willing to address those issues. It is a problem that life on the Indian territories seems to hold a very questionable future. Many of the Indian territories exist on a "welfare" economy, held up from quarter to quarter by the Bureau of Indian Affairs (BIA) and other federal grants and loans. An alarming percentage of the people are presently employed by the federal government or programs funded by the federal government.

Native communities in the United States and Canada possess a surprisingly low number of people participating in any form of material production. In most cases, people are not producing the things the community needs. They are on the bottom rung of the economic ladder, and they are trapped there by the enormous dependency on grants and the welfare system that is the reservation economy. Conditions may be better materially under the welfare economy than they were during the period of "benign neglect," but the basic problems remain unaddressed. Part of what has happened is that the motivation to address those problems has been removed for a lot of people. When asked about the future, most of the federally funded people respond that the United States has a "trust responsibility" to Indians. They think the federal funding will keep coming in forever.

Native peoples have also become captives of the consumer mentality. As with other Americans, many Native peoples are led to pine after every amenity in order to achieve happiness. Although many of us grew up dirt poor, we now want the most expensive toys for ourselves and our children. Money, and the things that cost money, are of value to us today, and independence, or things of quality that do not have a price tag, have come to have less value. There is not much effort in the Native communities directed at finding ways to meet people's needs that do not involve chasing after federal or grant dollars, as opposed to directly producing food, clothing, or other things that people need.

One of the things people need to address is: what will happen if by some chance the US economy falters? Almost the only people who think that will never happen are Native people who are living on federal program checks. What will happen if the US economy starts to fail, or if there is a Proposition 13 situation that impacts Indian Country? What will Native people do in the event that the dollars stop coming in?

In times of economic crisis, people seem willing to accept radical changes. The politics of the New Deal, which arose during the Great Depression, give an example of this tendency. Today, for a great many people, programs such as the New Deal, the New Frontier, and the Great Society appear to be a source of economic problems instead of the answers they once were seen to be. In the event of a deepening economic crisis, the indicators are that the American public is willing to accept a radical shift to the right.

There is every appearance that the United States is beginning a serious political shift to the right. Right-wing politicians, such as Jack Cunningham, appear to be growing in popularity. That trend is almost certain to impact Indian territories where it will hurt the most—in the area of federal funding. The same trend also poses a possibility of the total loss of the land base.

There are other factors that people should be aware of. The US economy is experiencing some crises that aren't mentioned very often. At one point, US industry was the most modern and efficient, and the US economy the most vigorous in the world. But now, the US gross national product has stagnated and is beginning what appears to be a decline. A lot of US industry is, today, obsolete, and other countries, especially Japan and West Germany, have very modern industrial facilities that are more efficient than their US counterparts.

The United States is losing its position as the unchallenged leader of the industrial world. US products and manufacturing techniques are no longer considered the best or most efficient. Because of this, and the accompanying realities that other countries are producing goods of the same quality at lower prices, the balance of trade is shifting seriously away from the United States, at least in many industries. Today, the major US exports involve weaponry, grain, and technology—specifically computer technology.

The weakening position in terms of the world trade balance, which has resulted from the relative decline of US industry, has been the major reason for the decline of the US dollar against the

West German mark and the Japanese yen. Some influential American economists are saying that what is needed is massive capitalization of US industry and the expansion and rebuilding of the transportation networks and other supportive structures that an industrialized country needs. There is not a lot of capital lying around for this purpose.

The politics of reindustrialization appear certain to trickle down throughout the society. It is undeniable that big-business moguls have an eye on the social services funds that the US government has been doling out in increasing amounts since the Depression. The people who see the "welfare state" as a competitor for investment capital have a broad base of potential political allies in the middle class, who sees their property taxes and income taxes are used for social welfare programs, which deliver services to the poor and minority groups.

In California, conservative politicians were successful in obtaining passage of a public referendum that altered the state constitution to create a ceiling on taxes and state spending. The amendment, called Proposition 13, should not be seen as an isolated incident. It could well foreshadow a popular national movement designed to reduce the amounts of public moneys allocated to social welfare services.

Conservative politicians are arguing that a reduction in corporate taxes will provide more money for investment capital. They say that reduction in property and income taxes will free more money for investment in the private sector and will stimulate the economy by making more money available for consumption of consumer goods. That will, they say, stimulate higher profits, which will mean more reinvestment, the creation of more jobs in the private sector, and a return to a more vigorous economy.

What that would mean is that the flow of dollars to communities for such services as alcohol abuse programs and summer youth programs, as well as a vast number of Comprehensive Employment and Training Act programs, Volunteers in Service to America, and other programs, could be drastically reduced. There is certainly a political movement under way in the United States that would accomplish just that.

It seems almost too obvious, at this point, that one of the program areas that would be slated for cuts, should there be cuts, will be the programs that impact the Native communities. In some Native communities, 85 percent of the people employed have jobs under some category of federal funding. There may be other kinds of communities that can show that kind of statistic, but the undeniable truth is that in the event of a political swing to the right and massive reallocation of funding priorities, the Native communities will be the first to suffer and will suffer the most. That prospect is not a dim possibility. The political processes in American life that lead that way have already begun.

There will be, predictably, exceptions to the rule. Those Native territories that possess substantial natural resources will probably continue to receive government programs at the same level or at even increased levels. The reason for this is that there will continue to be a need to create a dependent reservation infrastructure for the extraction of the minerals. On the Native territories where there are no, or insignificant, mineral deposits, it is probable that cuts in public spending for delivery of social services can be predicted.

The massive federal funding that has flooded into Indian reservations in recent years has created jobs and has brought accompanying social problems. On the Yakima Nation, everyone who wants a job has one. Yet, Yakima also has the highest adolescent suicide rates in the long history of that nation. People who believe that employment and employment alone is a key to solving social problems need to examine the record in Indian Country. The social problems bear a visible association with the increased federal funding.

It is much more difficult to see that the funding has added much to these communities' abilities at self-reliance. A quick review of the grant proposals will reveal that the federal dollars were intended to stimulate skill development and motivation that was supposed to lead to self-reliance among Native peoples. It hasn't worked. Indeed, even the attempts at real models of economic development have followed the route of efforts by the BIA and the Economic Development Administration to make reservations into tourist areas, efforts that cost staggering amounts of money and ended, in almost every case, in utter failure. The BIA policy of "self-reliance" has been, in the kindest possible words, unenlightened. For the most part, BIA bureaucrats see Native peoples as a potential cheap labor force that private industries can utilize during periods of expansion. Most often, "self-reliance" has simply been a rhetorical tool that the bureaucrats have used while designing programs that would draw the Native peoples into ever-deepening conditions of dependence on the bureau and other federal agencies.

What the BIA has accomplished is that many Native communities presently suffer almost total dependence on federal funding for their very existence. If the funding can claim any success at all, it is in the area of acculturation. Communities that forty years ago were almost entirely self-sufficient are today virtually assimilated into the US economy.

BIA/EDA policy brought to the Native peoples a system of industrial parks that were attracted to the reservations because of the lack of taxes and extremely attractive lease agreements, which allowed them to exploit Native credit and labor practically without liability or risk. When the Department of Labor and the Economic Development Assistance subsidies were discontinued, the companies fled to greener pastures in Taiwan and Korea.

Economic policies, such as industrialization, were introduced to Native communities with the full weight of the federal government. The major target of those programs was the replacement and destruction of the traditional economies, and to that end the programs were surprisingly successful. Today, the growing lands of the Pueblo lie fallow and abandoned, the grazing lands of the Oglalas are leased to white ranchers, and the fields of the Senecas are rented to commercial farmers—non-Indian commercial farmers.

Everywhere, most of the people buy their food at the supermarket. At last we know exactly what acculturation means. It means that peoples can't provide for themselves anymore. Acculturation is when peoples are not producing to meet their own needs. The federal funding has brought the people more than money—it has purchased their dependence.

Culture and economy are inseparable. A lot of people today have come to accept the BIA definition of *culture* as referring to music, dress, and language. But cultures are inconceivable without an economic base. Even spiritual life revolves to a considerable extent around the ways that people see their lives supported. Indeed, it is arguable that people's personal relationships, and their relationships to their environment, are molded by the ways in which they meet their needs, and the manifestation of those ways is what we call culture. In the absence of culture, there can be no economy. In the absence of economy, there is no culture. All that remains is the memory of culture. People who promote music and costume making in urban cultural centers are not promoting culture, albeit they are promoting the memory of culture. One of the alarming aspects of the loss of culture (of acculturation) is that in the absence of processes that meet people's needs, social disintegration occurs. That is why acculturation is associated with alcoholism, suicide, family disintegration, and all the other social ills that the federal government has programs to control. It is a model of the process of colonialism. First they create the problem, then they offer prescriptions as remedies. The destruction of the Native economy has one of the stated goals of the federal bureaucracies that deal with Indian peoples since the foundation of the United States.

The logical response to that process is that Native peoples must develop, or redevelop, their own economies. To develop a Native economy (and almost everyone is in favor of that, at least rhetorically), we are immediately forced to deal with overall questions concerning what is called technology. At the moment, technology is too often treated as a given. All technology, so we are told, is Western technology. If you are talking about providing housing, a lot of people think that there is only one technology that builds houses. In truth, there are many technologies and many kinds of housing. People who are serious about the need to develop a Native economy are faced with the problem of becoming familiar with the technologies that exist and then choosing technologies that meet their needs.

Stated differently, an economy involves the production and distribution of goods and services, and production requires techniques—tools and skills—as well as sources of materials. Before we can talk about developing the mechanics of distribution of goods or services, we must deal with the questions of what kinds of skills are needed and accessible, what kinds of tools are needed and accessible, and what kinds of materials are needed and accessible.

Technologies come in all shapes and sizes. There are many potential choices. There are capital intensive technologies, which require huge monetary investment and which often employ very few people. An example of such a technology is the coal-mining process on the Navajo lands or the proposed Navajo agribusiness project. Capital intensive technologies are out of the reach of most people because they simply don't have the money to purchase the hardware. That kind of technology is also not appropriate to community development, where the purpose is to help people to become productive, because such technology is designed to replace human labor with machine production.

What Native communities need is low-cost, labor-intensive technologies that they can afford and that help people to become productive. Any Native group that attempts to develop a local economy must be sophisticated in its approach to the problem.

For a technology to be really "appropriate," a number of criteria must be met. The technology must be low-cost and basically ecologically sound. The tools and skills should be under the control of the local communities, and they should use locally available resources, including materials. Those technologies should be flexible enough so that people are not locked into some kind of dependence—a reference to putting all of your eggs in one basket. And they need to be technologies that do not conflict with the cultural assumptions of the community. Technologies that do not meet these minimal criteria cannot be termed appropriate, although one is always advised to ask, "Appropriate to what end?"

Technologies can be conceived in two broad terms. There are hard technologies and soft technologies. *Hardware technology* refers to the physical tools and procedural skills of a technology. *Software* refers to the things that mold value systems and that motivate and stir innovation and invention of new technologies.

At this moment in history, soft technologies are at least as important as hard technologies in the Native communities. The problems Native peoples are facing will not be solved by simply sifting through a catalogue of existing technologies and selecting some that seem applicable to the purpose. What is needed is a process that brings to people an understanding of the problem and that motivates them to move toward a solution. A truly appropriate technology cannot be purchased. To a considerable extent, it must be invented—or reinvented.

People should be encouraged to rediscover old technologies, to adapt those technologies to present realities, and to educate people to their use. It may be found that there is a need to investigate what people call intermediate technologies—technologies that are neither traditional nor the most capital intensive. It could be that it is not inconsistent to use rototillers or older tractors, which are cheap but productive. Basically, what people need to do is to take control, once again, of their own lives. They need to discover, rediscover, invent, reinvent, and otherwise gain access to the technology that makes this possible.

The idea that Native peoples can adapt technology is not new, but there are lessons to be learned about the social impact of new technologies. Technologies can alter culture. Consider for a moment the introduction of the horse to the Native peoples of the plains. The horse actually arrived among many Native groups ahead of the Europeans. But the horse was an agent of profound cultural change.

But a number of Native groups that were primarily agricultural and matrilocal prior to the introduction of the horse were gradually becoming or became hunters, gatherers, and herdsmen, and the cultures became more patrilocal. There will be arguments about that assertion, but the evidence is that the horse provided a new technology on the plains, and its introduction made possible, and perhaps inevitable, some kinds of social change.

There is a need for social change in the Native communities today, but there are many pitfalls and problems involved. Native peoples need to adopt some new forms of doing things that provide an alternative to the federal funding system, which promotes environmental exploitation of a destructive nature and BIA paternalism. When we look into the arena of technologies, we find that the alternative grab bag is filled to the brim. There are so many technological possibilities that it staggers the mind. The choices must be made with an eye to goals, presumably the enhancement of community well-being, cultural values, and local ecology.

The horse keeps coming back to mind. It provided a new possibility for life on the plains. One must ask, what kind of technology is needed now? What would bring to Native peoples the possibility of a new life on the territories they now inhabit? What would revitalize and strengthen the people now?

If the technology of grant proposal writing has a questionable future, what could be developed to replace it? What kinds of things will be developed when Native peoples do begin to regain control of their lands and resources? What will people do for a living? There are proponents of what is called "appropriate technology" in other areas of the world who are simply seeking labor-intensive ways to force people to serve the world economy. If appropriate technology involves drawing people into an extractive relationship with the industrial centers, rural Native food producers could become a new kind of sharecropper for the multinational agribusiness firms.

The focus pretty clearly needs to be local production for local consumption. A given community of people needs to look at their resources with an eye to meeting their needs themselves. When we speak of technologies of food production, we must understand that the food that is produced must be intended for consumption by the group producing it. The prospects of the sale of surplus must be secondary. The same principles need to be applied to forest products, fibers, minerals. The need is to produce for ourselves with our own (or our adapted) techniques on our own territories. And we need to consider a lot of economic networking. There exist the materials on Native territories to build homes, heat those homes, grow food, and develop a wide array of locally produced products. Native communities don't need M16 carbines, they need food to eat. They don't need plywood factories, they need homes. And there is a need, on a very practical level, for people to begin to think small. We should readopt the theme "small is beautiful."

A great number of Native peoples today are looking to the US government for assistance in these problems, but there is a low level of understanding about the processes at work. People can't invoke Native sovereignty in one breath and demand that the United States enact its "trust responsibility" in the next. The trust responsibility is a policy that states that Native peoples are legal dependents of the US government. Peoples cannot enact sovereignty when they are in fact dependent on federal dollars for their every need, from housing to education to food on the table.

All of these issues are entwined. To develop economic self-reliance (or even economic independence), a people must exercise sovereignty. To exercise sovereignty, the Native nations must achieve economic self-reliance. To do any of these things, they must control all elements of their own lives. The true value of appropriate technology is that it can be the process (including both hardware and software) by which that control is practiced. Appropriate technology is appropriate to Native peoples only if it returns to them control over their lives. What Native peoples need to develop are technologies appropriate to the exercise of sovereignty. Returning to people's real control over their lives must be the primary goal of Native peoples if they are to survive in these times.

Technology As Enemy: A Short History

A number of years ago, a group of students were sightseeing with Thomas Banyacya, well-known Hopi Traditionalist interpreter and spokesman. The group was from SUNY at Buffalo, and the tour followed the Niagara Gorge to Niagara Falls, past the myriad chemical plants near the now-famous Love Canal, and out toward the Robert E. Moses Power Project. Thomas had given a speech the night before as part of a program to bring Native consciousness to the American public. He had told Hopi prophesy, and to the extent that such a teaching could be received by a college audience, the adventure was a success.

He was impressed by the sights of the day, as is everyone who first sees the gorge, the falls, the industrialization of the Niagara Strip. By late afternoon, we had left the falls and were where the highway signs announce the approaches to the Robert E. Moses Power Project. Suddenly, Thomas told us to stop the car. We pulled over, and he got out. For a long time, in silent awe, he stood beside the road, a few hundred yards from the gorge. Before him stretched the power transport network—the endless maze of cables that transport electricity from the Niagara Fall's generating plant to points throughout Western New York. He got back in the car, and we rode for a few moments in silence, past the transformers and the cable towers, which dominate the landscape. Finally, he spoke softly: "In the Hopi teachings," he began, "we are told that toward the end of the world, Spider Woman will come back and she will weave her web across the landscape. Everywhere you will see her web. That's how we will know that we are coming to the end of this world, when we see her web everywhere. I believe I have just seen her web."

He didn't mean that the Hopi world was coming to an end and that the power lines signaled an end of Hopi culture. He meant that the world was coming to an end, that the history of humans as a species was coming to some crisis and that the crisis was connected in some way to the appearance of those power transmission lines.

The teachings of Hopi culture are not easily translated into a way of thinking that is accessible to Western technological man. The Hopi Cosmology is an oral history of the Hopi people and the human species that interweaves a complex set of symbols in such a way that it illuminates a set of moralities that the West has generally found to be both confusing and inappropriate. But the Hopi Cosmology should be interesting to the Western mind in at least one category—it contains as a central element a "history" of technology. (I'm not going to apologize at this point because words like *history* don't accurately apply to the Hopi version of the past. The word *cosmology* isn't an accurate description of their teachings either. The language is deficient, not the Hopi mind.)

Technology, which is extremely prominent in Hopi ways of thinking, is virtually invisible in Western conventional histories. Since Western conventional histories shape Western conventional wisdom, it is really useless to talk about technology unless we can talk about history, and unless we can accept the fact that all of us are products of what is called conventional wisdom—those things that we accept to be true because "everybody knows" those things are true. The culture we were born into nurtured each and every one of us to a belief in certain premises, and our socialization in that respect is surprisingly complete. We are each of us "prejudiced" to certain beliefs, certain ways of seeing the world, and certain ways of being in the world.

If technology occupies a prominent place in the Hopi version of the human experience, the role of technology in shaping human events in the Western world is seriously downplayed. In fact, the historical force of technology is almost invisible in the West. If technologies have had an impact on molding Western history, then those versions of Western history upon which English-speaking people were all nurtured were woefully inadequate in explaining these forces. For a number of reasons that I don't want to talk about here, Western history has been written largely with an eye to expounding upon personalities and events in ways that leave the role of technologies, to say the least, secondary. In the following few pages, I am going to delve into a version of history that states that the evolution of technologies has been the major moving force in all of Western history, and that the **vectors** of that evolution give us some insights into where it all goes and what it means to the future of us all.

The beginnings of technological innovation can probably be traced to that period of time several million years ago when ancestors of our species climbed out of trees and began life walking erect on the ground. There isn't much that can be said about that period of time, so little is really known about that phase of evolution. It is certain that over long periods of time, our species evolved from arboreal creatures to erect creatures that eventually inhabited the semiarid savanna country of present-day Africa.

At some point, and it is not entirely clear at what point, protohumans evolved from creatures entirely dependent, as are most creatures, on the raw gifts of Nature and ventured from their natural habitat into an increasingly alien habitat to which they had not physically evolved. Human evolution took some revolutionary turn in the history of the world's creatures, not the least of which involved the human evolution of the development of culture as a means of surviving in environments to which the species was not physically adapted. As protohumans left their ancestral habitat, they evolved new ways of surviving that required they learn to do the things that Nature had not provided them at birth. As they moved into colder climates, they had to learn to fashion clothing to take the place of fur coats that other species evolved biologically. They had to learn to devise shelters, to eat what was available, and to shape and mold the things of their new worlds to their needs.

From the very beginning of "human" time, all things are products of "technology." There must have been many revolutionary technologies that enabled human populations to spread from their places of origin to inhabit nearly all places of the world, from the hottest and most arid deserts to the polar ice caps. Those technologies must have included such things as learning to work leather and to sew clothing and to fashion tools from wood and bone. It is not preposterous to imagine that an awl and a sewing needle were at one time revolutionary technological developments that enabled people to fashion clothing, which in turn allowed people to venture to and live in climates that had previously been too hostile for human habitation. It must have taken tens of thousands of years for some of these inventions to take place and to have an impact. Inventions that made it possible for humans, who do not possess the fierce claws or powerful jaws of most meat-eaters, to kill and eat large grass-eating animals were powerful inventions. Those kinds of inventions shaped human history. For hundreds of thousands of years, that cultural evolution was going on, and human populations evolved into creatures capable of expanding into many areas of the world, able to trap and ambush animals many times the size of humans, able to devise shelters adequate to provide survival in increasingly hostile environments, and having invented languages that made it possible to transmit from one generation to the next the group's accumulated knowledge.

All of that was going on long before the end of the Pleistocene. In fact, we have a lot of evidence to indicate that the concept of religion, the idea of a cosmological order of things, was pretty universal among mankind some seventy thousand years ago and may be one of the developments that set modern man apart in some ways from truly ancient man, although even that isn't entirely clear. By the end of the Old Stone Age (at the end of the Pleistocene), man's most complex and marvelous technological feat—language—had clearly evolved to fascinating proportions. The hunting and gathering culture had lasted through several ice ages and seemed to have survived the test of time. By that time, man had evolved so far from his origins that for all practical purposes there was no place left on earth where he could survive without his devised method of evolution—culture. And the culture of man—even in our archaeology textbooks—was defined by his tools and the way he lived in the space he occupied.

It was about ten thousand years ago that technologies started to evolve in new ways. The inventions associated with the New Stone Age took root in several places under varying conditions, but it is useful to look at the evolution of the West especially because it is there that the kind of technologies we must concern ourselves with were nurtured. It is entirely possible that at least some of the early technologies were born out of some kind of necessity. The hunting culture of the Old Stone Age comes to an end with the appearance of agriculture and animal herding. Those things probably were accepted only very gradually. The first crops were probably gathered and replanted because people were experiencing some kind of adversity—famine or near famine. Until people began sowing and cultivating plants, those plants were gathered, and it seems highly unlikely that people would have adopted the tedious and strenuous work associated with most agriculture unless Nature failed to provide the food they needed abundantly enough to meet their needs. Once agriculture took root, however, it probably seemed like a godsend to people who were in need.

As new technologies are introduced, human societies change in order to incorporate those technologies into their world. The introduction of agriculture seems to alter hunting and gathering societies in some relatively predictable ways. A hunting society is primarily patrilocal, and the spirits that people look to for their health and safety are largely animal spirits. Agricultural societies tend to be more settled, and women play a greater role in the society, which often becomes matrilocal and which looks to the spirits of plants increasingly for the same purposes. In the beginning, agriculture was a woman-based technology, and the society reflected that. In Europe, we know of the existence in historical times of Mother Goddess religions that have their origins in prehistory.

Sometime after the introduction of agriculture, at least among Indo-European peoples inhabiting the area known as the present-day steppes of Russia, animal herding was introduced.

A society's religion seems to be intricately related to its technology. The herdsman truly revolutionized the way humans saw the world, because he is a human who manipulates the reproductive aspects of the animals he herds and upon which the society depends for its food and clothing and, in many cases, for shelter. But if agriculture had a primary female bent, herding had a male cast. Males became dominant in the herding culture and, to a considerable extent, the same technology that is employed in herding is readily applied to societal organization. Herding cultures tend to be patriarchal, with women playing a secondary role. The religion of herding cultures tends toward male sky gods, whose attention focuses largely on the affairs of men. Animals had previously been thought to be sacred, at least to the extent that they possessed spirits that could assist or injure humans, depending on the respect shown to them. In the herdsman's experiences, the animal's spirit became less and less important.

Hunters and gatherers who become herdsmen tend to become more hierarchical than agriculturalists and in fact sometimes evolve into extremely patriarchical societies. Herding is not a technology that provides a more attractive way of life compared to hunting and gathering—it provides a more efficient way. The animal supply is under human control, easily found, and usually required less territory than hunting and gathering. Animal herding made it possible for human beings to live on the grasslands, which hunters and gatherers could not do.

Agriculturalists that lived in semiarid regions were probably the first to extensively practice water-use technologies and were the first to build settlements. It is extremely possible that the first irrigation ponds were dug by agriculturalists who were experiencing crop failure due to lack of rain and who invented irrigation as a way of resolving this problem. The early permanently settled villages could have grown up around the use of this technology, although it is also possible that villages in dry regions sometimes arise in places where water is available and where the availability of that water is so critical that groups of people really can't move around very much during long periods of the year. It is interesting to note that where towns appear we also begin to see the appearance of priest-classes, which not only control the religious life of the community but which also seem to be in control of the technology. Civilization (from the Greek *civos*) arises out of these roots, and it will remain constant that people will fashion their society after a model dictated to them by the technologies that define their material economy.

The evolution of civilization—in this case Western civilization—was a very complex process. The steps from settlements that arose because people needed a reliable water supply for crops to the population centers that we call cities was a slow process and technologies that reinforced that process were evolved all along the route. It seems not unreasonable when looking at the history of ancient Anatolia and the Fertile Crescent that a series of events took place in those early towns. The towns that produced crops, mainly grains, also invented ways to store and keep track of those grains. The culture seems to have invented writing for the purpose of keeping track of things like grains for the purpose of trade and also seems to have developed increasingly sophisticated kilns to make pots in which to store the grains against pests.

Eventually kilns developed that could produce enough heat to melt metal, and townspeople became the early producers of both clay pots and metal products. Metal was also useful for making weapons, and the technology of metalworking was a guarded military secret for a long time. Metalworkers need raw materials, and there was no copper or tin or iron ores in the towns or nearby. This development gave rise to a need to open trade routes to get these things, and the opening of trade routes meant a need for a military to protect the caravans. Since it is easier and more certain to own your own mine than to trade with somebody else, it became quite profitable to go out and colonize other lands and peoples to get the raw materials.

All this metalworking and pot making and mining and transportation required more and more supportive labor. As trade developed, towns became permanent marketplaces, and the markets generated needs for increased production that required more people employed in making both trinkets and tools. Those citified people had to have other people who would protect, feed, house, and supply them. In addition, there were others who were employed at managing the affairs of the town, its economy, and at seeing to other people's spiritual needs. Each step in this expansion of civilization required and motivated the evolution of technologies, a process that could be called technological dialectic. Technologies arose and became popular according to needs in every case. When the Natural World failed to provide (and the Natural World does not sustainably provide for civilized needs), some inventor came along and developed a substitute.

These technologies arose in response not to human needs, but to the needs of that peculiar form of human organization known as civilization. In the ancient world, the kind of pot that spawned the kiln that eventually smelted metal was not invented for the purpose of keeping a small family's grain safe from pests. It was invented to produce big pots that stored grains in the royal granary. Most of the technological innovations such as metal processing were invented for the benefit of the city's need for trade goods and weaponry and were not invented for the good of some now distant abstract called humanity. In time, civilizations would completely forget the distinctions, and they use the word *man* to refer to civilized man. The conventional wisdom has it that technologies, at least some technologies, benefit humankind. The historical fact is that technologies were invented to benefit civilization. There is a difference.

Civilizations (especially Western civilization) had the potential from the very beginning of being destructive to the point of being self-destructive. It is in the process of civilization that a region is exploited without regard to its material (ecological) limits. When humans become "civilized" they cease being "citizens" of a region, and they become actors in a process that disregards the reality of regionality.

The conventional histories to which Western peoples are exposed propose that histories are composed of personalities, battles, and dates of events. Those histories would have been more enlightening had people been required to look at the rise and fall of civilizations in material terms. How did each produce food, develop water resources, or provide people with clothing? What was the source of raw materials, and what were its sources of energy? What technologies characterized the various sectors of production? Did the technologies of these civilizations meet with crisis, did they ever cross over an invisible line at which technologies were doing more harm than good? Conventional histories never seem to concern themselves with these questions.

The conventional wisdom has it that great civilizations fell because of invasions of barbarians and the imprudent leadership of morally deficient kings and emperors. But the area that was once called the Fertile Crescent is today a desert caused by centuries of soil erosion and salinization, which were the long-term effects of technological innovations that once made the same area bloom. The conventional wisdom seems woefully incomplete. Barbarism and poor leadership may have been factors that appear at the decline of civilizations, but the causes of the erosion can be found elsewhere. Long before the barbarians reached the city gates, the limitations of technology had been reached, and the contradictions inherent in certain technologies had begun to take their toll.

Technologies have always defined cultures, and cultures have always had at least some impact on environments. Western cultures and Western technologies have been defined by the objective, inherent in the culture, of supporting overly large concentrations of population. The underlying driving techno force of the West has been expansion for the purpose of providing for the needs of population concentration. Decentralization of population centers is seen as the most serious of sins, for it is anathema to the culture, and the culture's technologies, en masse, are not adapted to that purpose. It will become clear as this discourse continues that the concept of an invisible line has to do with a given technology's purpose. All technologies serve a purpose. When that purpose is to support inappropriately large population centers, then that technology has gone over the line, and the contradictions of the purpose of that technology become visible.

It is arguable that the economy of a civilization—the market system—is the motivating force of the modern technological dilemma. In the modern world, technologies of agriculture, for example, are not in any way divorced from the market system. We are living in a time when the needs of Western economies have clearly stated priorities, even within the Western economy. Given a need for agricultural land versus a need for electricity, the culture of the West has clear priorities in favor of electricity. Food is merely a commodity in the marketplace and receives no priority consideration because of its role in sustaining human life. The land, and its life-supporting function, is expendable. Subsistence farmers, whose existence makes more sense in regional, millennial, and species-specific terms, are readily sacrificed to the needs of the urban centers. Lands that are flooded for hydroelectric projects are considered regional or national "sacrifice areas."

Western culture experienced critical periods of change that gave rise to these kinds of priorities during the first millennia AD. The so-called Dark Ages were a period of major technological change. The ancient world was powered almost entirely by direct sun energy. Beginning around the fourth century, power-driven machinery appeared as the result of the development of windmills and waterwheels.

Such inventions enabled the introduction of power-driven bellows, which enormously increased the potential for the production of iron. Iron production required huge amounts of charcoal, which was produced from hardwood trees. Iron also provided a material for tools that cut down the European forests. At this same period, the iron plow was introduced that was now pulled by horses, which were made more efficient for this purpose by the invention of the harness. The axe-cleared forest could be plowed and cultivated through the use of this technology by far fewer people than had been required previously, and the increased efficiency of this mode of production made it possible that more people were freed for more functions in the system of feudal estates, which this technology made not only possible but inevitable.

All of this was unfolding as the motivating force behind the spread of the Christian techno revolution. Christianity is an ideology of technology because the Christian message is that the indigenous, animistic, so-called pagan gods and spirits of the forests, mountains, streams, and so forth are false gods and that streams and rivers aren't really sacred. Christianity paved the way for the philosophy that there is nothing wrong with taking an axe and a plow to the forest and reducing it to so much charcoal and so many acres of cropland.

By the fifteenth century, feudalism had spread through Europe, its cities were established, and the people were suffering from the plagues that accompanied the incredible filth that characterized that long period of history. The forests were largely eroded. The symbols of that period are a man and a tool and the Four Horsemen of the Apocalypse. The by-products of medieval technology were the pressures that led to the European-settler expansion into the Americas, Africa, and Australia.

The technologies of ship construction and navigation probably "saved" European society as we know it. Those developments made possible the mass transport of populations from Europe to the rest of the world (and mass transport of food and materials from the rest of the world to Europe) and ushered in the modern world. New technologies enabled that process to take place at an even faster pace. The inherent crisis of urban techno society was delayed for several centuries by the "discoveries" of new lands, resources, and the adaptable technologies of non-Western peoples.

The nineteenth century saw the development of fossil fuels, which delayed the crisis that was developing when the hardwood forests were becoming depleted. The use of fossil fuels led to entirely new dimensions of population growth and concentration. It is hardly remarkable that technology became a kind of religion in the West.

People had long ago abandoned "faith" in God as a way of life. Christ's admonition to people to trust in God (read: Nature), when he said that God provides for the birds and will provide for the faithful as well, was entirely disregarded by the Christian world. It was considered, in a manner of speaking, advice for the birds. In fact, the West has developed more food-storage technology than any other people to guard against the possibility that God might not provide for the future. The true religion in the West was better expressed by the sentiments that "God helps those who help themselves," and the more ways people invent to help themselves, the better.

At each point in crisis in Western history, the invention of new technologies can indeed be said to have "saved" the culture. So much for faith. Have faith in technology, it works. At least, it has always seemed to have worked because there has been some new resource to tap when the old resource was exhausted, and because the West conveniently forgets those historical periods when no resource could be found and the technologies depleted people's resources and left them stranded.

In the twentieth century, we are viewing the continuation of the drama of Western man in his quest to stay one step ahead of disaster. Until now, the West has continually adopted technologies with disastrous results, but for more than four centuries it has been possible, whenever things went wrong, to simply move on to new frontiers.

Ever since the West embarked on this path, necessity has truly been the mother of invention. What has changed has been what was necessary.

Some years ago, a comedy film sequence circulated that depicted a man who had spilled ink on a rug. To remove the stain, he had to get some ink remover, but the bottle cap was stuck. To open the bottle, he got a pair of pliers, but those were rusted together. To fix the pliers, he had to get a can of oil, but the oil wouldn't flow out of the can so he needed a pin to open the hole. And he couldn't find a pin.

Something similar to that has been happening to technology over the past two centuries or so. The Industrial Revolution set in motion some entirely new processes and brought forth some new problems. Industrial technologies that the conventional wisdom said benefited everybody also produced dangerous by-products. Paper mills produced a lot of paper but also produced a lot of effluence and the people of Minneapolis had to build eighteen water-purification plants to put the water into a condition that people could stomach. The cheap technology was never developed that could remove all the chemicals, and if everybody's drinking water was filtered through activated charcoal filters or distilled, true water purification would cost more than the entire dollar benefits of the industries that polluted the rivers in the first place. The problem with most technologies since the Industrial Revolution is that they involve the production of some kind of toxic chemical—lead emissions from cars, sulphuric acid compounds from steel mills, carbon oxides from just about everything that burns—and the scale of those toxic chemicals has reached cataclysmic proportions.

Civilization-supportive technologies have always been ecologically destructive. We are now reaching a crisis whereby modern technologies have made much larger cities possible and have speeded up the process of habitat decay that in Mesopotamia took millennia. In fact, the industrial age may last only a few centuries before acid rains and chemical poisons of many types condemn all complex organisms in the Northern Hemisphere.

The technologies of the twentieth century need to be approached with the same kind of materialist critique as was applied to the economics of the nineteenth century by writers like Karl Marx. How much does a certain technology—say, coal-generated electrical power—cost the society when all the costs are included, including the costs of acidified land and forests, fish life and fuel transportation costs, acid runoffs and strip-mined land? Can we begin to evolve a methodology—a technology of social critique—that weighs things in terms of Hopi thought—i.e., biomass costs? If we take a simple "essential technology" of the 1980s world, and we then apply a regional analysis of its cost in biomass terms, we may find that we are rapidly eroding something that may be termed the Life Supportive Index (LSI) of that area. And if we analyze the present technologies and their impact on North America, we may find that they are uneconomical in the LSI balance book, even if we apply a price tag to the resources in dollar terms. It seems inevitable that we will find that the kind of society we live in today is in fact a physical impossibility over the long run (the centuries-long run) and that what will be possible will require, out of necessity, an entirely new approach to the purpose of technology.

Right now, we are looking at the possibility that this culture will designate all the Northern Hemisphere as a "national sacrifice area." The present technologies have the ability to destroy the life-support potential of huge areas of North America to the point that no culture, as we know it, can survive in those regions affected.

The television images of the future that are being pumped into the head of America's children offers the version of a future holocaust with total or near total destruction of the Natural World. The survivors of that holocaust, according to these TV writers, will be those techno aristocrats who find some answers in the form of man-produced and man-controlled environments. Their scenario seems to be about half right. The holocaust part seems logical, and the idea that different technologies will be employed by humans thereafter, but will that process (assuming human survival) produce the automatic-door–controlled-environment city that we are presented in popular science fiction?

Highly complex technologies have tended to disappear with past civilizations. The Etruscans developed incredibly sophisticated ways of fusing tiny gold balls into decorative patterns more than two thousand years ago. Modern science has been able to duplicate the effect, but we're still not certain how they did it then. People built great pyramids in Egypt and in Mexico, and Peru, but the technology of stone cutting and moving was lost for hundreds of generations. There are numerous other examples of lost technologies, but one must ask why techniques of doing things could become forgotten.

Perhaps it was because those techniques of doing things cost those societies more than they could afford to pay. We should consider those questions when we look at technology from the perspective of the twentieth century. Technologies that generate centralization and that support that centralization are the very ones that pose a danger to the LSI of our environment, just as similar (and now antiquated) technologies for the same purpose destroyed the LSI of civilizations past.

When the West makes an error, it tends to compensate for that error by continuing to make the same mistake, only at an accelerated rate. Those TV writers have it all wrong. They are telling the children of North America that supercivilization technology got us into this mess, and super-supercivilization technology will get us out. That's crazy.

The Hopis are right. The power lines are a symbol of the end of this world as we know it.

Small, Indian, and Beautiful:
Development through Appropriate Technology

Not too long ago, I visited the Native Self-Sufficiency Center (NSSC) in upstate New York. The NSSC is an effort by some Iroquois people to develop practical alternatives to reservation life as it exists today. They have built houses—a log house and an underground house with solar orientation. Photovoltaic cells charge batteries that operate lights and other utilities, and wood is used for heat for the houses as well as for the water. They are planning fruit production and animal husbandry projects.

There are few places in Indian Country where the discussions at the dinner table are as positive as they are here. Have you seen the latest plans for installing a hydraulic ram? What about small-scale production of electricity on-site using water power? Discussions about alternative technologies, cheaper ways to build things, possible cottage industries, and food production are the standard fare here. Many of the items discussed are actually tried on the site, and many of the attempts are successful.

The enthusiasm and overall direction of the NSSC is badly needed in Indian Country. Indians suffer the lowest per capita income of any group in America. Although they own apparently significant areas of land and resources, they are not the primary beneficiaries of the wealth extracted from their lands. A few tribes, for example, own significant coal deposits. On the average, Indians realize about 4 percent of the dollar value of the coal taken each year from their lands. The other 96 percent accrues to the huge energy companies that mine the coal under lease arrangements that were approved by the federal government. Those with oil and gas deposits do little better: about 13 percent versus 87 percent to the corporations.

Nine out of ten reservations, however, have no significant mineral or energy deposits. On most reservations the primary resource is agricultural lands. Indians reap only about 36 percent of the dollar value of the agricultural production of their lands. The rest accrues to non-Indian farmers and ranchers.

The result is an Indian per capita income of about $1,850 in 1980 compared to a national average per capita income of $8,773. A major contributing factor to this numbing poverty is the fact that Indians have been unable to develop their resources (their agricultural potential) and are therefore impoverished. There are a number of reasons for this impediment to self-development: lack of capital, lack of access to markets, the realities of the American market economy, federal policies that directed energies elsewhere, bad advice, to name a few.

Conventional farming appears to be a logical solution, but it has been an abysmal failure on the reservations. A part of the reason is that it is a failure in America generally. Small farmers and even medium-sized farmers face bankruptcy every year. American agricultural policy favors the big farmer to the detriment of the small farmer and everybody else, and Indians fall into the category of small farmers.

The current agricultural markets are inaccessible to Indians. America is drowning in surplus food: cheese, wheat, corn, dried milk, etc. It has been estimated that if all the surplus food were loaded in boxcars on a single train, that train would stretch from Bangor, Maine, to Kansas City, Missouri. Paradoxically, premium prices are being paid for "organically" produced foodstuffs because such foods are in short supply.

Organic foodstuffs are produced by technologies that are generally not conventional. They are produced by organic farmers who do not use chemical fertilizers, herbicides, or pesticides and who increasingly do not use big machinery or necessarily large acreage. Organic farming is part of an alternative farming movement, one which implies and supports various alternative lifestyles.

Indians could adopt the mentality necessary to begin to produce the kinds of agricultural products for which there is a market. They could, if they became self-reliant enough to break away from the standard prescriptions of government and industry and all the institutions that discourage that direction. And, if Indians looked to "appropriate" technologies they could conceivably lead the way in that direction.

Appropriate technologies could be a path to support a self-reliant lifestyle. The list of possible adaptations is long; it includes owner-built homes incorporating energy-conservation principles. New houses in America now cost in the range of ninety thousand dollars, but owner-built units can cost one-fifth as much. People in rural areas don't have the income to support the conventional costs of either construction or maintenance of such houses. Nothing on the horizon, not government housing, heat-assistance programs, or food stamps, is available to adequately meet people's needs for shelter, heat, and food.

"Alternative energy sources" in practice means developing alternatives to high wintertime electric and oil bills. Alternative agricultural technologies would be those that produce the food for which there exists a market. Alternative lifestyles could mean ways of life that are controlled by the Indian people.

Alternative technology as applied to agriculture may hold the key to a prosperous lifestyle for Indian peoples. It could mean use of solar and solar-assisted greenhouses in food production, the use of organic compost, wide-row planting, double-dug plant beds, and the many other techniques that may enable Indians to produce the kind of food for which there is no surplus and for which there is a market. In addition, some of these technologies do not require a huge capital investment. And even if the potential for market gardening is limited for many people, small-scale food production for family consumption has advantages of saving money at the grocery store and providing very good food and the pleasures of physical activity outdoors.

It is absolutely certain that in most areas of the country food can be grown organically. The technology exists for water conservation in arid environments. There are techniques for growing significant amounts of traditionally labor-extensive crops on small acreage. Many things are possible. Indian people need to begin cultivating a self-reliant mentality. This is not to argue that people need to bootstrap their way to prosperity, that people are poor because they are lazy, or because they have given up. It is to state simply that one of the requirements for a solution is self-reliance, and self-reliance includes a mental attitude. That mental attitude will be very hard for people who have been so poor for so long to acquire, but it is necessary if we are to see the emergence of economic growth in Indian communities. Beyond this desired attitude, people will need an array of supportive services, including training in ways to do things, help in finding funding to do even the minimal task, and help in skills ranging from bookkeeping to electronics. Some models, like those presently found at the NSSC, need to be built so that people can see these things working for themselves. Economics need to be integrated into lifestyle: it is not enough that we devise ways to make money, we must also lead the way in learning to conserve our resources, including money.

I can't predict where the self-reliance mentality of the people at the Native Self-Sufficiency Center will lead. What I can see is the potential. A potential market for organically grown produce that could be organized on Indian lands. A potential for Indian people to take hold of technologies that could help them save money while affording a comfortable life. It is self-reliant thinking that offers the potential for positive change in Indian Country. That, and a developed ability to find ways for Indian people to use the resources they have to enter into the market economy to the extent they find the market economy necessary to their needs. Appropriate technologies seem an inevitable part of that formula.

Part III
Nation and Governance

The "Disappearing Indian": Twentieth-Century Reality Disproves Nineteenth-Century Prediction

Thomas Jefferson was among the first to express the expectation that the Indian nations would disappear as a result of progress. Jefferson expected the Indians to melt away at the approach of American settlers. This tradition of American nationalism evolved into Manifest Destiny, a kind of utopian ideology suggesting that some irresistible higher power was clearing the Indian from the land as part of a divine plan. This idea evolved into the imagined "disappearing Indian," but history indicated that the Indian was not disappearing fast enough—and this disappearance would require some assistance. Two phenomena occurred almost simultaneously: the policy of forced assimilation and the myth of the vanishing race of Indians.

In 1889, Supreme Court Justice John Marshall Harlan summarized the idea of the disappearing Indian in a lecture at George Washington School of Law:

> [The Indian race]…is disappearing and probably within the lifetime of some that are now hearing me there will be very few in this country. In 100 years you will probably not find one anywhere. It is as certain as fate that in the course of time there will be nobody on this North American continent but Anglo-Saxons. All other races are steadily going to the wall. They are diminishing every year.

In 1879, Captain Richard Pratt, a major in the US Army who had dealt with prisoners of war, extended his sense of combat to the schoolroom when he founded the Carlisle Indian School. It is not surprising that Indian boarding schools have been compared to the Nazi concentration camps given certain similarities: trainloads of children arrived at a strange place, their hair was cut, and they were forbidden from speaking their own tongue and punished if they did. They were dressed in military-style uniforms, subjected to the regimented indignities of military prison life and directed to become Christians. The purpose, famously stated by Pratt, was to "kill the Indian, and save the man." In a sense, it was here that the Indian, paradoxically, had finally come into being and embraced the idea of being Indian. He was, it turned out, a product of oppression.

In the spring of 1971, Thomas Banyacya, spokesperson for the Hopi traditional councils, was invited to speak at the University at Buffalo. He was a short, stocky, soft-spoken man who almost always wore clothing that identified him as Hopi. He was a man of outspoken convictions. "*Hopi* means 'peace,'" he would say, and he lived by that. During World War II, when confronted with the military draft, Banyacya refused to go and was sentenced to prison for his actions. He did not talk about that, but to know the man was to understand what a prisoner of conscience is. Banyacya was, in his quiet, peaceful, nonprovocative way, a man of great courage, conviction, and integrity. Above all, he believed in and acted on the Hopi way.

While in Western New York, he asked for a tour of the Niagara Frontier. We took him along the Ontario side of the river to Niagara Falls, then crossed back to New York and went along the gorge to the Robert Moses Dam. This is where public electricity was first created in the United States. The region is a study in the archaeology of industrial technology. Arriving at the power dam, Banyacya asked us to stop the car. He got out and studied the remarkable maze of gigantic electrical transmission wires. Most of us had seen transmission wires before, here and in many places around the country, including the Four Corners area, where Banyacya lived. But these were, in his eyes, somehow different. After a long time, he finally sat back in the car and asked us to proceed.

"It was prophesied a long time ago," he said, "that in the future, in the beginning of the final days, there would appear on the earth spider webs. When we see these, it is time for the Hopi to go forward and warn the world that the balance of nature is being destroyed and that there are very great consequences for humankind when that happens." He had seen the fulfillment of that prophecy in the power complex at the Niagara Reservoir. He had seen it with Hopi eyes. Most Americans would look at that scene and see progress and the necessities of the good life. To Banyacya, it was a warning about a world headed in a dangerous direction. Most of us can understand something of the sentiment he expressed, but few would feel the way he felt that day.

Culture provides the lens that lends meaning to what we see. Through the Hopi cultural lens, one sees something quite different from that seen by a person with an Anglo-American lens. Our cultures tell us what things mean, and meaning is of primary importance.

The identity of the Indian has always been and continues to be an enigma to the Western mind. When Christopher Columbus set sail across the Atlantic, he was hoping to reach the spice islands of Indonesia—the Indies. When he arrived off the shores of Santo Domingo in the Caribbean, he thought he had found them and mistakenly dubbed the peoples who lived there "Indians." To his dying day, he never admitted that the people he encountered might not be the people he thought they were. At the same time that he projected a mistaken identity on the peoples he met, he also started renaming the mountains, rivers, and islands after places in Spain and Spanish history and mythology. The process of colonization involves the imaginary transformation of the unfamiliar to the familiar. In the eyes of the European, the Carib or Arawak, once named Indian, could be whatever the European imagination made him to be. All that was known of him for certain was that he was not European, but the new name made him a European invention. The Indian was a fiction—another people's fiction at that.

The term came to be applied to peoples representing thousands of cultures, speaking hundreds of languages, from the Arctic Circle to Tierra del Fuego. These peoples represented a vast cultural diversity and did not think of themselves as one people or a category of people within all the others that inhabited the hemisphere. Each of these peoples had a version of its own religion (or spiritual traditions), a history unique unto itself, and a wide range of cultural markers ranging from foods, clothing, geography, and even alliances with other peoples. They were and are distinct peoples.

These peoples were never confused about who they were. Each had a name for themselves and an elaborate network of stories that existed to give themselves, their institutions, and their land context and meaning in their own languages. Most, if not all, of these peoples had elaborate and ancient rules about membership in their nations. The eastern woodlands peoples had ceremonies and customs with the force of law to bring people into their nations including requirements that they enjoy sponsorship, have at least some knowledge of the language and culture, and renounce membership in other nations. To be "adopted" into the Mohawk Nation in the seventeenth century involved a whole change of identity, including a new name, clan, family, nation, language, and set of laws. Once this transformation was completed, it was the custom not to mention one's nation of origin. Membership rules were even more elaborate than contemporary notions of citizenship in the United States or many other nation-states. In their own languages, under their own rules and practices, the identity of the members of indigenous groups was generally unambiguous and positive.

The early Europeans usually came into contact with individual indigenous peoples through introductions by other peoples, often peoples with whom they were at war or at least in competition. Many Indian nations thus have names that were given to them by their enemies or their hostile neighbors, and those names were adopted by Europeans. Thus we have the Navajo, the Sioux, the Mohawk, the Seneca, the Chippewa—all names common in European languages but not the names these peoples had for themselves. The identities of many indigenous nations became flawed early on as a result of the hegemony of the English language.

Flawed interpretations continue today as some people have begun to give English definitions to indigenous terms. One example of this is *Haudenosaunee*. This was originally an Onondaga term intended to distinguish peoples who lived in settled villages and groups of longhouses from peoples who moved from one hunting camp to the next. It means, "the people who build [permanent] longhouses." The English designated these peoples as the Six Nations; the French called them Iroquois, a derivation of an Algonquin term meaning "black snakes," "real adders," or "snake people." The term *Iroquois* came to be used as the collective name for the six tribes of the Iroquois Confederacy or the League of the Six Nations, an umbrella that referred to the member nations now known as the Seneca, Cayuga, Onondaga, Oneida, Tuscarora, and Mohawk in the English language. Over time, *Haudenosaunee* came to be used interchangeably with *Iroquois, Iroquois Confederacy*, and *the Six Nations* when describing those member nations. Today, uses of the term *Haudenosaunee* raise some interesting questions.

Since before anyone can remember—except for the Tuscarora, who joined the confederacy in 1722—these peoples were united under a constitution, known as the Great Law, and acted as a single nation in their dealings with all other nations. Those parts of the various Seneca, Cayuga, Oneida, and other member nations who have separated from the confederacy can claim membership in their nations but not in the Haudenosaunee, because although they continue their ethnic identity (Cayuga, Oneida, etc.), they uphold new invented political entities, which are not recognized to have membership in the confederacy. This is the case linguistically as well as under Haudenosaunee law and custom.

If a modern group within these nations is separate and distinct from the Haudenosaunee but distinctly a people who were once part of it—a Mohawk community, for example—what is the most accurate way to describe who they are? The Mormons, for example, claim to be indigenous—arising in North America—although they are not indigenous in the sense of existing in North America since time immemorial. They are, in a very definite sense, a new people. But what about a similar group with connections to the indigenous? Let us say there was a Mohawk group that was entirely Christian and had lost their language, their stories about which they are, the continuity of their political traditions, and everything that identified them in 1492. Would they not be, like the Amish, a new people? And although they might have a claim to being Mohawk, an English term, can they also claim to be Haudenosaunee? They could make claim to being a part of this grouping, if *Haudenosaunee* was a word with an English definition. But if it is an Onondaga word, as the Onondaga define it, then they would be "outside the circle" according to Haudenosaunee custom—meaning no longer a part of them. The only meaningful way they could become Haudenosaunee, under the customs and traditions of that group, is if they endeavor to learn the language, carry out the customs, and follow the laws—because that is how the Haudenosaunee define themselves. This is not a moral or legalistic definition but a linguistic and cultural one.

Today, there are dissident factions within Iroquois communities that are diametrically opposed to the Haudenosaunee, yet they make a claim to being traditional and to filling under the banner of the Haudenosaunee. These attempts at redefining the term *Haudenosaunee* pervert and diminish the meaning of the word as it is understood and defined by the traditional Onondaga people.

Identities are part of the creative process of human cultures, and people are continually inventing and reinventing themselves. This is especially true in America and is true of tribes. People can pretend to be who they claim they are, but the claim is not always valid. Some groups are motivated to make a claim based on some perceived benefit, reward, or property right. The hypothetical Christian Mohawk group might think that claiming to be Haudenosaunee enhances claims to sovereignty and enhances legitimacy, but the claim itself may not be legitimate. The Haudenosaunee vigorously deny that they follow a religion. Christian Mohawks might claim that traditional Mohawks are simply one of a number of religious groups within the overall definition of who is Mohawk. But the Haudenosaunee claim that theirs is a specific way of life, with a tradition of laws, customs, and languages—and not simply a religion or a particular governance structure.

The argument that a way of life is distinct from a religion is compelling under inspection. "A way of life" describes not what a group or person believes but what they do or do not do, giving a much clearer definition of what it means to be and what one claims to be. Identity in many ways reflects cultural understanding and engagement. One gains one's social identity partly by how one reveres and respects the opinion of others. The children in the boarding schools were challenged with forming an identity all the while removed from the laws and customs of their own people.

Today, nearly two centuries of acculturation policy has altered and eroded collective Native identities with state and federal laws and policies and the legacies of institutions such as the boarding schools. Through no fault of their own, Native people have been distanced from the laws and customs that define them as distinct peoples. This loss of culture, much more than intermarriage or education, is the source of identity confusion in Indian Country. Many indigenous groups have begun to reevaluate the regressive impact of colonization and the psychological denial of colonization on their peoples.

The Indian has not disappeared, but his identity has undergone many changes, as external forces prompt tribes and Native individuals to reinvent themselves again and again. Native efforts to reclaim indigenous identities with meaningful, cultural engagement will ensure that the Indian does not disappear. The issue of identity is among the most daunting matters that need to be addressed in Native communities—but this is a positive and spiritually enhancing step on the path of discovery.

The Future Is the Family

A few years ago, there was a religious convention at the Tonawanda Reservation in Western New York. I think of that time often. One of the oldest men of the Six Nations was there, and we talked for a long time. He was a speaker and leader of the traditional religion, a soft-spoken and sincere man, whom I remember best for a gentleness that was a part of him. There was a quality about him that isn't common any longer: he had a strong and honest place in his heart for the People.

He came to me that day and said that he had heard that I was trying to learn about our religion. The religion of the People of the Longhouse is a very complex one. There are many skills to learn, many explanations, many stories, much music. I am certain it is one of the most complex in the world, for it is the oldest, or I should say it belongs to the family of oldest religions. We still carry on ceremonies that archaeologists today say were carried on by human beings seventy thousand years ago. Our religion contains activities that are similar in some basic ways to the ways of Native people in Australia and Africa. It involves, according to our tradition, the original teachings, passed down from generation to generation, from a time when all human beings in the world were hunters and gatherers. We call these teachings "our original instructions."

"Our religion is really a way of life," the elder said. "It is one of the hardest ways to follow. There are few of us now who really follow that way."

I know he was right. He was one of the people who had turned my mind to that way of life. I wasn't attracted to him because of his words, although I liked his words. What drew men to him and his ways was his strength. In his nine decades of life, he had seen the world turn around and yet he remained compassionate and responsive, and his thoughts were always about the People.

"Why is it that way?" I asked. "Why do the people no longer follow the old ways? Even today, a lot of people say they were good ways. But people don't follow those ways anymore."

What he told me was something that many people would not wish to hear. My friend had grown up in a different world from the one I knew. He was raised in the old ways, and he knew as much as anyone alive about the People. He knew the secrets of our culture, and was one of the headmen of the Six Nations religion. To my knowledge, he lived up to that which we had been taught to expect from a man in his position. As long as I knew him, he never harbored a negative thought for anyone.

"In those days, most of the people here raised their own food. People didn't have much, but it seems that they got along all right. We came here to hear the religion. In the afternoon, the people gathered together in the longhouse to talk about what they had heard. I was a young man at that time, I was just learning about these things.

"Some of the people here told us about a problem they were having in this community. There was a woman here who had been brought to our attention. They told us that this woman had been all around the community, that many of the men had known her. It was a thing of great concern at the time. The people here said that such a thing was unknown among the [Longhouse] People.

"The people talked about it that afternoon. They said that what has happened is that our People are taking up too much of the European [sic] ways, and that if this continued, we would lose our own ways."

I know what he meant. He wasn't talking about morality; he was simply stating a fact. We had talked many times and I knew that he felt that many of our People no longer really lived the old ways, with their high dose of respect for truthful relationships. But he always had hope whenever he saw young people who might try to be Iroquois again. He knew that as long as there were a few young people really dedicated to following the old ways that the culture would go on and that possibly the People would come back to it someday.

He wasn't saying that the woman was evil or that our people didn't know about adultery by both men and women. The religion talks about such things, and such things went on in earlier times. But until that time, the community was able to exert some kind of sanction against such behavior. This time, the Longhouse was admitting that it no longer had the power it once had to deal with family problems that, in the past, it could have affected.

When we talked about the decline of our culture, the old people pointed to the evidence of the decline of our families. Only a short time ago, our People had large, strong families. It is much less true today. Probably less than one-half of the children under five years old are living in the same house with their natural fathers. Young people are not well advised and marriages do not last. The family, and with it the old ways, are under tremendous pressure.

The thoughts of the old people are strong. They said that all people needed to be happy was to learn to appreciate the things we have, to be grateful. And they pointed out that there was much to be grateful for. (Years later, I found myself looking up a dictionary definition of *happiness*. It was defined as "a feeling of good fortune.") And one of the truths that the old people stressed was that the quest for material goods makes people unhappy. All you need for a good life, they said, was a strong belief that the Creator had provided for the people, a good mind toward the people, and a will to help others.

Over the past seventy years, it seems that fewer and fewer people are in pursuit of that good life. The result, logically, has been a great deal of misery, which is arguably a contemporary reality. It is as though something enormous has happened and that somehow people have been sold a bill of goods, to the effect that everywhere we look we can see that people really aren't living natural ways.

There are a few sincere people who will argue that natural ways are not good ways. The natural way means living close to the earth. It means eating foods that are natural to the region you are living in and that have not been processed. It means avoiding the use of harmful chemicals, such as refined sugar and food preservatives. It means plenty of exercise and fresh air and much attention to the well-being of the body. The natural ways require an abstinence from such things as alcohol. Ask anyone who knows anything about health—those ways are good for you, they will add many years to your life. Those ways will keep you fit and physically active much longer and help to keep people's minds healthy.

Most people in North America do not live those ways any longer. Over the past century, there has been a tremendous propaganda campaign to convince people that there are other, better ways. Since birth, most of us have been subjected to an argument that we should be drinking soda pop and eating canned spaghetti, and the effort has been successful enough that such things dominate our food culture. The reality is that most people have been motivated by advertising to be consumers of unnecessary and even undesirable products of modern technology.

We have always been told of the advantages of modern society. There is more wealth, more goods, more services, more ease, less work. We have rarely been told the costs, in terms of people's lives and misery, that modern society has extracted from each of us, even those people in North America who have seemingly benefited from all the "advances." The modern age and its consumer values have altered, in very basic ways, the very structure of human society.

Most people agree that the modern family is an institution that is presently under a great deal of stress, although people disagree somewhat about the source and nature of that stress. Most people can probably agree, however, that the family in modern society has undergone great changes over the past century, and it might be helpful to look to the nature and history of changes for sources of the present conditions.

The most significant change that the family has faced has been in the area of functions. Those changes are mainly attributable to that process in modern history known as the Industrial Revolution, a process that truly revolutionized much of the basic structure of the society. The Industrial Revolution reduced drastically the number of functions that the family traditionally performed. Prior to that time, the family was the major unit of production, at least in most rural and agricultural societies. It is fairly clear that one of the first things that happened as a result of the Industrial Revolution was that the function of production gradually left the home, and thus the family gradually ceased to perform much of that function.

In order for the extended Indian family to survive, before layering into other systems it must perform at least five basic functions for its members: production, reproduction, education, judicial, and religious/psychological functions. Societies—for which the extended family is foundational—that are vital and functioning entities are those that have some means of producing the food, clothing, and shelter that its members need and that also have means of controlling the social organization of those functions.

In addition to the obvious needs of production, societies must also provide ways for members to reproduce and replace the population. The social organization that surrounds and controls reproduction includes societal rules concerning marriage: who can marry whom and when, as well as questions concerning the rate of population increase and decrease, questions of adoptions, and so forth. A society that fails to be able to deal with these questions must eventually cease to exist.

Societies must also provide for the education of its members. A vital society must provide a means of socialization that instructs people in the skills and required code of behavior necessary for the material and social production of that particular society. Such skills include proficiency in the society's particular language and an ability to function within the social institutions of the specific group. The dying members must be replaced through this socialization process, and education that provides the function of training people in the skills necessary for the perpetuation of the group or nation. Thus, education must be seen as a socialization process, for that is the function that the educational process performs for societies.

There must be some way of settling disputes within any group for it to continue functioning in a productive way, as a group. That means, ultimately, that some people must function in roles as judges, referees, advisors, and so forth, and they must have the power, either through force, persuasion, or a combination of both, to enforce their decisions. In that respect, the judicial function (and many societies manage the judicial function spoken of here without courts or legal systems as are common in the West) inevitably infringes into the other areas of societal life. There are many ways in which people have handled this function, but all vital societies have, in one way or another, done so.

Finally, societies must provide some sources of psychological support and/or spiritual direction for their members. This, too, takes many forms. Basically, people need to have some sense of identity, some feeling of purpose, and some sense of integration into the society as a whole, and traditionally societies have organized ways to provide support of that kind.

A century ago, for the majority of American people, and certainly for rural Indians, those five needs were met, to some degree, by the institution known as the family. Nineteenth-century American life was largely rural, composed of agricultural family units. In that setting, the family was the major unit of production. The rural family raised its own food and produced much of its own clothing, even in the period when it bartered for cloth. The family members produced their own tools, built homes, and to a comfortable degree provided at least some security for its older members.

It is also true that, to a considerable extent, agricultural societies tend to support extended families (three or more generations) rather than nuclear families. They also extend laterally in the incorporation of aunts and uncles and generations of cousins. The point is that, prior to the Industrial Revolution, the societal institution that we call the family was far more functional than it is today and that it performed, at least on some level, each of the five functions that a a larger society must perform if it is to survive. The family of the nineteenth century functioned to meet the needs of its members.

This can be readily seen in the area of marriage. Families during the last century probably had much greater influence in the area of mate selection than is generally recognized. The young man who went courting most often fell under the scrutinizing eye of his prospective bride's parents and/or grandparents, and they were interested primarily in his history in the area of stability and level of responsibility and were able to exert a great deal of influence in the matter.

Some sociologists believe that societal institutions have vitality and power in direct relation to their ability to be functional. When the West was an agricultural society, it is true that the family functioned to meet its members' needs, and vice versa. Parents and grandparents were largely the teachers and advisors of the young. In the area of socialization (education) there was a high level of interaction between mother and daughter, father and son, children and grandparents. The relationship, at least ideally, was cooperative and symbiotic. Children were needed and welcome because they helped to increase overall production (in such societies, children are viewed as definite and necessary assets and are not viewed as burdens) and also to provide security for the parents in old age. Parents functioned as friends and teachers and also often settled internal disputes and acted as advisors in a great many areas. However we view the period, it must certainly be concluded that families were generally far more functional than they are at present and that functionality was a major factor in the stability of the family.

As was mentioned earlier, the Industrial Revolution changed all that. During the Industrial Revolution, production was removed from the home and centered in factories. The process did not take place over night, but it seems fairly clear that the process of industrial production became the major cause of the decline of the family in the West. As adult members (and at some periods, even children) left the home to work in the factories, the family ceased to function as a productive unit and became increasingly a unit of consumption. As the process evolved, the functions that formerly served to unify and stabilize the family were gradually replaced by other institutions that were created because those functions were being neglected.

The education system, as we know it, was a product of this time. Today, education is largely concerned with transmission of skills necessary for industrial production and generally does not produce a socialization process that would support stability in the family. As the family ceased to be the major production unit (and at the same time became increasingly a consumer unit), it ceased also to be able to control and influence the behavior of its members in many areas. Marriages became increasingly unstable because people were no longer socialized to support the family, and that happened because the family's functions and ability to function were greatly decreased by the changes in culture brought on by the Industrial Revolution.

The Industrial Revolution forced the creation of a number of institutions of modern society that were designed to provide the functions that had once been the providence of the extended family. As people moved into expanding urban areas, it became necessary to create agencies that provided security in case of lay-off or the death of an employable member of the nuclear family. Thus, welfare agencies were created. As the remains of spirituality declined, and as people found themselves increasingly isolated from their own roots and from their own people, there arose a need for psychological-support specialists, and during this period we see the development of modern psychology as a response to this need.

There also developed needs for child psychologists and marriage counselors. Industrial society has found that its people still have the same needs that people have always had. But the process of industrial society has been centralization for the production of people's needs. The result has generally been that there has been enormous production of services in all of these areas, but that most of the needs people have are subjective in nature, and the best efforts of sociologists have been unable to respond to those subjective needs. A social service agency can provide people with the means to obtain food, clothing, and shelter, but it cannot provide the satisfaction people derive from productive work, and that satisfaction is also a great motivation for a wide range of positive behavior. A child welfare agency can see that a child is placed in a situation that provides safety and a degree of material comfort, but such agencies cannot provide the love and sense of belonging that is clearly a necessary part of the socialization of stable adults. And a social security system can provide old people with a means of subsistence, but it cannot respond to the reality of loneliness and the feeling of rejection that is so common in this society among the elderly.

The point is that although modern industrial society has created ways of meeting people's needs, those ways do not always achieve successful results. Today, the family is seen as a unit that primarily functions to meet people's needs for psychological gratification. This is part of the reason that love is presently so widely the sole criteria for marriage. The high rate of divorce and unhappy marriages suggests that the modern family is failing, in a large percentage of cases, to perform that function. One reason that the family is becoming a nonfunctional institution, even in this area of psychological gratification, relates to the selection-of-mate process and to the fact that many of the forces that keep the family together no longer exist in most people's experience.

It is probably true that the nuclear family has never been completely successful at meeting its members' needs. For one thing, it cannot adequately perform many of the five necessary functions simply because if its size, and it is highly vulnerable to accidents such as injury or death. The agricultural extended family was probably more successful at meeting its members' needs, although it suffered weaknesses also, especially in the West.

Native Peoples are the greatest victims of the processes that are presently working to the destruction of the family. Approximately one out of three Native children born this year will be placed in non-Native foster homes. What is happening to Native Peoples has the same effect as if some invaders from Mars arrived and demanded one-third of all the schoolchildren of the United

States to be taken back to Mars, educated there, and forced to become, for all functional purposes, Martians.

The conscious destruction of the Native family is a persistent policy of American people. Native People (especially traditional Native People) lose their children to welfare placement agencies as a result of purely racist policies. If Native People try to raise their children in traditional ways (ways that would, by the way, stabilize the family) the children are removed because they are not meeting white education requirements and because the "standard of living" does not meet that of the administrators.

Native Peoples in the Americas developed societal units of great diversity. The Iroquois, for example, functioned as clans that were kinds of permanent, very large extended families that were not subject to the same weaknesses as were the patriarchal Western extended families. As a societal unit, the clan functioned to meet all of its members' needs. It provided for production and extensive control of reproduction, contained a working judicial system, and practiced its own spiritual traditions. And, of course, it controlled the socialization (education) of its members.

There are, of course, many other forms of societal institutions. In fact, the Western nuclear family is far from the norm. Of the hundreds of cultures in the world, the West may be the only culture in which the nuclear family is considered the norm. The Western family is unique. It also is not functioning very well.

Those Native People who are in some stage of adaptation to Western culture often lose their children because their families are unstable for the same reasons that American society's families are unstable. But Native People are generally poor, and poor people have less chance of being able to exercise any kind of control over their lives.

The Western lifestyle and the Western legal systems are combining to destroy the Native People, and the primary victims of the attack, as in any war, are the children. It is no accident that activists of the Native movement are calling for the strengthening of the family as a way of reversing the processes destroying Native nations and Native People. Last year, at a conference in Manitoba, Mr. Thomas Porter, a spokesman for the traditional people at Akwesasne, said:

People have been asking about the Indian ways. Those ways are not hard to understand. We are supposed to be taking care of one another, of our young, and our old people. We are supposed to plant, to raise food for one another, to help one another. And we are supposed to be faithful to one another.

When there is a woman who is standing with a baby in her arms, there is supposed to be a man next to her, to help carry the weight of that baby. And the two of them are supposed to climb into a harness, just like a team of horses, and pull together, all the way through life.

The family is not disintegrating only because it has lost its functions. Functional decline explains a great, and is, perhaps, major cause of the problem, but is inadequate to explain the specifics of people's behavior.

The older traditional people of the longhouse say that the real ways of the People are nature's ways. And how do we come to know those ways? By observing Nature, by watching the birds and the animals and the other beings of nature. It is an interesting method of viewing the world and one that I am confident will stir mixed reactions among Western people.

The wolf, for example, is a hunter of the deer herd. He is monogamous, taking but one mate throughout life. And he is known as a very family-oriented species. It is said that the wolf family is very close and affectionate, that they look to the well-being of their cubs as their first priority. It is also said that they raise cubs in a kind of group effort and that they practice a kind of birth control. The old Indian people say that the wolf is a very intelligent animal and that he possesses something that, in English, we would call a noble character. He is a follower of the natural ways.

People have a domestic cousin of the wolf in many households. The domestic dog, however, bears mostly a biological relationship to the wolf. The dog's behavior, from birth, is specialized to serve humans, not its own species. And the dog is not monogamous; in fact, it forms no real families at all. The dog is a total slave to humans and cannot survive in most cases without humans. But whenever the domestic dog escapes, it begins to run in packs, form dens, and form something like families.

I point to the analogy, not to state that people should live like wolves, but to emphasize that the natural ways support behavior that promotes the survival of the species. Of course, the survival of the species depends on the survival of the young. The wolf's behavior is specialized to the survival of its young, the dog's is not.

People in modern society have a similar kind of problem. Their behavior is no longer specialized to the needs of the human species specifically. Their behavior is specialized to the needs of modern technological industrial society. That is why people today are such consumers. It is why they cannot move toward natural lifestyles. It is why families are not stable.

Modern industrial society does not require stable family more than people require dogs to have families. In fact, the society is based on the need of children to learn highly specialized skills and to leave the home to practice those skills wherever the jobs may be. That is why the society is so mobile.

The traditional people urge the reestablishment of natural ways of life as a way of strengthening and promoting family unity. It is, as so many have attested, a hard life, but one that has true rewards. And it is a road that requires that we reconsider some of our most cherished fantasies, especially in the area of love between mates.

Love has an appreciative quality. The spiritual ways are based on the belief that every living thing wants know it is wanted and needed, including people. Love can be a thing to lift and motivate the spirit. But for love to be real, the things that are needed and appreciated need to be real also. Most love in our world is fantasy. It is based on things not real but apparent (appearance). But it can be real. It can be based on things that other people do that support our lives and on the feelings derived when we do things to support other people's lives. For it to be real, we must be functional human beings and not simply consumers. We must be producers and not people who acquire. Love requires that we become specialized in our behavior to serve the needs of the people in our lives and not be in the service to the abstract, distant industrial society. We must, in short, relearn to serve our own species.

The old people said that the natural ways are the ways of Real People and that if we leave those ways our children will become confused, and there will be much suffering. They also said that if we leave those ways, we might destroy all life on this earth. Whenever I think of those teachings, I am always faced with some unnerving facts. When the US government or the big corporations tell us not to worry about the drought or the oil shortage, they are telling us not to worry, to go on buying food and gasoline. They have something they want to sell to us.

But the traditional Native People don't have anything to sell. When they tell us to follow the Creator's ways, to have families and to be good to children and to be faithful wives and husbands, there is nothing to buy, no buttons to wear, and no music in the background. When they urge us to live the right way, I know what they mean. And in this crisis-ridden time, it seems to be the best advice on the market.

Indian Nations, the United States, and Citizenship

In the beginning, the question of how to view Indian nationhood and citizenship wasn't a question at all. We are reminded that how things came to be the way they are evolved in a history entirely outside the control, and indeed outside the view, of the indigenous peoples of the world. We are further reminded that the evolution of the idea of citizenship, and its application to indigenous peoples, is an idea that has been created and molded to suit the needs of people other than the subjects.

In some areas of Indian Country, the concept stirs deep passions. There are many among the Haudenosaunee who deny that they are citizens of any country other than their own Native nation, while some, notably Oklahoma Indians, assert dual citizenship regularly. Still others are confused about their citizenship and regularly reply that they are US citizens, without thought of their indigenous nation.

The reason for this state of confusion lies not so much in the absence of information as in the fact of vagueness about how and why indigenous peoples of the Americas were confronted with the idea of citizenship. Citizenship was, and for many Indian peoples remains, an alien idea, and for good reason.

Lawyers can argue about the exact legal definitions, which cloud the term. Social historians can affirm that at the time of the Columbian encounter, at the end of the fifteenth century, citizenship as practiced on the European continent was predictably different from the concept as used today. The world's indigenous peoples are, of course, a special case, even though indigenous peoples worldwide suffer similar problems coping with the intrusions of states. Throughout the history of the European expansion and subsequent invasions of the Americas, Asia, and Africa (as well as numerous places, such as Australia and islands without number), European imperialists encountered distinct indigenous peoples all over the globe.

It is extremely enlightening, for the purpose of determining the identity of the indigenous nations (as opposed to the extent of the rights and obligations of "citizenship"), that we begin our tale at the beginning. The most interesting work on the subject of European law, as it existed during the centuries leading to the

Columbian era, is by Harold J. Berman entitled *Law and Revolution: The Formation of the Western Legal Tradition* (1983). This work covers a lot of territory but, on the subject of citizenship, Berman points out that during the centuries prior to Columbus, legal customs had arisen on the continents that spoke to the issue of citizenship.

In feudal Europe, there arose a peculiar way of viewing the land. In some sense, land and country were indistinguishable. England was, in the custom of the day, the sum of its parts, and its parts were Sussex, Essex, etc. The people who represented those parts were the aristocracy, thus York was not only a geographic area, but also a person. When the king ordered, as he sometimes did, "Go and fetch York," everyone in the kingdom knew who he was talking about. Feudal relationships define humans as assets that belong to the land or "go with" the land. The centuries have blurred our ability to understand that in twelfth-century France a person was born to a place, that place was ruled by an aristocrat, and the aristocrat was, at least in theory, beholden to a sovereign.

Thus, the sovereign owned the kingdom; it was his to do with as he pleased, in theory, or as he could get away with in practice. A serf born to a district was perceived as a person who "went with" the property. He was, in effect, little better than a chattel slave, a person owned by a military aristocracy, which, during some periods, held unlimited sway over his life and property. Beginning about the eleventh century, this began to change in some parts of Europe.

One of the elements of change was the rise in Europe, during these centuries, of cities. The cities were unlike the rural subdivisions of the kingdom in that gradually they obtained a degree of autonomy from the system of feudal lords. In time, the cities came to be, in practice, havens from the arbitrary and sometimes brutal rule of the aristocrats. A practice arose that enabled a person who found his way into the confines of a city and who was able to survive for a year and a day to become a citizen (literally, from the Greek, meaning "a person who lives in a city"), and, in time, citizenship meant that the city-state guaranteed that person certain rights. Predictably, the first right was against capture and forced reenslavement at the hands of his former master. (This is a very general treatment of this somewhat complex and highly variable subject, but then this is a short paper. Berman goes into it at length.)

Thus far in this story, there are no indigenous peoples. Although there are numerous distinct peoples on the European continent, and although at one time in European history it can be successfully argued that some of these peoples were indigenous in the sense they occupied the land as a distinct people prior to some colonization, for our purposes there were no peoples who were indigenous in the modern sense of that word on the European continent following the Crusades. *Indigenous peoples* is really a term we were forced to invent to distinguish the peoples that occupy a landmass at the time of the European invasion from other peoples, some of whom do not exist at the beginning of that invasion.

The first modern indigenous peoples were the Guanches of the Canary Islands. The Guanches are almost forgotten in American history, but certainly belong in the introduction to any history of the invasion of the Americas. When the Spanish (with some French assistance) first landed on the Canary Islands in 1402, there was a population of about eighty thousand Guanches. The wars to conquer them lasted until 1496, when their final stronghold fell. They were as much victim to the epidemic diseases of Europe as to the Spanish arms, but they were unquestionably victims. Some historians have argued that their descendants can be found on the Canary Islands and the Azores islands, but the Guanches are not identifiable as a distinct people. The Guanches, it can be said, had no rights.

The history of the indigenous peoples of the Canary Islands is a very neat package. It has a beginning, a middle, and, for all practical purposes, an end. The Portuguese discovered an uninhabited island they named Madeira because it was covered with forest. They colonized it with some volunteer settlers. Within a short time, they cleared the island by burning it to the ground and a few years later were raising enough sugarcane to become the number one exporter of refined sugar in the world. Money flowed to the Portuguese crown and a very profitable investment called colonization had been born. Before long, it became clear that to make this investment truly profitable there needed to be a source of cheap labor. The cheapest labor at the time was slave labor, and that's where the Guanches came into the picture.

The Guanches were attacked because they possessed islands that were thought to be potentially profitable possessions and because they were a source of slave labor. The attack on the

Guanches was pure theft and slavery. No one, not even the Spanish, bothered to explain it in terms of advancing Christianity or bringing the benefits of civilization to the benighted. In that regard, the history of the Canary Islands is as refreshingly blunt as is the fact that their conquest and annihilation was brutal.

Christopher Columbus was married to the daughter of one of the governors of one of the Azores islands and is rumored to have engaged in the slave trade. The Guanches, as was mentioned earlier, mostly succumbed to diseases like smallpox and, like the indigenous peoples to follow, didn't make satisfactory slaves because of the death rate. The Spanish quickly adjusted by importing slaves from Africa, where smallpox, chicken pox, and a score of other childhood diseases were already known and where the peoples had developed some immunity to them. A fairly thorough discussion of the Spanish behavior in these eastern Atlantic islands is found in Alfred W. Crosby's excellent book *Ecological Imperialism: The Biological Expansion of Europe, 900–1900* (1986).

From the Canary Islands and the Azores, Columbus set sail for the Asian mainland and landed, instead, on the islands of the Caribbean, where he encountered, we all know, a people he mistakenly dubbed Indians. A pattern of behavior that had been established during the war against the Guanches was then initiated by the Spanish against, first, the peoples of the Caribbean, and then the indigenous peoples of the mainland. The results were, of course, devastating. On some of the islands, the entire population was wiped out, or at least virtually wiped out, by the twin demons of European-introduced epidemic diseases and Spanish cruelty. A pretty good account of that story is found in Karl Sauer's *The Early Spanish Main*.

The Indians presented an interesting dilemma when a dispute between the clergy and the military arose around the identity of the Indians. Bartolomé de Las Casas, a priest, circulated accounts of Spanish cruelty that were published in western Europe and eventually became a source of embarrassment to the Spanish Crown. The Crowns then ordered a debate before the Council of the Indies to settle the question of whether the American Indians were indeed human beings possessed of a soul and, therefore, rightfully the charges of the Holy Roman Catholic Church, or, as some conquistadors asserted, subhumans who had no rights whatever.

The conquistadors hired Ginés de Sepúlveda as their attorney. He argued forcefully that Indians are subhumans. Las Casas argued they had souls and intelligence and could be socialized to be servants of both the Crown and the church. (The best short telling of this story is found in *Aristotle and the American Indian* by Lewis Hanke.) No one argued the Indians are distinct peoples possessed of rights against both church and Crown, and no one questioned to whom the lands belonged. All understood under the doctrines of that time that the land was Spanish land. Somewhat consistently with this line of thinking, centuries later when Spanish colonies became states, most of them included the indigenous peoples as their citizens immediately, in their first constitution.

The English colonization had a slightly different history from the Spanish in both flavor and on the subject of citizenship. The English were watching and envious of Spanish success at plunder in what they called the New World. English adventures across the Atlantic had to wait. By 1565, Spain was the most powerful country on the Atlantic, commanding an empire greater than Rome at its zenith. When a French colony was attempted in Florida, the Spanish arrived and massacred everyone.

The English were undaunted. Beginning about 1565, entrepreneurs sold stock in London to finance a venture to invade Ireland. The source of wealth in Ireland was to be the forest products said to be in abundance there and the lure to some of England's landless poor (victims of a growing process known as enclosure) of an adventure in a foreign land. In Ireland, the English encountered their first indigenous people. The rural Irish were Catholic, a folk who continued to possess a number of cultural traits of their ancestors. Before long, the invading English discovered that the indigenes were seriously flawed in their national character. They were, according to reports flowing into London, pagans in spirit, probably not Christians at all, and rumored to be cannibals.

The purpose of these slanders against the Irish was to provide an excuse to do violence to them in order to drive them from their lands. One of the complaints against the Irish was that they did not improve the land as Englishmen did, and therefore, did not have as much right to it. If the Guanches were to provide Spain with practice in their treatment of the Indians of Latin America, the Irish provided the English with practice in their treatment of

the Indians of North America. An excellent history is by Nicholas
P. Canny, *The Elizabethan Conquest of Ireland: APattern Established
1565–1576.*

The English arrived in what they called New England a generation or so after the defeat of the Spanish Armada in 1588. They
immediately proceeded to take the land in a way that was, at that
point, wholly English. Instead of arguing about whether Indians
were human or not, they concentrated on the land itself. Indians
were unfortunately in the way of English possession of the land.
Every conceivable excuse was mustered to dispossess the Indian of
this land, excuses that had worked during the enclosures in England and the wars in Ireland. Acre by acre the Indians were driven
from the land just as the poor in England had been (and continued
to be) and the Irish had been (and still are). There was not much
discussion in this early phase of history about citizenship, pro or
con. An excellent account of the English in early New England is
found in William Cronon's *Changes in the Land: Indians, Colonists
and Ecology of New England.*

The invasion of North America is told almost entirely from the
eyes of the invader. During the early years, when the English, the
Dutch, the Swedes, and the French were weak, the Indians insisted
on treaty relationships, on a separation of law and territory. Thus,
the earliest agreements have the air of treaties, and the earliest
treaties reflect Indian thinking about cultural diversity and the
right to continue as distinct peoples. Earlier treaties are the now-
famous Two Row Treaty between the Dutch and the Haudenosaunee (Iroquois) and the original Silver Covenant Chain, both
of which declare that the relationships are equal to equal, or, in
modern terms, state to state.

The Europeans were pragmatists. If treaties served to cement
relations, then treaties were to be made. Although it took nearly two
centuries for the colonies to become established enough to challenge
the Indians, English colonists doggedly coveted the land. Unlike the
Spanish, who coveted Indian labor and subservience, the English
coveted mostly land. There are exceptions, but generally this was
the flow. The Spanish debated whether the Indians were human.
The English simply accepted that the Indians were not English.

Thus, not only were the Indians not seen as citizens, but also
the idea never really gained much currency among the colonists

that the Indians would ever be English citizens. The Indians belonged to America, not to England. America was not England, not its land and not its people. That ideological underpinning of British governmental organization and ethnocentrism was to be a major factor that would stimulate the American Revolution.

Pragmatism ruled the day, however, and the English were pristinely pragmatic when it came to doing whatever was necessary to liberate the Indian from land. An excellent account of the transmigration of European thinking to the Americas, especially North America, is found in Francis Jennings's *The Invasion of America: Indians, Colonialism, and the Cant of Conquest*.

It has been argued (see Jennings's early trilogy) that the Seven Years War was the first world war. Jennings argues that the English Crown claimed France had invaded British territory by building a fort at Duquesne because the land in question was part of an Iroquois empire, and the Iroquois empire was British territory. The Crown never claimed the Iroquois were British citizens, however. Land and citizenship are clearly separate under the conditions created by overseas empires and an evolving theory of law that finds the states coming to ownership of the idea of citizenship for their own purposes.

At the time of the American Revolution, there is no question the Americans viewed the Indians as distinct peoples and that they, at least, viewed the Indian nations as distinct nations.

Both the Articles of Confederation and the Constitution of the United States reflect this reality. The new constitution was sought and organized primarily to advance the imperialism of a new republic. It was, on the one hand, a reaction to tax revolts, and on the other hand, to organize an effective army that could deal with issues surrounding what it euphemistically calls the "western lands." The western lands, let us be clear, was Indian Country. The first major American military engagements were against Indians by armies invading Indian nations.

The history of US treatment of Indian nations during the nineteenth century is long and complicated because of the number of different Indian peoples involved, but fundamentally simple in terms of the process that was repeated hundreds of times across the United States. The US government deployed military garrisons on the edge of Indian territories and encouraged frontiersmen to enter and start conflict with the Indians. When the conflict arose, the army reacted by attacking the Indians. The best account of this process I know is found in *A History of the Indians and the United States* by Angie Debo. The Indians were attacked and killed, enslaved and abused, their land seized and their children forced into alien schools solely because they possessed land other people wanted.

The US Constitution treats Indians as noncitizens, and Indians remained noncitizens until 1924. From the time of formation of the United States to the present, the issue of citizenship for Indians has been dealt with by the US government entirely to its own interest. With the possible exception of early court decisions, later ignored, that Indian nations were legitimate in the eyes of the law, the United States has generally acted as though Indian nationhood is simply an inconvenient anachronism of history. Indian nationhood is inconvenient because if the Indian nations are legitimate, US designs for Indian land and labor are not legitimate. Thus, US Indian policy has ignored Indian nationhood whenever possible, even to the point of simply declaring Indian nations no longer exist during the fifties termination era.

During the nineteenth century, when the problem of how to steal Indian land without appearing to steal it was a major consideration, the United States passed laws that enabled non-Indians to sue Indian nations for damages arising out of acts of violence during these conflicts, but denied Indians the standing to sue non-Indians. Indians were clearly noncitizens during this century and, so long as an Indian continued to maintain his rights as an Indian, he was considered a nonperson in the eyes of US law. It was possible for an Indian to become a person. He need only take an allotment of land and renounce his Indian citizenship. Once a citizen of the United States, an Indian was no longer considered an incompetent because he was no longer an Indian!

The US government even constructed a legal concept that Indians, as Indians, are incompetent to manage their own affairs. And the federal government has a responsibility to manage their affairs for them. This insult had the practical application that it allowed the government to transfer the use of significant amounts of Indian assets to non-Indian hands. It became the much vaunted "trust responsibility" theory, which some Indian lawyers seized upon as a way to channel federal dollars to Indians (and Indian lawyers) during the 1970s, and which was put to rest during the Reagan years. The "trust" responsibility is really an insult. To benefit from it, Indians are forced to plead diminished capacity on the basis of race.

Indian nations, on the other hand, have become mystified about their own legitimacy. Most Indian leaders act unaware that over the centuries a few states (about 177 at last count) now claim to own the entire globe. They have a conspiracy among them that whatever goes on inside the territories they claim is nobody's business but their own. Thus, Brazil claims as citizens Indians who have never heard a word of Portuguese and have never heard of Brazil. Other countries of the world, such as Indonesia and India, have been recruited into the scheme of things. Thus, indigenous peoples have no rights in the world because nation-states simply have declared them to be illegitimate and thus have declared all the theft, murder, dispossession, oppression, cruelty, and coercion directed against indigenous peoples, past and present, to be legitimate actions that are wholly the internal affairs of the state and not a cause for complaint at the international level.

In addition, citizenship has become the excuse these criminal states have used to justify their actions. Just as Sepúlveda argued it was acceptable behavior to enslave Indians because enslavement also brought the benefits of civilization, states today argue it is acceptable to take Indian land without due process of law, to deny recognition to an Indian nation as a nation, and to do whatever it wants, in the name of plenary power, and in the name of international law, which effectively bars Indian nations from bringing actions in international forums for even the most outrageous crimes. Although the idea of citizenship may have started as a limitation on the powers of an aristocracy to seize persons and force them to servitude, by the nineteenth century the idea of citizenship became solely owned by the states that were in an international conspiracy to possess the planet at the expense of all the indigenous peoples.

The question is probably incorrectly drawn when framed around whether Indians are citizens. The question should not be whether Indians enjoy the rights under US law, but whether and when Indians enjoy rights under their Indian nationhood. Indian nations are denied legitimacy solely because they committed the crime of owning land somebody else wanted and surviving after the land was taken. Having failed to physically disappear, the Indian nation is now urged to disappear legally, culturally, and psychologically.

The question about citizenship should center on the rights the Indian nations and citizens (if that's the proper term) had prior to the colonization and subsequent reservation period. Certainly Indians enjoyed standing as persons in their relationships with all peoples prior to that time. Certainly Indian individuals were viewed as full adults in the eyes of whatever decision-making process they engaged, and even peoples of different cultures never discriminated against each other in the fundamental ways Indians suffered discrimination and racism at the hands of the United States.

The law around Indian citizenship came at a time when the empires of the world were at their zenith. When the League of Nations was formed, imperial states were faced with the enormous problem that they had militarily occupied most of the world's population, but had not defined membership or nationhood in a satisfactory way. It became popular to declare that everyone born in the world is entitled to citizenship in some country or other, an idea embraced by the Wilson administration. Subsequently, the people of Puerto Rico were granted US citizenship in 1917. The Indians were even more problematic, being neither a colony nor a territory from which the United States had any intention of ever evacuating or withdrawing from and comprising peoples who held a potential claim for very large portions of the claimed US territory.

The obvious answer satisfied both the Indians and the liberals who wanted to see "better" treatment of the Indians. Making the Indians citizens opened the road to correcting a long list of injustices around standing in court and civil rights and also opened the door to the forced assimilation policy, which came to be known as termination. The Indian Citizenship Act of 1924 is worded in such a way it can be construed to confer on Indians the *rights* of US citizenship—specifically rights against unlawful seizure, the right to due process, habeas corpus, to travel overseas, to be a person in the eyes of the law—but does not diminish the Indian's individual rights under his Indian citizenship.

Those rights are not well defended by the Indian leadership in recent years and have not been clearly defined as a political agenda. International forums have debated the issue with only incipient input from the legitimate Indians. Indeed, pretenders have represented themselves as Indian leadership while the legitimate Indian leadership stayed home. Indians logically have a right to all the rights and privileges they enjoyed prior to the armed robbery that characterizes US/Indian relations of the past, and Indian leadership should move to identify those rights and press for them. Indian leadership needs to understand that when they stand as Indians for Indian rights, they are often in direct conflict with US aspirations, and that an Indian allegiance to the United States can be secondary to their allegiance to their own nations because the former, by nature, seeks to eliminate the latter.

Review: *The Spirit of Regeneration: Andean Culture Confronting Western Notions of Development*

The indigenous cultures of the Americas are characterized by a great range of diversity and creativity. One might expect such cultures to generate sophisticated and eloquent critiques of Western colonization, and there have been some, but certainly not as many as might have been expected. There have been resistance movements for the entire period since 1492, of course, but there has not been much in the way of systematic in-depth critiques of Western culture from indigenous intellectuals. There are, to be sure, sentimental reflections and idyllic projections, but few that defend and promote living cultures. This has been true even among indigenous academics.

Until quite recently, few indigenous peoples of the Western Hemisphere had been exposed to the level of education that commands respect on such topics. When India was decolonized, the country was left in the hands of peoples indigenous to the Indian subcontinent, and its educational institutions produced people capable of engaging in an informed critique of Western thought and practices. In the Americas, not a single state government is in the hands of its indigenous people. Spain, for example, left its former colonies in the hands of cultural descendants of the conquistadors who had little connection to the indigenous cultures and, until the 1960s, little interest in exposing indigenous individuals to the fine points of a Western education.

Peru was among the countries to recruit indigenous individuals to universities in hopes such people could solve the daunting problems defined as underdevelopment in the rural countryside. Some of these individuals became dedicated scholars, some became leaders in development initiatives directed at transforming rural indigenous populations, and a few became completely disillusioned with the ideology of Western notions of development. Some of these people founded the Andean Project on Peasant Technologies (PRATEC).

Dr. Frederique Apffel-Marglin's *The Spirit of Regeneration: Andean Culture Confronting Western Notions of Development* is a book by and about PRATEC, a group of Andean intellectuals who have come to identify development as a process that advances the goals of Western colonialism while impoverishing the people, degrading the environment, and attacking the spirit of humanity in indigenous Andean communities. Although its founders are individuals with indigenous backgrounds, their work is not specifically an indigenous revitalization movement or even an indigenous rights movement. PRATEC embodies and intends to share principles with peoples across cultures and continents, and it makes no pretensions about reforming any indigenous culture.

There are, to be sure, individual North American indigenous scholars who address some of the same types of issues—Professor Vine Deloria Jr. comes to mind—but there are no indigenous organizations that have addressed an integration of such varied topics as defending and promoting indigenous agricultural techniques, encouraging biodiversity, promoting cultural practices, critiquing mechanized and chemicalized agriculture and critiquing Western technologies and ideologies as part of an overall program of cultural affirmation. PRATEC's members do all this and more. They believe Western forms of colonialism cannot and will not work in the Andes, that the period of Western domination can be viewed as similar to a plague that has peaked and is now receding and that indigenous cultural practices are the wave of the future. They make an extremely powerful argument that this non-Western point of view deserves careful and reflective evaluation. *The Spirit of Regeneration* is a collection of six chapters written by PRATEC members and a masterful introduction to their work by Apffel-Marglin, a well-published author and member of the Smith College faculty. The introduction—worth the price of the book— provides a necessary context that is clearly intended as part of the text, in keeping with an analysis of the problematics of professionalism she embraces. Other contributors included a founder who passed away in 1996 (Eduardo Grillo Fernández), Grimaldo Rengifo Vasquez, a current PRATEC director, Julio Valladolid Rivera, a former professor of plant genetics, and Greta Jimenez Sardon, a consultant in gender, agroecology, and sustainable development.

The PRATEC organization offers a popular course each year that is attended by numerous teachers from all over Peru and, increasingly, all of Latin America. The message of the organization is thus spreading from the Andes to the peoples of the Americas. Although members of PRATEC have written numerous books in Spanish, this is the first introduction of their works in a book in English. It is a must-read for indigenous scholars and, indeed, everyone seeking a fresh and energetic theory of indigenous resistance that has potential to support a reindigenization of the hemisphere.

Review: *American Indian History: Five Centuries of Conflict and Coexistence*

Robert W. Venables's meticulously researched two-volume survey of Native American history, *American Indian History: Five Centuries of Conflict and Coexistence*, develops a narrative within the context of two bipolar themes. One is the "crowded wilderness." Many European immigrants mistakenly thought that they were discovering a largely empty land that (in the words of more than one Puritan theocrat) had been swept of whatever humanity it had contained by the Puritans' God, for their use. In reality, as modern scholarship has been revealing, the "wilderness" was nearly as crowded in some places (at least before the invasion of smallpox and other diseases) as Europe and Asia. The second duality is "conflict and coexistence." While Venables details the often-bloody nature of the European conquest (and the collective amnesia that today often abets denial of these details), he also describes the synthesis that grew out of the encounter.

Venables's narrative begins with the Spanish conquest. One wonders why the lights should come up at this point in an account meant to provide a Native view of history. Beginning at Columbus's arrival seems to reinforce a view that history did not exist until Europeans arrived to validate it. Why not begin with Native origin accounts, as well as recent findings in archaeology that have steadily moved backward in time the dates that are academically acceptable for first evidence of the first peoples in the Americas?

An author, however, has the right to choose his own historical frame of reference. The history that Venables writes, he does very, very well. Venables takes the reader to the scene, quoting Bartolomé de Las Casas on the Spanish conquest as "essentially anti-Christian."[1] The Spaniards sometimes hunted Native children with specially trained dogs and worked their parents to death in mines, meanwhile singing psalms to their God. "Surely God will wreak his fury and anger against Spain," thundered the priest Las Casas, "for the unjust wars waged against the American Indians."[2]

Often God was called upon for justification of land transfers from one group to another. God has been invoked as a real-estate agent so often that in our time we sometimes forget the remarkable ideological twists and turns required of those who invoked such a justification for conquest. The Spanish and the English knew exactly what they were doing, as Venables points out when he quotes from a sermon by the Reverend Robert Gray, speaking in London during 1609, when he gave his blessings to the Jamestown colonists. In so doing, he raised the basic question that underlies the entire five centuries that Venables surveys so ably: "By what right or warrant we can enter into the land of these Savages, take away their rightful inheritance from them, and plant ourselves in their places"?[3]

Gray then answered his own question. If "gentle polishing will not serve," said Gray, then "old soldiers" should square and prepare them to our Preachers hands."[4] In other more often-invoked words: might makes right. And, as might was making right, the Puritans sacked Native graves and survived off food stored by peoples so recently killed by European pathogens.

The often-bloody nature of this history may be news to students raised in the warm bosom of collective denial. Venables takes us, for example, to ground zero for the Pequots—Mystic, 1637, where a thatch fort was consumed by facing flames, killing perhaps seven hundred men, women, and children. "It was a fearful sight to see them thus frying in the fire and the streams of blood quenching the same," observed William Bradford.[5] During the Sullivan campaigns in Iroquois Country (1779), patriot soldiers skinned two dead Haudenosaunee "from the hips down for boot legs, one pair for the major [Daniel Piatt]; the other for myself [William Barton]."[6]

This narrative concentrates on the history of the Haudenosaunee (Iroquois), Venables's specialty (Venables taught at Cornell University). It offers some needed correctives to long-held academic doctrines. One of these is the widespread belief that the Haudenosaunee Confederacy was founded between 1450 and 1600. Iroquois elders have long maintained that the confederacy formed earlier than that, and now they have scholarly support (cited by Venables) assembled by Barbara Alice Mann and Jerry Fields that the founding actually occurred during the 1100s. Mann and Fields use astronomical data to pinpoint the solar eclipse that occurred as the Senecas (the last nation to join) finished debate on the issue in late summer 1142. This new knowledge, first published during the mid-1990s, has been working its way into mainstream academia.

Some of Venables's account is well-known military history. Even here, however, he provides correctives to the usual.

In European-centered versions, Native nations often went to war against each other in rivalries that were encouraged by the British. They were very concerned about the potential power of pan-Indian military alliances of the type that, for example, Tecumseh built shortly after 1800. Land speculation sometimes preceded and always followed the advance of the military. Venables provides a list of land speculators that reads like a who's who of the American revolutionary generation.[7]

The military narrative is livened by other material. Chapter six, on slavery and women's roles, is original and very enlightening. We are reminded that Native women's authority often surprised Europeans, but that even with their gender stratification, Europeans of the time had women leaders, of which Queen Elizabeth and Queen Isabella were two very notable examples. European soldiers sometimes were paid in Indian prisoners, women and children included, by cash-poor governments. Venables points out that the prisoners were readily salable as slaves.

As an alternative to conflict, a desire for coexistence sometimes provoked emulation. As the United States and the State of Georgia prepared to remove them from their homelands, for example, the Cherokees established a republic that was so much like the United States that it denied women the vote (this in a culture that traditionally had been matrilineal). Before they were exiled to Indian territory, the Cherokees owned 22,000 cattle, 7,600 horses, 46,000 swine, 726 looms, 2,448 spinning wheels, 2,943 plows, 172 wagons, 31 grist mills, 62 blacksmith shops, 18 schools, 1 newspaper, and—again emulating their Anglo-American neighbors—1,277 black slaves.

Some of those slaves were owned by the Cherokees' best-known leader, John Ross, who was one-eighth Cherokee. Ross also owned a sizable home and land before the Removal Act authorized its seizure. The seven-eighths of him who was European in heritage (mainly Scots-Irish) didn't get an exemption. As Venables points out, the US Constitution prohibits establishment of a state inside of another without that state's permission.[8] Georgia and its land-hungry citizens were not in a permission-granting mood. As usual, ownership of land was the issue.

This book is strongest east of the Mississippi—foremost among the Haudenosaunee (Iroquois), but also in describing the Cherokees, Creeks, and Choctaws, especially during removals. Venables's narrative of the Cherokees' removal is riveting, ending with commentary by Ralph Waldo Emerson: "A crime is projected that confounds our understandings by its magnitude, a crime that really deprives us as well as the Cherokees of a country...[T]he name of this nation, hitherto the sweet omen of religion and liberty, will stink to the world."[9]

This book's focus and energy does not reach the West Coast, which is barely touched. The California gold rush's impact on Native societies gets one page.[10] Settlement-related conflict in the Pacific Northwest is covered briefly and nearly entirely restricted to conflicts attending the missionary Marcus Whitman.[11] The Nisqually Chief Leschi, who was hanged after leading a revolt that briefly threatened the young city of Seattle, is not mentioned. Chief Seath'tl (Seattle) and the relationship of his people, the Duwamish, to the citizens of the city named for him (probably against his wishes), also does not appear in this account. (Modern fishing-rights conflicts in the area are mentioned briefly.)[12] Other Northwest Coast peoples (which are among very few high cultures to evolve without agriculture) also have been ignored, although the Russian-American Company is discussed.[13]

A history of conflict also may become a stage for coexistence. Our remarkably bloody history also is laced by stories of cooperation, even in the nineteenth century. In one such episode, told masterfully by Venables, the citizens of Omaha, then a frontier city, rallied behind the Ponca chief Standing Bear and his people during the late 1870s after they were wrongfully deprived of their homelands. In this spirit, Venables concludes that "an acceptance of perpetual diversity can evolve into a truly pluralistic society, stable in its multiplicity. An America—and a world—of contrasts, crowded as it may continue to be, is preferable to a barren cultural, political, and spiritual wilderness."[14]

Notes

1. Robert W. Venables, *American Indian History: Five Centuries of Conflict and Coexistence*, vol. 1, *Conquest of a Continent: 1492–1783* (Santa Fe, NM: Clear

Light Books, 2004), 25 (hereafter *V1*).

2. *V1*, 33.
3. *V1*, 69.
4. *V1*, 69.
5. *V1*, 94.
6. *V1*, 293.
7. *V1*, 255.
8. US Constitution, art. 9, sec. 3.
9. Robert W. Venables, *American Indian History: Five Centuries of Conflict and Coexistence*, vol. 2, *Confrontation, Adaptation and Assimilation: 1783–Present* (Santa Fe, NM: Clear Light Books, 2004), 163 (hereafter V2).
10. V2, 181.
11. V2, 181–183.
12. V2, 345.
13. *V1*, 166.
14. V2, 381.

Part IV
Native Rights

The Confusing Spectre of White Backlash

Stories are appearing across the wires of international press services that tell of a rising tide of white backlash in America, a white backlash aimed at American Indian peoples and their attempts to assert sovereignty over their lands. The reports say that this is a popular movement against Indian rights, based on people's fears generated by land claims in the East, fishing rights in the Pacific Northwest, and fears of tribal jurisdiction over nonwhites in states with large Native territories and populations.

It is tempting to simply report the so-called backlash organizations and their activities, and to analyze, one at a time, the legislative bills that have been submitted to Congress to give the whole affair something of the same treatment that it has been receiving in the press and elsewhere, and maybe to say a few words about how racism is the culprit fanning the fires of anti-Indian feelings in the United States. But somehow that approach seems unsatisfactory. The facts, weighed against the assertions, leave some unsettling questions—questions that must be answered.

There are, to be sure, a number of "citizens' action" groups that are pressing for legislation that would extinguish Native rights in a number of areas. A group of farmers and ranchers, mostly in Montana and South Dakota, formed an organization that calls itself Interstate Congress for Equal Rights and Responsibilities (ICERR). Although that group talks about rights, their objective is clearly an effort to deprive Native peoples of land and resources and also an effort to destroy whatever Native identity has survived past efforts of this nature. They would like to see an end to the reservation system and they make it clear that their reasons are because they feel that *they* and not the Indians are the victims of unequal laws, even though all historical evidence points to the contrary.

A group called Civil Liberties for South Dakota Citizens is largely composed of people who own or lease at least 75 percent of the Pine Ridge Reservation in South Dakota. Their group has about one hundred members, mostly ranchers. They talk a lot about law and order, are heavily armed, and possess fairly sophisticated equipment usually associated with law enforcement agencies. As a people who have penetrated the reservations and who have a property interest in Pine Ridge (a property interest that was sponsored by the federal government and that is intended to remove land and resources from the use and control of Native people), they are petty colonists of the classic mold. But they are not very great in number. They do find allies among John Birch and minutemen types around the country. Their motivations are clear—the treaties and federal court recognition of even some vestiges of Lakota sovereignty are visible barriers to their absolute control of the area of Pine Ridge and the people living there.

That environmentalists are opposing Native people in the struggle for land and sovereignty (and often just for a little human dignity) points to one of the powerful effects of colonialism. It is strange at first glance that the Sierra Club, the Friends of the Earth, and the Isaac Walton League should be at work preventing Native peoples from obtaining lands that are rightfully Native lands (not many are seriously arguing that point) and that Native people have occupied for centuries with little visible destruction of the environment.

The Native people, specifically the traditional Native people, have both religious and cultural roots in the conservation of the land and its animal and plant life, which are so deep that they are generally incomprehensible to most of the environmentalists. But many of the environmental conservation groups operate on a concept of Nature that has man somehow separated from all of Nature's processes. They are embarked on a program of separating man from Nature on the thesis that because Western man is always destructive of the environment, so must it be with all humans. Thus have environmentalists opposed allowing the Havasupai to remain on their ancestral lands in the Grand Canyon—pressing for the removal and disruption of a people who have occupied that place since time immemorial and who have, incidentally, every moral and human right to remain there.

But the environmentalists, at least in this instance, are somewhat blinded by their own cultural history. They are moving to conserve Nature in its abstract purity, and that abstract purity translates to mean wilderness without human beings. The Native people, at least the traditional Native people, carry the process of respect for nature a step further. Rather than viewing the land romantically, as a virgin wilderness, they view it as a loving mother, productive, protective, and sacred. They interact with the land. Somehow, the same old conflicts are there. And the same results: the Native people and their way of life is threatened by invaders who have another plan.

Then, of course, there are the sportsmen. Basically the sportsmen's position is that all Native rights to fishing, hunting, and gathering under the treaties should be extinguished. Their purpose, however, is not preservation of the wildlife. They see the wildlife as their own private property, paid for by their hunting licenses. They want to preserve this wildlife so it will be available to them on weekends as trophies. (In England, a few centuries ago, the king would get really upset if any of the peasants "poached" any of *his* deer.) Although Indians account for very little of the game taken in this country, and even less of the fish, different regional sportsmen's groups (especially in the state of Washington) and the National Wildlife Federation have been urging the termination of Native hunting rights under the treaties.

It should be mentioned at this point that Native hunting and fishing rights were reserved under many treaties and also that Native people have never really been able to exercise those rights. The taking of Native hunting rights, in most areas, would simply make legal the situation of illegal arrests and seizures of Native peoples, which has been going on for many decades and was, for all that time, promoted to be legal.

There are a number of political organizations that would like to extinguish the concept of Native existence also. Any number of towns, townships, and even a couple of cities have expanded into or grown up on Indian lands, which were either leased or on which title was under a cloud. Many of these governmental organizations have neither a legal nor a moral leg to stand on. They simply encroached on Native lands, and now they want to stay there. What they don't want is a recognition of Native jurisdiction in the areas that they have encroached upon.

And then, of course, there is the publicity that has been given the land claims. The story is circulating that there are a large number of federal court decisions that will result in the return of great amounts of land to Native nations; that the return of such lands is a great moral wrong because private landowners bought the land in good faith, and now they are threatened with the loss of their homes.

But that view is not supported by the facts. There have not been a huge number of Indian victories resulting in the successful pursuit of land claims. There have been a few very minor victories in the federal courts, and at this writing, no lands have been won in this way. This is especially true in the much-publicized Maine land dispute.

The Maine land dispute concerns the Passamaquoddy and Penobscot claim to a large area of the state of Maine. It is based on a Supreme Court ruling that stated that a 1790 Nonintercourse Act was violated at the time that the Commonwealth of Massachusetts negotiated the land transfer, a fact that is undisputed. But will the United States "give the land back to the Indians," as has appeared in so many press headlines?

Hardly. In fact, that is not even in the list of possibilities, as it affects homeowners in Maine. The Indians have agreed to forego their claim to the areas that have population centers. They are interested in pressing their claim to lands owned by the state and also by eight large landholding corporate families in Maine. And they are a long way from pressing a successful claim to even that. The legal strategy of their attorneys is based on a return of land to the federal trust responsibility, a legal maneuver that would mean that even if the Indians won the suit, they would have less than total control of the land. In fact, it would be very much less than total. If the Native people did win any land back in Maine, it would be won from the hands of powerful corporate interests there.

The headlines leave us with the impression that there is a groundswell of anti-Indian movement among the grassroots American people, and such headlines are certainly geared to create such a backlash, but generally, support for Native causes seems to be growing rather than shrinking. The Native struggle for land is not a struggle for the land of American homeowners generally. That struggle has, however, been used as a tool to frighten people into opposing Native movements, especially in the area of land, and the strategy extends to include opposition to Native sovereignty.

The list of reasons that there should be a public groundswell of anti-Indian feelings in the country is long, but it is not a convincing list. Certainly there are no reasons that there should be a widespread reaction to injustices against non-Native people in the areas of court jurisdiction when there have been no real cases of abuses in those areas. The reaction against Native people having and exercising sovereignty over their own territories just doesn't justify the present climate in Congress, which is fairly certain to result in the passage of laws that severely limit Native control over Native territories.

But Congress is considering such legislation at this very moment in history. The reason has nothing to do with hunting and fishing (the conservation of the game and fish), and it has nothing to do with the rights of homeowners in Maine, either. The reason is that a long-standing strategy of controlling the resources on Indian territories is being countered in some instances by Indians who do not want development in their country and who are taking steps to halt that development.

And the beneficiaries of the legislation proposed by Representative Lloyd Meeds are neither the Indian people nor the local citizenry. The Meeds Bill is in fact a study in hypocrisy, in its statements about "protecting" the rights, etc. What the Meeds Bill is intended to do is to see to it that the Indian people in the Southwest do not use water that would go to the interests of corporate ranches and industrial uses. It is also intended to protect the exploiters of Native lands from taxation in the northern Great Plains. That is the reason behind legislation that limits Native sovereignty. Native jurisdiction could pose a threat to such development, a threat that big business is moving to eliminate. And the only way that threat can be successfully eliminated is by passage of legislation that would limit Native jurisdiction.

But it would not be good public relations if that were the way it was presented in the press. And so, it is necessary to manipulate non-Native groups and organizations to press the charges in other terms—in the areas of somewhat obscure rights against prosecution under Native jurisdiction on the theory that Native people always abuse non-Native people in courts.

And the other strategy is to blame the Native people that it is happening. Indians have gone too far, they have asked too much, according to Meeds. But the Native people have not gone too far. In fact, they have not done very much at all. Most of the Native governments have generally been little more than rubber stamps for federal policy since the days of the Indian Reorganization Act. What is changing is that there is emerging another era of gross theft of Native resources, and that process is threatened by the potential of Native peoples exercising their rights over their resources.

There are major pieces of legislation before Congress that would extinguish Native rights in a number of areas. The Cunningham Bill is probably best seen as a smokescreen for the Meeds Bill. The Cunningham Bill is a piece of straight termination legislation, intended to stir up some amount of response from the Native people and their supporters, but which stands little chance of passage.

The Meeds Bill, however, sounds, on the surface, much more logical. They would serve most of the purposes of the Cunningham Bill. Most specifically, they would freeze Native peoples' access to water at a point prior to one at which most Native communities would actually have use of much water (HR 9951). The proposal concerning criminal and civil jurisdiction would place outside Native jurisdiction all activities by non-Natives in Indian Country immune to criminal and civil action by the injured community. It is the same as if the United States passed a law saying that US citizens who commit a breach of law in Nigeria could not be tried by Nigerians, but instead must be sent home to an American court and tried before an American jury. This law is considered following a decade of relatively unsuccessful attempts to secure prosecution for crimes (including murder) against Native people (Remember the murder case of Wesley Bad Heart Bull?). The statement can't be avoided after all—racism is a powerful tool in this piece of legislation and a tool that clearly serves the people with plans for expansion in Indian Country.

This then, is why the Meeds Bill has a good chance of passing in Congress. The powerful multinationals do not want to deal with the spectre of Native peoples' efforts to tax and zone, to set up court systems that could regulate their access to water, that could regulate their effluence, and that could "interfere" with issues of coal and uranium mining. In short, they don't need Native people to be exercising sovereignty that might cut into profits.

And they have a powerful ally on their side. They have the ally of two hundred years of confusion. Confusion on the part of the environmentalists, who have trouble seeing that the commercial interests are a hundred times more destructive to the land than all the humans in the world and that removal of Native people pushes forward commercial interests in the long run.

Confusion on the part of the American public, which has not been told, and at any rate is reluctant to believe, that the Native people are pressing for the lands that are held, not by the common people, but by the huge aristocratic landholders of the Northeast, the same people who own some 85 percent of the land in this country.

Confusion on the part of the Native people who still see the white Americans as the enemy and who have not come to understand that the white Americans are a people who have been dispossessed as they are being dispossessed. And, their continued confusion as they look to the system of colonial governments that have made them victims of the exploitation of their lands and, increasingly, their labor.

As I said in the beginning, it is tempting to report this issue as one that is simply another legislative ploy, to find out who is the beneficiary of that ploy, to analyze the conflicts, and to let it go at that. But somehow, that is not the whole story; the message at this point is not complete.

Colonization is an extremely complex process. It is a process that truly makes the colonized dependent, even for their information about the nature of their colonization. The big corporate interests are the beneficiaries, in a primary way, of the legislative effort to limit Native peoples' sovereignty. And their arguments in favor of those limitations are interesting because Native people are held to be trying to assert superior rights simply because, if they have any rights, if they can assert any rights, they are almost the only people who would be able to do so in North America. The problem is not that Indians want too much sovereignty, jurisdiction, or whatever you call control over your life and the world you live in. The problem is that the rest of the population has too little control over those things.

The colonized are always also colonizers unless they are active, total resistors of their own colonization. And that is wherein lies the great contradiction that has been so hard to unearth in this drama. The Native people are resisting, in some instances, a major part of the colonization process evident in their communities— arrival of coal and uranium-mining interests. And they are opposed by an array of non-Indian organizations who think they are acting in their own self-interest in limiting another people's control (sovereignty) over their lands and peoples. That is the great problem in this culture. People have a great deal of trouble seeing where their real interests lie because they are dependent on exactly those things that are in opposition to their own real interests. And they have trouble seeing and acting on that fact.

Colonialism is everybody's problem—everybody's enemy. That is the problem here. What is clear, at least in this instance, is that opposition to the Meeds Bill is a positive strategy in opposition to that process. And support of Native sovereignty is a strategy in opposition to that process too. From there, maybe it will be possible for people to see the need to support local people's right to self-determination wherever definite communities can be seen to exist. Whenever we struggle, or assist in the struggle, against interests that are external to those of the people who live in the place that is affected, we are moving in a direction that supports the development of human rights—of resistance to colonialism. That is the message here. That is what people need to come to understand.

The Great Bowhead Controversy:
"We Are the People of the Whale"

It all began last June, when the International Whaling Commission (IWC), meeting in Australia, passed unanimously a resolution setting a one-year zero take limit on the bowhead whales. The action set off a storm of controversy because the only country that presently allows hunting of bowheads is the United States. The United States claims jurisdiction, in international affairs, over the lands and waters that for thousands of years have been home to the Inupiat (Eskimo) people. These Native people have been able to survive in the Arctic regions of Alaska because of the existence of the bowhead. As a result of Inupiat efforts, a compromise of sorts has been reached—the IWC has agreed to the taking of twelve bowheads this year. But according to Inupiat spokesmen, the issue may not be settled.

The IWC is composed of representatives of the countries of the world that hunt whales commercially. It was formed in response to the fact that whales are migratory mammals and that whales are presently threatened with extinction because whale populations have been nearly exhausted by commercial whaling fleets. The whale said to be closest to extinction is the great bowhead whale, a giant animal that sometimes reaches sixty feet in length. Bowhead hunting has been illegal in US waters since 1946. The US Marine Mammal Protection Act of 1972 and the US Endangered Species Act of 1973 stopped all but subsistence hunting of this species.

The IWC met last June and unanimously approved an international agreement to ban killing of bowhead whales for a period of one year because of reports that the bowheads were nearing extinction. Reports reached the commission that there remained a worldwide population of only 1,000 to 1,500 bowhead whales. The United States abstained in the voting because the only allowed bowhead hunting in the world takes place in the waters of Alaska under special provisions of US law that allow whaling of the species for subsistence purposes by Native peoples of the Arctic. The bowhead is the only great whale that comes close enough to shore to be taken by harpoon from ice floes on shoreline craft.

The Inupiat people have been hunting bowhead whales for at least three thousand years. For all that time, the bowhead has been essential to their way of life. Commercial whaling initially depleted the world's population, and few dispute the fact that historically it was commercial whaling that created the present crisis.

It is ironic, in many respects, that the Inupiat are accused of complicity in the depletion of their environment. When oil was discovered in Prudhoe Bay, the Inupiat people mounted a serious defense of their homeland and have consistently attempted to guard against irresponsible exploitation of their country.

The Native people had established an organization called the Alaska Eskimo Whaling Commission (AEWC), comprising leaders of the communities that are dependent on the bowhead. When word of the ban reached the Eskimo communities, the AEWC filed suit against the US State Department to force them to object to the ban. That lawsuit went all the way to the Supreme Court, where, this fall, the court found in favor of the State Department.

But the issue didn't end there. Public pressure began to mount almost immediately following the IWC announcement. Some environmentalist groups initially supported the ban, and then reversed their position. The State Department sided with the IWC; the Interior Department took the Inupiat position. The issues are several and, as is becoming common in these times, complex.

Many of the Inupiat people continue to be subsistence hunters. They argue, and quite convincingly, that a ban on bowhead hunting would bring an end to their culture. The bowhead whale represents a major element in the Inupiat spiritual life and is a cornerstone of the economy.

Inupiat spokespeople contend that bowhead hunting is essential to the survival of the people of the Arctic. They point out that the Inupiat are the only people who are able to survive in the Arctic region using only the resources available in the region. They say that in their climate, there is no nutritional substitute for the whale. The bowhead, and only the bowhead, sustains human life in the Arctic. Mayor Eben Hopson, of the North Slope Borough, former special assistant on fisheries to Alaska governor William Egan, has charged that the ban on bowhead hunting was a form of genocide. "We are the people of the whale," he said.

The Native people of the Arctic look to muktuk whale meat and blubber as an important, indeed essential, source of vitamins B, D, and A and as a source of iron. A single bowhead whale weighs forty to fifty tons and provides enough food and raw materials to sustain a small village from one hunting season to the next. Some estimate up to one-quarter of the nutrition of some villages is derived from the bowhead.

They also argue that their communities have little cash economy and they cannot afford costly imports of substitutes such as pork and beef. The economic consideration in the Far North is a serious matter. Milk sells for $6 a gallon; eggs cost $2.35 a dozen.

The controversy extends even to questions of whether the bowheads are actually as close to extinction as government estimates would indicate. Inupiat people say that the bowhead population has increased in recent years. Native whale hunters have estimated the bowhead population at around ten thousand, nearly ten times the US Marine Fisheries Service estimate. They have charged that official estimates are based on whale counts taken by people who are totally unfamiliar with the North and suggest that the estimates are totally unreliable.*

Nationally, the question of subsistence hunting of the bowhead whale began to take form when the US Commerce Department called a hearing to decide whether the United States should object to the IWC's ban. Court action arose out of the disagreements that followed.

Conservation groups appeared confused at first. Then many, such as the Sierra Club, reversed initial positions and came out in support of the Native people. By the time of the December IWC meetings at Tokyo, there was a general consensus that the environmentalist groups could live with a limit of ten to twenty bowheads taken by Inupiat next year.

President Carter's initial position supported the ban, causing the AEWC to issue a statement saying, "We naively assumed that when President Carter was faced with the choice between human rights and the rights of animal-loving, man-hating conservation groups, he would opt for an action which maximized protection for a people within the borders of the US. But we were wrong."

The Inupiat have plenty of critics among the non-Native population. Some people argued that the bowhead hunting isn't really

---

*In 2008, Canada attested the Inupiat position by admitting consistent professional undercounting of bowhead whales. The bowhead population has rebounded in the past twenty years.—Ed.

necessary now that the Native people have settlement moneys following the discovery of oil on their lands. Others said that modern Native hunters hit three whales for every one they beach and that many of these escape mortally wounded.

Another criticism was that the Native people are no longer real Native hunters. They said that today whales are hunted by men carrying shoulder-held harpoon guns fired from boats or ice floes. They paint a picture of senseless slaughter of the bowheads by modern and insensitive Natives.

At the beginning of the century, the Native populations took an estimated ten bowheads a year in the entire Arctic. That number was no threat to the species. It has been estimated that bowhead kills have since increased and that there were an estimated twenty-nine bowheads taken per year over the past decade.

Critics are also quick to charge that some of the bowhead are taken for commercial purposes. Whalebone carvings are valuable items, as are other by-products of the whale. Finally, it was charged that an estimated forty-nine whales were taken last year (1977), and that number of whales from a small population has pushed the bowhead to the head of the endangered whale species list.

On November 1, North Slope Borough mayor Eben Hopson met with Vice President Walter Mondale at the White House. Mondale indicated that the United States would try to convince the IWC to lift its bowhead subsistence whaling moratorium at a special meeting on December 6 in Tokyo. There were some indications that the Japanese wanted to bargain increased sperm whale quotas for a bowhead subsistence quota. The IWC had utilized biological data from the more depleted South Pacific sperm whale population, and the result was a quota reduction from 7,000 whales in 1976–77 to only 763 for 1977–78. That figure would wipe out the Japanese and Russian Pacific whaling industry.

Although bowhead whaling has been outlawed by the United States since 1946, American law contains special provisions that allow for subsistence hunting of the animals. At Tokyo, the United States found itself in a difficult position. The United States has been a leader among whaling nations seeking international agreements that restrict taking of the great sperm and other whales. But at Tokyo, the United States found itself in the position of potential opposition to a complete ban on the taking of possibly the most endangered species because of a population of Native people who depend on that whale for subsistence, indeed survival. The Eskimo people sent their own representatives to appeal their case before the IWC. There were fears that Canada, France, New Zealand, and Australia were likely to oppose the US position on the restoration of the bowhead subsistence hunt.

The Inupiat requested that the ban on subsistence bowhead hunting be lifted and that subsistence hunting be subject to domestic regulation. The American position was that the nutritional needs of the Native people required twenty-four whales, but that fifteen whales landed might be tolerable, assuming availability of other food sources.

Initial suggestions to lift the ban were rejected by the commission, and it became apparent that the general body could not reach an agreement. The matter was then referred to a technical committee.

The Soviet Union put forth a suggested limit of eighteen whales landed, but that figure was rejected. Finally, the United States offered the figure of eighteen whales struck, twelve landed. That figure was also rejected until Norway suggested the same figure. The commission voted 10–3 to allow Eskimo whalers to strike eighteen bowheads and land twelve.

Tom Garrett, US deputy commissioner to the IWC who was also a Washington, DC, lobbyist for the Defenders of Wildlife, had written a seven-page letter criticizing the US government's bowhead conservation program. The letter repeatedly charges of wasteful whaling practices that he felt were not being addressed by the government.

One of the allegations was that the Eskimo whalers were taking lactating females. The Inupiat whalers were asked how the AEWC would prevent their crews from taking females and calves. Arnold Brower, Barrow Whaling Captains Association president, pointed out that the taking of females with calves was unusual because such females customarily traveled together in the third run, which usually occurred when the ice turned rotten. He said that this run occurred far offshore and was not customarily hunted by Inupiat whalers. Thus it would be easy to prohibit the taking of lactating females. Lactating females do not travel through the leads in which all bowhead whaling is conducted in the spring, when most whales are taken.

The debate over lactating whales has been identified as a turning point in the discussions. What emerged was the understanding by the US delegation that the true experts on the life cycles of the bowhead whale are the Inupiat people and that any successful effort to practice bowhead conservation would be unproductive without the cooperation and participation of the AEWC. New AEWC regulations restricting the use of the shoulder gun to whales already secured with a harpoon would eliminate whatever struck and lost problems that might have existed.

Under the gavel of Mr. Thordur Asgeirsson of Iceland, the technical committee began a debate that soon made it clear that the IWC nations were generally annoyed by the United States and that there was a greater hunger for revenge than for justice. The Canadian government planned to oppose the US position and in any event would have no Inuit (Eskimo) delegates to the IWC. But Sam Raddi and Randy Pokiak from the Canadian Inuvialuits' Committee on Original Peoples' Entitlement (COPE) arrived and were added to the Canadian delegation at the last minute. Denmark did not send any Native Greenlanders to Tokyo. Canada had been pressured to include the Native delegates and nevertheless steadfastly opposed the Inupiat interests in the conflict.

Canada had planned to introduce and promote a new bowhead subsistence quota of just six whales, and they had also planned to urge that this had been approved by the Canadian Inuit. Raddi and Pokiak's presence discouraged that latter strategy. Both men protested Canada's position on the whale limits shortly after their arrival in Tokyo.

Canada also attempted to introduce a resolution that would have restricted the Inupiat communities from any increase take of beluga whales, a species that is not a great whale and that is not an endangered species. The beluga whale is an important subsistence species hunted along the entire Arctic coastal range of Alaska, Canada, and Greenland. There is a heavy concentration of beluga hunting at Mackenzie Bay, where the Canadian government and Dome Petroleum have announced that there has been a significant oil reserve discovery.

Mr. Rod Moore, representing Alaska, Congressman Don Young, and the House Committee on Interior and Insular Affairs stated, "They just picked an arbitrary number. That was the basis for this twelve whales." Observers at the proceeding complained that the commission acted without adequate technical information. Said Moore, "It was evident on everybody's hands that the scientific committee did not have all the data it needed."

The Inupiat expressed great disappointment at the compromise. They had lobbied for a limit of eighteen whales. Many conservationists agreed that twenty or thirty bowhead whales could be killed each year without perceptibly reducing their number. Following the meeting, Inupiat spokespeople announced that the United States had never fully supported their position.

During the proceedings, Inupiat whalers learned that the US Marine Mammal Commission has long advocated bringing the beluga whale under the jurisdiction of the IWC, although not a word of this had ever been mentioned to the Native community of Alaska or Canada. Eben Hopson vigorously protested this attempt to extend IWC jurisdiction to a species about which there was no evidence of depletion, and which was taken only for subsistence use by the Native people. The major result of the meeting was that the IWC had confirmed its claim to be able to regulate Native subsistence whaling, something that it has been secretly urged to do since 1970 by an axis of US civil servants and the Washington, DC, conservationist lobby. The other result was that some of the Inupiat people were able to see more clearly the people and organizations that were in opposition to their interests.

The Arctic North is one of the places on the earth that has been spared serious penetration from the West until this decade. There are good reasons for this—mean annual temperature is ten degrees Fahrenheit, and during winter, chill factor readings reaching seventy below zero are not uncommon. For sixty-eight days a year, the sun remains below the southern horizon, leaving these communities in near or total darkness.

The Native people of this region have proven to be fairly astute politicians, even though they are playing against a stacked deck. Following the discovery of oil at Prudhoe Bay in the 1960s, they organized an impressive lobby to press for a fair settlement. What emerged was the Alaska Native Claims Settlement Act of 1972, by which the US government agreed to pay the Native people nearly one billion dollars over twenty years for parts of their land, and which guaranteed them continuing possession of millions of acres of their ancestral territories.

But Native wealth in the Far North appears to be more of a mirage than a reality. The extraction of natural resources from this area requires competency in a wide range of modern technologies that are possessed by few Natives. For the most part, skilled technicians have been imported at high wages for these jobs— a mechanic can expect to make $18 an hour, schoolteachers are often paid $25,000 a year. Most of the modern manifestations of wealth—running water, electricity—are enjoyed by the newcomers from the south. But the Native people often live in shacks in small communities, and few enjoy the conveniences of prosperity or the jobs that seemed promised by development. Although wealth in the form of dollars appears to be everywhere, most of that wealth is siphoned off and, like the natural resources, goes south. Each family has received no more than several hundred dollars from the Alaska Native Claims Settlement. The land of the Inupiat is experiencing the pains of colonialism.

The process has brought many problems to the people. Some of those problems include increasing use of alcohol and rising racial tensions. Many more problems seem to loom for the future, and some of these center around the age-old dependence of the Inupiat people upon the bowhead whale.

The North Slope Borough was incorporated six years ago, in 1972. Its mayor is Eben Hopson, who resides in Barrow, Alaska, the largest Eskimo village in the world, with a population of 2,200. He is one of the most powerful officeholders in rural Alaska. Much of remote Alaska has been divided into regional corporations owned by Native people. The Arctic Slope Regional Corporation is the largest and probably also the wealthiest, covering 88,000 square miles. It has 10,000 inhabitants.

Following the Tokyo meeting, Hopson stated, "At the present time, I'm thinking along the lines of filing a jurisdictional suit against the IWC. If our argument wins, then there can be no more moratoriums or quotas imposed by the IWC." He has called upon the US government "to reject the unjustified action by withdrawing its membership in the IWC."

Later, in an interview with the *Tundra Times*, he said, "I have repeatedly said that we plan to continue with our spring hunt. There is a possibility that the quota itself may be violated."

(Thanks to *Tundra Times*, *The Washington Post*, *American Indian Journal*, and *The Arctic Coastal Zone Management Newsletter* for much of the information contained in this article.)

The Longest Walk: Vignettes of the Day*

They formed an impressive line. There were twenty-four people in all, young men and women, and older people. They were dressed in their traditional dress. It had been explained to us that some of the older people did not speak English. The occasion was historic—for the first time, a group of Navajo people had come to Onondaga to a Six Nations Council.

An older woman spoke and introduced herself. She spoke through an interpreter, a younger woman who spoke flawless English. She said that she was very happy to have been able to visit our country. Then she said that where she came from they were told that there were no Indians to the east of the Mississippi.

"I didn't even know there were any Indians at all here," she said. "But now I know." People laughed. The atmosphere was relaxed and friendly.

"We came here from the Longest Walk," one of the younger women said. "Our elders have come with us. My grandmother here," she said, pointing out one of the older women, "when she first joined the walk she saw that the people were running. So she ran too! In fact, we couldn't even catch up with her. She ran a couple of miles!" Everyone laughed. The older women laughed too.

A young, powerful-looking man in a huge cowboy hat stepped forward to speak. "We are called Navajo by the non-Indians," he said. "But we do not call ourselves Navajo. That name was given to us by the Spanish. We call ourselves Diné, which means 'the people.' That is who we are." The people gathered in the longhouse nodded.

○ ○ ○

We were camped in a park in Maryland, just outside of Washington, DC. The place of the camp was a large field, and around the edges of the field were pitched tents and tipis and a few army tents. The Maryland National Guard was there, administering field kitchens. The water supply was in military water tanks, which were mounted on small trailers. The national guard people ran the

---

*In summer 1978, in response to legislation that would abrogate treaties, thousands of Native people marched from California to Washington, DC.—Ed.

camp stoves and pretty much maintained a low profile.

It was one of those hot, sunny days, and the people were gathered in a great circle to discuss their problems. Vernon Bellecourt had called the assembly. "We want the people to gather around here," he said, "so that we can discuss our problems. We want the people to speak out, to tell us what is happening. That's what we are here for."

Various people were introduced, a pipe was passed among the people who had led and participated in much of the walk. A few speeches were made. The people sat on the ground patiently, listening, watching.

Late in the afternoon, one of the Diné came forward to speak. "My grandmother has a few words she would like to say," he said. Then an older woman came forward. She was dressed, as they all dressed, in the colorful clothing of her culture. She wore a great squash-blossom necklace.

"Where we live," she said, "the United States government is interfering in our affairs. The say that there is an argument between the Hopi people and the Diné people, but there is no argument among us. The argument has begun because of the interference of outsiders, of non-Indians."

"Now they are coming and telling me that I have too many sheep and that I must get rid of some of my sheep. And they are saying that we must sell or move away from our homes. Without my sheep and without my home, where will I go? What will I do? What will become of me?" There was silence after she spoke.

That night, we went to the Diné camp. They had a fire and had cooked mutton stew, good mutton stew, and fried bread. Roberta Black Goat stood alone at the edge of the light. She is an older, very soft-spoken woman. She speaks English.

"Some of the white people came to my house and they asked me how I felt about selling out and moving away," she said. "I told them I was against it. They said I was the first one they had talked to who said that they didn't want to sell."

She folded her arms in front of her.

"I told them I wasn't interested in selling. I told them that it is the same with us as it is when you have an old tree, and it is in your way. If there is a beautiful old tree, and you dig it up and move it, do you think it will continue to live? Even if you do everything you can to prepare new ground for it, do you think that old tree will live? No, it won't live. And it is the same way with us. When they move us away, we will die.

"I won't take even one dime for my home. That house is not simply a house. That house was made with our prayers. When we built that house, we prayed every step of the way. It is more than a house. It holds our ways. I won't take any money for my house because it doesn't really belong to me. There are many prayers and songs in that house—it means more than money.

"When I talked to those people, what I said got back to the newspaper, and my family came out from the city and they said, 'Boy, Grandma sounds really mad this time.' So I told them that I wasn't going to sell because of them, that someday they will realize that they need that land, and I don't want them to say that they have no place to go because their grandmother sold it."

o o o

We were gathered on a Friday night just outside of Washington DC, in Greenbelt Park. We were over near the Lakota camp. It was a hot night, and it was very late. Russell Means was speaking.

"We have talked to the people at the White House," he said, "and they tell us that President Carter is in Europe this week and that he won't get back until Wednesday or so. When he does get back, he'll have a lot of work to catch up on, and they tell us that he won't be able to see us."

A man standing nearby said, "When he gets to Germany, some people will demonstrate there. While he talks about human rights in the Soviet Union, they will tell him to go home and talk to the Longest Walk."

"Carter won't see us," Means continued, "but Mondale is going to meet with us after he's been briefed on Wednesday."

"Carter doesn't want to talk to us," someone else said. "He doesn't know anything about Indians anyway."

"I know it's against our usual ways," Russell said, "but they want a list of the names of the people who will be meeting with Mondale. They need that list fairly soon."

One of the Diné people stepped forward. "My grandmother wants to speak. I will translate."

An older woman stood. She said that she and her people have walked for months and that they came here for a meeting with Carter. She said she was in no hurry, and that she and her group would be willing to wait. She felt that the Indian delegations should meet with both Mondale and Carter at the same time and suggested that they could stay at the park until they were granted a meeting.

Quite a few people agreed, but it was clear that Means didn't expect to see Carter.

It was nearly 2:30 AM, and there would be prayers at dawn.

o o o

The final leg of the Longest Walk came on Saturday. We were a little late getting started. Someone ran through the camps announcing that there was to be a bus ride first, then a twelve mile walk into Washington. The buses were about a mile from the farthest camp area.

As we walked toward the buses, it became obvious that the trees hid from view a much larger camp than was generally visible. Down the long paths they came, people from the northern Great Plains, the Pacific Northwest, the deserts, and the woodlands of the East. As we walked toward the park entrance, the trickle of people became a steady stream, then a river. It was obvious that there were a lot of people. We walked quietly. There were white people, and black people. And Indians. All kinds of Indians.

A woman ahead asked, "What are we supposed to do this morning? What's first on the agenda?" A man walking with her looked up at the cloudless sky overhead. "The first thing," he said, "is that we take part in the Hottest Walk into the city. Then we're supposed to go to a park in the middle of town where there is a rally."

"And what about after the walk?" she asked. "What do you think will come of it? Even after we go there and we tell them about what we want, that we want our rights? What do you think will happen then?"

"The Longest Wait," he said.

We kept walking. The buses came into view, and a large crowd of people. There was a row of buses to the right. We went that way. They were all filled. We came back. More buses came. They were parked at a roadway entrance, and they stretched out as far as you could see in either direction. We walked to the back of the row of buses. They were mostly filled.

The buses stopped somewhere outside of Washington, and people lined up along the side of the road. There was an organizing period while some instructions were passed, and finally after maybe twenty minutes, people began lining up behind the banners that had been brought for the purpose. The final part of the journey was under way. There were quite a few banners—survival schools, nations, regions. Security tried to keep the people four abreast.

A group of Buddhists brought up the rear. They were from Japan. Their heads were shaved. Someone said that they marched in support of peace. They had walked from California. They were dressed in orange robes, and they were highly disciplined. As the day's walk began, their drums set the cadence.

As we started over that first mile or two, I could see the banner that led the march. It was perhaps a hundred yards in front of us, the Buddhists maybe eighty or so yards behind us.

From the beginning, as we walked, people came out of their homes or stood along the sidewalk to watch. Soon the streets were lined with onlookers. It was hot. The people at the front of the procession carried pipes, the people at the rear carried drums. It was, if nothing else, one very colorful procession.

People lined the sidewalks. The hot Washington sun turned the street into a frying pan, and the humidity was oppressive to people from different parts of the continent. Some people were carrying babies.

As we neared the city limits, the crowds thickened. People seemed to stop work to come to the street to watch. By that time, the front banner was more than two hundred yards ahead. The crowd was swelling. Bit by bit, Indian people joined in from the sidelines. People with cameras and news crews with videotape equipment walked alongside the crowds. Security tried to keep the marchers in line.

As we entered Washington, we heard a man singing alongside the road. It was Grandfather David from the Hopi Nation. He was singing his song, and he danced, and he couldn't go on. He stopped and he cried. He couldn't go on.

The streets were emptied of traffic as we entered what was clearly a black section of the city. The previous night someone had mentioned that today we would be walking through their country. This area of Washington, we were told, is more than 90 percent African American. We had received nothing but hospitality from the black organizations. In 1972, when the BIA occupation took place, the only accommodations offered to Indian people came from a black church in one of the poorest parts of the city.

The black community stretched for miles. Longest Walk posters were in many shop windows and on some of the masonry walls. People came outside to watch. We walked.

The Indian movement and the black movement have not communicated well over the years. Black people who are conscious of their own oppression are sympathetic, but whenever the question of cooperation is raised, someone is always able to bring up a long list of differences between our peoples. Every atrocity committed in history was committed against both of our peoples, and those atrocities continue today. Black people have been the other major target of the sterilization programs of US institutions. It could be that we have more in common than we generally acknowledge. And today, Native people are headed for Malcolm X Park.

As we walked down Sixteenth Street, more people joined the march. There was a standing crowd on both sides of the street now, and an increasing police visibility. People rushed ahead with jugs in their hands and full water jugs passed through the crowd. Others came with bags of ice. Soon we were passing what were clearly office buildings and institutes.

We turned down one of the large streets heading toward Malcolm X Park. By that time, the banner in front was close to three hundred yards ahead. We walked slowly.

Somewhere in front, a drum started. It was the American Indian Movement anthem. Overhead was the sound of a helicopter, passing back and forth over the tops of the trees. In the rear, one could hear the sound of the chanting monks and their drums— ONE TWO THREE FOUR, one two. It was an incredible mixture of sounds. A woman next to me said something, but I couldn't hear her over the din.

I looked to the rear, but at that time, the end of the line, which now stretched behind the Buddhists, was not in sight. We saw the front of the line disappear around a corner, and many more people joined in the walk. We came down through the center of the city, an increasingly curious mixture of people, a spectacle never before seen even in this, the most jaded city in the world. We didn't see the front of the line again until we reached the park.

There was something about that walk that people who were there will never forget. The sound of the drum and the song of the northern plains, a rallying song now for all of the Indian peoples of North America, mixed with the chants and the drums of a Buddhist people most of us had never seen before. And overhead, the helicopter.

People came out to the street, non-Indians, and applauded. Many stood alongside with their fists raised at first, but the line was so long that they couldn't hold the pose long enough for even a fraction of the people to return the salute.

Somehow the significance of it all began to take on a new perspective on that hot summer day in Washington. I remembered reading a journalist's report, filed more than five years ago, in reaction to a news story that Richard Oakes had been shot to death in California by a YMCA camp employee. Richard was one of the people who had led the occupation of Alcatraz. The journalist wondered aloud where a movement like this one would go, and he came pretty close to announcing its death with the passing of one of the people who started it all. There were a relative handful of people at Alcatraz—things have changed.

I looked behind me at the crowd. There was a line of people as far as one could see. If he had lived, Richard would have been elated.

People began pointing out a white-haired man who joined the procession. He was walking alongside Vernon Bellecourt. It was Marlon Brando. Muhammad Ali was also there supporting the Indians.

Finally, the people crossed the street and turned into Malcolm X Park. We walked up the center of the grounds of the park. I looked at my watch. We were more than two hours late. The people who came had waited. It was a small park, but it was filled. As the marchers filed in and approached the speaker's platform at the far end of the park, there was a great cheer, and then applause. There were a few moments while the sound equipment was made ready. We looked around the park. There were many supporters and many of them were black. We had walked for perhaps three hours. Our destination was to be the Washington Monument.

"Only about two more miles to go," a man nearby said.

"We have a lot further than that to go," another man replied. Then the speeches began.

o o o

As we pulled out of the park, the line grew enormous. We walked into the heart of Washington, DC, past some of the most impressive-appearing real estate in the world. The words, the purpose, and the ultimate reason behind this gathering of people were growing. We marched into the center of one of the United States' most impressive displays of wealth—a march that included what are undisputedly among the poorest and most powerless people on the continent. Police were everywhere now photographing the marchers, sitting on their motorcycles. We passed the Organization of American States building, and the White House. If the crowd was large when we entered Malcolm X Park, it was much larger when we came into the center of the city. People came out of their offices to watch. Some stood silently, almost disbelievingly, while others applauded. But everywhere the people came to watch, along the sidewalks, or from the windows of offices along the route.

Estimates of the size of the march ranged from a low of a few hundred to a high of nearly thirty thousand. I don't know how large the crowd was. I only know that from the middle, it was not possible to see either the beginning or the end of the line and that as we entered the Washington Monument grounds, the line was probably five deep and could have stretched out for two miles or more. I had seen more people on demonstrations during the anti-war movement days, and even a week earlier, a hundred thousand people had demonstrated in support of the ERA.

But for the American people to put the same percentage of people in the streets, they would need a demonstration with about six million people. And I knew, from looking around for those I would have expected to see, that there were many, many who had not come, even among the leadership. It wasn't out of apathy or lack of brotherhood, but many had not come because there is important work to be done at home.

We stopped in the shade of some trees to one side of the Washington Monument. People were tired. Some had dropped off along the way. Generally there was a good mood, a feeling of accomplishment. We had hoped there would be support among the Indian people. There was. The event belongs on a calendar somewhere: July 15, 1978—date of the strongest demonstration of Indian unity this century. So far.

○ ○ ○

All day long at camp, people had been meeting in their various areas. Some of the camp areas didn't wait to follow the schedule that had been posted, and a number of people expressed a sentiment that indicated the futility of going into Washington to talk to the people representing the US government. Some of the daytime meetings were excellent—the people were talking. There was a growing sense of participation. Things had the appearance of change. It was good.

It was nighttime on Sunday and we were sitting at one of the small camps, around an open fire, talking. The group was young and they had met each other really perhaps for the first time this week. But they knew each other. They had all come in by caravan from the same reservation.

"I think I know how to explain it," a young woman, perhaps twenty, was saying. "The thing is, it was among the traditional people that I first learned how to pray. I mean really pray. Oh yeah, I knew how to do that 'Now I lay me down to sleep' thing." The group laughed.

"But what I mean is, well, this year I really learned how to pray—when it meant something. I went out west, where they have sweat lodges every few days. And when you're in a sweat lodge, when you are in there suffering and you have to come in there to suffer, to share something with the other people, to touch them, that's when you first come in touch with yourself."

"And I think I know what they mean about the right way now too. I have seen some of the right way. The right way to pray, so that it means something. The way to be among your friends, so that they mean something to you. That's what I've been learning."

A young man carried their thoughts. "The right way means to live by the way our ancestors lived. That was the right way. A pure way of life. One mind with the Spirit. I learned, too, how to pray, how to be. Now I only have to find a way to live the right way."

"But our people don't want to live that way, at least most of them don't," another young man said. "Most of our people have never prayed, really prayed, in their whole lives. And they don't care that much about anything or anyone. Just so long as they have a little money and they don't have to work too hard."

"Yes," said another. "But don't forget. They can't help it. They were sold a bill of goods just like we were. They were taught that they were following the right way, when in fact what they were given was just the opposite from a spiritual way. I can see that now. But they can't see it. Not yet. But now that we know, what can we do about it?"

There was a silence.

My mind wandered to a meeting we had had this spring in Louisville, Kentucky, while on a Voices from the Earth trip. We had been invited to a dinner with a group of people who lived in a community house in the city. They called their organization Ananda Marga, and they were a spiritual people who found their teacher in a man and a movement that has its roots in India. They practiced a strict personal discipline, and their philosophy was based, as is our own, on principles of charity.

Before we ate, a young woman took a guitar and she led a song, a beautifully done song: "We are one with the Spirit. We are one in a unity," it began. "We will show them with our love. With our love, that God is living in this land!" They know, I thought. And now these young people, they are beginning to know too.

o o o

It was late and we had invited the people who had walked the entire distance into our camp to share a meal. Afterward, one of the men took a guitar and he sat down near the fire. "I want to sing you a song," he said.

He played his guitar, and he talked and sang. He said, "We came through the mountains in the wintertime, and it was cold up there. Fifteen below, maybe colder. And some nights there was no place to sleep, except in the snow. And one night, one of our men, he stayed all night in his truck, way up on the mountain, because he was carrying the Pipe. He wasn't going to bring that Pipe down into that town, because he knew the Pipe was sacred, and he didn't want to bring a sacred thing into that town. He could have come down and slept where it was warm, but he didn't. He didn't. So I want to sing this song for my brother, because he stayed strong."

"Walk on, long walkers, we got many miles to walk on!"

"Walk on, long walkers, we got many miles to walk on!"

He sang for nearly an hour, and we heard that he didn't sing all of the song. "The Longest Walk," which is the name of the song, is also the longest song.

"I learned the right way on this walk. At least, the right way for me. I fell in love while I was on this walk. I fell in love with my Mother Earth. And I'll never forget it. I have tried many things—booze, marijuana, heroin, religion—you name it, I've tried it. But I have never known anything like Mother Earth.

"And I know now that the Pipe is sacred. I know what that means. My brothers taught me about that on the walk. That Pipe is powerful. It is so powerful, because we are powerful.

"You know, I believe the Spirit was with us on this walk. And we saw, we saw. The Spirit, he doesn't care for money. A lot of people came on this walk with money, and while we walked, they rode. But you know what? None of them made it, because money is not what the Spirit is all about. I saw that. The Spirit doesn't care for money. What he cares about is what you are made of."

He spoke articulately and with feeling. "You know, this walk has brought so much to me. Now I know what the Mother Earth means to me! And you know what? When my grandmother from the Diné in the Southwest says she needs my help, because the man has come to rip off her land, you know what I'm going to do? I'm going to go down there and help her!"

"Now I'm going home and I'm going to tell my bothers and sisters about the power of the Pipe. Everywhere I go, I'm going to tell about this thing. I have seen it, on this walk," he said.

It was an extremely powerful speech. He is one of the Native people from the south of the imaginary line, in the land known on the maps as Mexico.

o o o

We sat in the shade near one of the camp cooking areas, talking with one of the chiefs of the Six Nations delegations. "One of the younger men was telling," he said, "of some of the things that happened at the beginning of the trip, when they came through the mountains."

"I guess it was a miracle that they survived. He told that it was very cold, and he was carrying a pipe, and running down the mountain. He said that although it was very cold, he had his shirt off and he was sweating. Later, when he stopped, he found that his hair was frozen."

"Anyway, as he was running, he said that one of those mountain goats came down off the mountain and ran alongside him, but it stayed off the road. Then an elk joined in, and a deer. Pretty soon, an eagle came down and flew above him."

Later, a group of people was riding in one of the vans, talking about the events of the trip. "Did you see the animals as we walked into town?" a young woman asked. "All the way, the horses and even a bull ran up to the fence, and then walked along the fence with the walkers. All the animals were acting funny. Did you see?" The others nodded. They had seen.

The Iroquois Land Claims

The American Revolution ended with a victory for the revolutionaries, which was something of a military miracle involving innovative tactics and the assistance of French arms. The Treaty of Paris, which ended the war between the United States of America and England, failed to mention the rights or interests of those seen by both as England's Indian allies. The ensuing treaty between the United States and the Haudenosaunee, or Six Nations, produced at Fort Stanwix, left the Six Nations angry over land cessions the negotiators were not authorized to make. The Six Nations government on numerous occasions exclaimed that the Haudenosaunee had lost lands due to coercion or deceit. In the Mohawk Valley, some Indians who had fled during the confusion of war returned to find their homes and farms occupied by supporters of the Revolution, and they tried using the courts to regain their property. These two types of complaints—from (1) Indian warriors and government complaints to officials and (2) individual Indians seeking return of assets through the courts and petitions to the legislature—were the earliest Indian land claims following the Revolution. The Indians, for their part, have never missed an opportunity to press their claims.

The new republic had won the war but was immersed in a sea of problems that started to rise even before hostilities had ceased. A significant problem was the English military's continued occupation of a string of forts: Fort Stanwix, Fort Oswego, and Fort Niagara in New York, and others in present-day Ohio and Michigan. The British occupation encouraged resistance to encroachment into Indian Country. The new United States was in many ways exhausted, its currency inflated, and its ability to enforce its laws challenged internally from every side. It did not want another war with England. The US government, the states, and private land companies all viewed the "western lands"—a euphemism for Indian lands—as a source of dollars to repay their debts and to finance their needs. These three sectors approached Indian nations with offers of money and other assets in exchange for land cessions. Some states, including New York, began selling parcels of land in areas long recognized as belonging to Indian nations even before negotiating a sale or other conveyance from them. During the years following the Revolution, and while the US government operated under the Articles of Confederation, it was not clear how such transactions would be handled. No one knew which ones would be legal and which not, or what could be done in the event of fraud or disagreement. Under the Articles, the central government had almost no power to enforce its laws, and the states sometimes acted as though they had little or no obligation to act in the interest of the whole, especially when that interest conflicted with their own. The test of whether the central government would be able to survive and the union flourish came on two fronts: Indians and taxation. (The taxation issue would be settled in a conflict known as the Whiskey Rebellion.)

Indians had lived side by side with non-Indians in the Mohawk Valley for more than a generation. Problems had arisen because in incidents of conflict, the courts were not available to the Indians; Indians were not permitted to bring suit or even give testimony against an Englishman. The only workable, peaceful solution was in the form of government-to-government agreements—treaties. This reality greatly enhanced the influence of men such as Sir William Johnson, the British Indian agent who skillfully represented the interest of the Crown, prior to the Revolution, in negotiations with the Indians and settlers. With the defeat of England, the Indians turned to negotiations with Albany and Washington in search of a way to expel squatters and other intruders without resorting to violence and ultimately war. Some officials at Albany talked about expelling all Indians from New York, but this was not realistic because of the British forts guarding British and Indian interests in Central and Western New York.

In 1787, the confederated US government passed the Northwest Ordinance, a historic step toward asserting central control over lands not yet part of existing states. The ordinance created rules in anticipation of the admission of new states and helped to raise money to pay the national debt. The ordinance, however, had the effect of offering for settlement lands that had not been purchased or otherwise obtained from the Indians. When settlers moved to occupy these lands, Indians attacked and harassed them.

In 1768, the "Line of Property" had been established running south from a point about seven miles west of Rome, New York. No settlement could be made west of the line without a formal cession by the Indian owners. By acts passed in 1783 and 1784, New

York State created a commission to obtain cessions of land from the Indian nations. The Six Nations, as a confederacy, responded to the first message from the commission, saying the Six Nations desired to make peace with the United States as a whole. Despite this, the state proceeded with plans to deal with each of the Six Nations separately. The so-called treaties that resulted have never been accepted as valid by the Indian nations.

In 1789, the United States adopted a constitution that concentrated far more power in the hands of the federal government. US forces, including local militias, moved to punish the Indians in the Ohio region for the raids that had caused property damage, injuries, and death on disputed lands. President George Washington and Congress resolved to implement a fair treatment policy in regard to the Indians, to retreat from bribery and coercion and move toward offering market value for the land. Although the federal government appeared to be in favor of fair treatment of the Indians, many states were not. The history of the Indians' subsequent attempts to regain lands lost through fraud or coercion or other unfair means would confirm that while fair treatment occasionally was reborn as a federal policy, it was rarely invoked in Albany or other state capitals. This is essentially why Indian land claims in New York have lingered for some two centuries.

American forces suffered two military defeats during this period, including a defeat of General Harmar's forces in 1790 and a disastrous loss of an army under General St. Clair in 1791. President Washington asked General "Mad Anthony" Wayne to create an army to defend US interests in the Ohio region. Wayne was to march into the Miami River country to engage the Indians while avoiding military conflict with the British, who had built a fort there.

At this point, the states, including New York, had interests that were distinct from those of the United States and had the potential to interfere with federal policy. President Washington invited a delegation of Six Nations chiefs to Philadelphia. They complained bitterly about fraudulent treatment of Indians at the hands of the states, including, obviously, New York. Washington promised to do what he could, and Congress subsequently passed what is now called the 1790 Trade and Intercourse Act, a promise that the federal government would guarantee that Indians would not be cheated by the states in dealings over land. By the summer of 1794,

Wayne's army was marching toward the Indian towns in Ohio, and President Washington's envoy, Timothy Pickering, was assembling a treaty conference at Canandaigua, New York. Wayne's victory at Fallen Timbers—the first field victory of the US army—secured the federal government's position of power over the states.

The Canandaigua Treaty was one of the seminal documents in US history because it confirmed the federal triumph over state assertions of rights to land transactions with Indians. Had state militias defeated the Indians, and had the states been able to assert control over the future of land dealings in the territories to the West, US history might have been very different. This is particularly apparent when considering the Louisiana Purchase, the Indian resistance organized by Tecumseh, the War of 1812 with England, the Mexican War, and the Civil War.

The 1794 treaty also was a defining document for Indian nations because it established a federal responsibility to guard the rights of the Indians against the ambitions and abuses of the states. It would not be lost on the Indians that this historically arises as a government-to-government arrangement, not one engineered by lawyers in courts.

Nevertheless, in the decades following this treaty, New York aggressively followed a policy of dealing with the individual nations of the Six Nations, and even with unauthorized individuals, to obtain land sales and cessions in defiance of the 1790 Trade and Intercourse Act. The only recourse open to the Indians against abuses was in the form of appeals for justice to the federal government. But the United States was hardly open to such appeals, because it was locked on a course dominated by warfare with Indian nations across the continent.

In 1838, the US Senate ratified a treaty quickly found to be fraudulent (the Buffalo Creek Treaty), and a long line of Indian law cases affirmed that claims could not be brought against the United States without a special act of Congress. In addition, the courts would not question the validity or fairness of a treaty that had been legally signed and ratified by the United States. The courts were not open to Indian nations to make claims against New York. As a result, no court would hear the most important claims of the Six Nations. The Indians had no recourse to assert their claims that their lands had been taken—although most Americans at the time acknowledged that the Indians' lands were stolen—through political or judicial means.

The first case under the Trade and Intercourse Act was decided in 1920 and is known as *United States v. Boylan*. This involved thirty-two acres of Oneida land that was seized for nonpayment of a loan, which the court held could not be seized because it was protected under federal law. This revelation led the New York Legislature to create the Everett Commission to study the question of Indian title to lands in New York. Assemblyman Edward Everett concluded the Indians had been subjected to very serious abuses, but his final report was rejected by the legislature, and Everett was treated as an outcast.

In *Deere v. St. Lawrence River Power Co.*, another case brought under the 1790 Trade and Intercourse Act, the court ruled that such cases were barred because they did not technically arise under federal laws. This ruling was overturned in 1974 by the Supreme Court in the first Oneida land claim to reach the US Supreme Court, *Oneida Nation v. County of Oneida*. This decision and the 1985 Supreme Court decision in the same case made it possible at last for Indian nations to seek justice for their land claims in the US legal system.

In 1946, Congress passed the Indian Claims Commission Act, which authorized certain Indian nations to bring claims against the United States. However, the commission decided claims could only be brought for money, and the amount of recovery was limited to the dollar value of the land at the time of taking. Because the law restricted the lawsuits to actions against the federal government, it was not applicable to a whole category of cases in which the states or county or individual landowners would rightfully be the defendants, such as exists in New York.

Until 1974, the Indian nations of New York, including the Onondaga, Cayuga, Seneca, Tuscarora, Mohawk, and Oneida nations, never had a realistic opportunity to pursue claims for lands illegally taken some two centuries ago. These modern land claims are merely the latest attempt by the Haudenosaunee nations to secure the fair treatment that Washington had promised. History will judge whether this country will or will not finally fulfill this promise to be fair.

The current wealth that is enjoyed in New York—and the country as a whole—was built on a foundation of illegally taken land and stolen natural resources. The Empire State was created when the state government violated federal law and illegally obtained 98 percent of the Native lands and forced 95 percent of the Haudenosaunee people to flee from their aboriginal territories. These claims test whether this theft will be acknowledged and at least partially paid for.

The nations of the Haudenosaunee have persevered through these many decades, sustained by the words of a Seneca prophet who, in the early nineteenth century, predicted that although times would be difficult, the nations will survive. They have survived awaiting the fulfillment of a policy advocated by the United States' first president, George Washington. Fair treatment, the first order of the new country's business, has been a very difficult path to follow.

Rights of Indigenous Women
Are Advancing on Several Fronts

Indigenous women are found on every inhabited continent and suffer from the same kinds of discrimination as do nonindigenous women but are arguably the most disadvantaged of the world's populations. In addition to the disadvantages societies place on their gender, indigenous women often face a variety of social disadvantages including discrimination, forcible or economic displacement from their lands, and public policies that exclude them from the mainstream society's pathways to power and prosperity because of their race and ethnicity.

Indigenous women generally existed in societies that valued them, and in most cases, they played an important role, along with men, in the decision-making process. With the advent of colonization, indigenous women were marginalized in both the dominant society and the colonized indigenous society. Their traditional roles in society were often systematically ignored and reduced, and they were relegated to conditions of powerlessness and poverty. Even in societies that took pride in upward mobility through education, indigenous women in particular did not and do not thrive because the dominant society's plan of education for them is intended as a way to sweep them into the mainstream at its lowest levels of income and power.

In recent years there have been some signs of change in attitudes and ways of thinking about priorities that hold potential for indigenous peoples, in general, and indigenous women, in particular. The first is a very ancient struggle. Practically since the evolution of civilization, dominant societies have infringed on others in a search for land and resources in a process of dispossession and transformation known as colonization. Until recently, little thought was given to this as a problem that demands a solution. The twentieth century brought experiences that demanded that this change.

The experience centered around genocide. Genocide is not a crime against individuals. It is a crime against a group. A grant of civil rights, which guarantees people a right to participate in the political, economic, and social life of the nation-state, can benefit individuals but does nothing to curb genocide. Nation-states, including the United States and Canada, are far more comfortable conceding rights to individuals than to groups. Massacres of people, ranging from the attempted extermination of the Armenians in Turkey in 1915 to the holocaust of the Jews in the 1940s, stunned the world, and the realization that such horrors could be repeated in vastly distinct societies such as Serbia, Croatia, Kosovo, and Rwanda has rekindled the discussion about what genocide is and how it can be met.

Obviously, distinct peoples need protection against those who would take action to destroy them. Genocide can be accomplished without hate, and it is clear that the industrial world has underestimated its collaboration in this regard. Some distinct peoples—who possess a language and a distinct history and who occupy an area of land—have been rendered extinct as peoples through such developments as hydroelectric dams, access roads and subsequent privileging of settlers, logging and mining. If a state takes an action or permits an action that has the impact of destroying a people, is that not genocide? Do outcomes matter?

This essentially means that development must become a human rights issue. Many of the issues of human rights and reproductive rights impact indigenous women. In much of the world, the remaining natural resources are on lands occupied by indigenous peoples—land and resources coveted by multinational corporations. Those corporations, if able to extract the timber, water, oil, fish, or whatever they want, will create conditions that will inevitably lead to the disappearance of the indigenous peoples. Indigenous women have become increasingly visible and vocal in the international community and are demanding the right to survive as distinct peoples. They have formed numerous organizations in many countries of the world and are determining for themselves what their needs are and demanding that their rights to a continued existence as distinct peoples be respected. Such demands are reshaping the very concept of human rights.

The antidote to cultural and physical extinction, in the eyes of many indigenous women activists, is the empowerment of women through giving priority to women's education and training and through informing women of their rights so they can improve their standard of living and can increase their independence. To survive, they must have information about the impact of the development projects that approach their territories and an ability to resist schemes that will take from their communities the things needed for survival. Indigenous women have looked to international law in such forms as the International Labor Organization Convention No. 169, the United Nations Working Group on Indigenous Populations and the Organization of American States.

Indigenous women have also entered the culture of world politics. The first and most famous was Rigoberta Menchú, Nobel Peace Prize winner from Guatemala, but many others are now doing this work. Mary Simon is an Inuit who was recently appointed Canada's ambassador for circumpolar affairs; Lois O'Donoghue is an Aborigine who is chairperson of the Aboriginal and Torres Straight Islander Commission; Eulalia Yagari is an indigenous woman of Columbia who is a member of the Provincial Assembly of Antioquipa in northwest Columbia. These are but a few of the growing number of indigenous women who are working on the most pressing need in the world: the need to address the survival of distinct peoples everywhere.

Part V
Political
Philosophy

Traditionalism: The Wave of the Future

Not so long ago, it was possible to pick up any number of newspapers, journals, magazines, and other publications and to read analyses about how the world was being threatened by some kind of mass conspiracy. That conspiracy, we were told, took the form of the mysterious and dreaded Trilateral Commission and was headed by tremendously wealthy families such as the Rockefellers and Cabots and so forth. We were told that we were all victims of something called world monopoly capitalism and that we needed to organize and to struggle against its dangers.

There are fewer voices today issuing this clarion call. Many of the Left's newspapers have fallen victim to inflation and the apathy of a readership that has grown weary of reading the same tale week after week, month after month. The political Right has taken the offensive. Following Reagan's election to the presidency, there seems to be a widespread feeling that the political atmosphere in America is such that the liberals and the Left have all but disappeared.

In the Indian movement, things aren't a lot better than in the continent at large. A revitalization of the traditional Indian movement took place in the late 1960s. Those of us who were there can remember the spirit that began to be stirred during those early years—the Spiritual Unity Caravans, the rebirth of interest in Native cultures, the movement toward Indian-controlled Native studies programs and colleges, Alcatraz, Pit River, the founding of the American Indian Movement, the rise to media prominence of some traditional and movement Native leaders.

It was a new movement in the sense that it sought to establish a Pan-Indian politics. It was based on a widely shared, but poorly articulated ideology that saw a return to the old ways as a goal but that never was able to agree on what the old ways really looked like or how to bring about a return to those ways. The ideology of the Indian movement, circa 1970, was extremely abstract.

As the movement grew, the sense that there might be some concrete goals grew with it. Indian politicians joined the rising voice of a movement that demanded more legal sovereignty, educators joined a movement that demanded more classroom space and salary lines, community workers in urban areas struggled with each other over whether the ideology of the programs delivering services was to have a traditional flavor or the color of a tool of acculturation.

The early days of the movement were an inspirational time. The movement, more by popular acclaim than as the result of any specific charismatic leadership, identified itself as "spiritual," a term that many non-Indian supporters and detractors alike seized upon as meaning apolitical. But the Indian movement (and it is properly titled the traditional Indian movement) was and is anything but apolitical. It offered to the world the concept of the synthesis of the emotional and psychological functions usually associated with religion, with the need to organize in specific ways to struggle with political realities. It pointed to the hard technologies of the West and stated that such technologies threaten life on this planet and create undesirable social conditions, and it offered a path toward cooperation with nature. There was the spark of the development of a kind of Native liberation theology, one with a true grassroots leadership located in the Indian communities. There existed the potential for a real cultural revitalization based on a sort of loose coalition of peoples who shared similar spiritual beliefs and objectives across the Western Hemisphere.

The definition of a Native cultural revitalization, given the nature of oppression suffered by Natural World peoples, is that it must be a political movement that seeks to analyze and counter those forces that are responsible for the destruction of Natural World cultures. It would not be a political movement as we have seen such movements. It would be directed with a priority to give rise to power at the grassroots level, and not at the level of government or quasi-governmental organizations.

In short, it would be a movement that would seek to empower the people first, not a movement to empower a party or a government. It would empower the people at the grassroots through reestablishment of economic and social institutions that benefited and were controlled by the people. Power would rise from the people to their leaders and would not flow the other way. It would mean that organizations would be created that would function to grow food or to manufacture building materials, and the organizations would be composed of workers who would be responsible for designating leadership very much in the same way that clans and villages once operated under precolonialist linear organization patterns. It would be a traditional economic organization that would function in the modern world.

The strategy for that change required the rebuilding of the Native spiritual community, not on a national level, but on the local level in such a way that Lakota communities would remain and become stronger Lakota communities, and Apache communities would devote their energies to the strengthening of Apache ways and customs and lifestyle, and so forth.

While that vision, or at least aspects of that vision, was vital and central to the movement, the movement grew enormously in strength among the Native people. The best evidence of that growth and its direction was seen at the Longest Walk in 1978, when tens of thousands marched on Washington in support of Native rights. At that gathering, the people issued a position statement to the US government in which they mostly demanded that the United States get out of Indian Country. The man who emerged as a leader of that gathering was appropriately Phillip Deere, a man who represents traditional values and lifestyle and who has an unblemished record and reputation in such traditionally valued characteristics as truthfulness, material simplicity, sobriety, humility, and dedication to the well-being of the people.

The traditional movement, in order to be successful, must be informed of developments in the world. The people and peoples who are involved in the movement need to be conscious of the fact that they are today part of a struggle against developments that threaten to destroy peoples and cultures globally, and that all the forms of oppression are interrelated. The most profound stories, and the untold stories, of this half of the twentieth century are the stories of peoples, cultures, and communities all over the globe that are struggling to survive in the face of an assault by transnational corporations and nation-states that seek to exploit their lands, waters, forests, and labor—in short, all of their resources. The result of that exploitation is necessarily the destruction of whole cultures and peoples, the despoliation of the environment, starvation, dislocation, despair, disease, and mass poisoning. The only defense against that kind of onslaught is the revitalization of cultures that can not only resist the assault but also develop enough strength to make gains against it.

Those now-defunct radical newspapers that talked about the existence of a mass conspiracy in the West were right. Almost everyone who reads newspapers today is at least vaguely aware that a very small number of people control most of the West's oil, gas, and coal reserves, and the term *energy czars* appears in even conservative media. Most people also know that there is a virtual monopoly in the areas of newspaper ownership, magazine production, and electronics communications media and that although it is not a complete monopoly (contradictions exist), it is clear even to most of the American public that big business has a lot of influence on television, movies, newspaper chains, and the American government.

People who have some knowledge of Native affairs know that transnational corporations and vested private interests have been responsible for driving Indian peoples off their lands in Latin America to make way for plantations and oil and gas exploitations, and that Indians are threatened by hydroelectric power projects, mining interests, energy corporations, and the possibility of nuclear waste mining and dumping on their lands. Everywhere, the activities of these interests are forcing people off their lands.

Less well publicized, perhaps, is the fact that transnational corporations are following strategies that promise to lead to world food shortages, if such shortages are not in fact already present. Although the media promotes the myth that there are too many people and not enough land, the fact is that there is enough food produced in the world now to feed its entire population, but productive lands are increasingly in the hands of corporations that seek profits and are not organized for the purpose of producing food for people.

The process is affecting non-Native people as well as Native peoples. While food prices are rising at an alarming rate in the grocery store, some five hundred American farmers go out of business *every week*. At the present rate, it is estimated that in twenty years, 1 percent of the farms will produce over 50 percent of the food that reaches American markets and that the average, medium-sized farmer will need two million dollars in capital to go into business.*

The reason is that a very small number of people who control huge amounts of capital have been able to exercise enough

---

*These figures are from the mideighties.—Ed.

influence in government to create policies that favor monopoly in practically every area of the economy, and the small farmer has been all but driven from the marketplace. The price of food at the consumer level will continue to rise at an alarming rate. The same process is driving farmers off the land in Ohio and Indians off their lands in Guatemala, and essentially the same interests are opening uranium mines in South Dakota and raising the price of milk at the supermarket.

The Native peoples and the average American have a lot more in common than most of them know, because by the end of the century, unless things begin to change, urban dweller and reservation Indian alike will be suffering from the effects of a society nearly totally held captive in the embrace of a world where practically every aspect of life will be controlled by very powerful cliques of corporate managers. There are almost certain to be other, more spectacular effects to this evolution: mass starvation, wars, incredible repression, ecological destruction, disease—you can probably add to the list as you grasp the dimension of the problem.

The struggle to maintain cultures and communities, to exercise community self-development and economic self-sufficiency, is a struggle against the growing power and control of international monopoly. That is why the Native traditional movement is part of an international movement in solidarity against the abuses of the transnational corporations and toward the redevelopment of lifestyles on a human scale. The redevelopment of culture on a human scale is the only practical way that people and peoples can regain control of their lives and their destinies. It must be the primary goal of the traditional Indian movement, and other (often, as yet, unnamed) movements as well. The Native people have called that goal sovereignty, the international community calls it self-determination, and a number of American people refer to it as self-sufficiency, and all of these terms express in some way the nature of the goal.

The redevelopment of culture on a human scale—that's the goal of the traditional Indian movement. By its very definition, including its spiritual objectives, the movement must organize toward that goal. All else will lead to the extermination of our peoples. Any move that is contradictory to that goal is simply not a part of the solution and is too often a part of the problem. The strategies by which that redevelopment can and must take place will require some changes and sacrifices among those people who are of the movement. We are engaged in struggle, and it is a struggle for social change that is not much different from the kinds of social change efforts that have met repression in many countries in recent years. To be successful, Indian people need to be aware that discipline has characterized successful struggles in recent years. One element of the struggle waged by the North Vietnamese is especially important to study. The North Vietnamese made a conscious decision that their soldiers would not be responsible for atrocities committed against the civilian population, and although there has been some propaganda to the contrary in the United States, they in fact developed the image among the Vietnamese peasant population that their soldiers did not wage war against the people.

That was very important. Integrity among both the leadership and their following was a foundation of their struggle. Had they not emphasized discipline among their ranks, they would not have been successful in winning the hearts and minds of the people.

The traditional Indian movement needs that same kind of integrity. People are not going to support social change promoted by people who abuse other people. People aren't going to support a movement when its leadership is reported to have engaged in fist-fights in barrooms or to have threatened physical violence against elders who were in disagreement with them. Rip-offs of any kind simply can't provide leadership to a movement that seeks to revitalize spiritualism to attract the hearts and minds of the people. That kind of activity doesn't lead to the goal of redevelopment.

Integrity. It is an essential element of a traditional Indian struggle. Those of us who have experienced the movement know that a spiritual movement does not necessarily require charismatic leaders. The principles of the movement are able to motivate the people even if no leaders arise to represent those principles. The essential thing that must happen in such a movement is that the principles of traditionalism must be shared among the people and the politics of those principles be widely accepted. Once that is accomplished, the major objective becomes organization of the grassroots community around those principles.

The beauty and strength of a traditionalist movement is that it allows the formation of political/cultural organization at the community level in a way that seeks to empower the people in the place where they live. Simultaneously, it offers a set of shared principles that crosses cultural lines, making possible the existence of a national or Pan-Indian movement, because peoples across a vast geographic area share the same politics and can support the same issues. The traditional movement can act as a national entity even though it has little or no formal organization.

A small circle of very powerful interests (which in North America is called the ruling class) is pursuing policies that enrich themselves and that dispossess and impoverish people. The North American Indian peoples are but one specific group of victims of that process. The political forces among Indians that resist that process can line up in the traditional Indian movement.

The traditions of the peoples urge that the communities be strengthened through a spiritual practice that preserves their distinct nature. Traditionalism is not the wearing of beads or feathers or a unitary appearance at the Sun Dance or the Antelope Dance or any other kind of dance. It is the effort to establish community identity and the internal strengthening of the community with an emphasis on the preservation of those aspects of precolonial Indian life that makes those communities distinct. It is the recognition that individuals have a responsibility to be active members and participants in the life of their communities.

Traditionalism is not the act of seeking power for oneself. It is the effort to empower the community and through the community, the nation. Our ancestors were not in the habit of raising up dictators as chiefs and medicine men. The Indian people of old prized individuals who were givers to their community not takers. A good citizen of those societies was a man or woman who acted to benefit others. A great hunter was an honored man because he brought home meat to feed the people, not because he could kill a buffalo barehanded with one blow. A great woman was honored because she saw to the needs of the people, not because she could rabbit dance seventy-two hours without a break.

Traditionalism means the development of the community and thus the nation. The word has very specific trappings in Hopi or Cree or Onondaga communities, but in all of our cultures it is the politics of community development. The term has been vulgarized in any other context. Traditionalism is not the effort to develop powerful men; it is the effort to develop strong peoples. Powerful medicine people come from strong spiritual communities, not the other way around.

The effort to develop strong communities demands that we act in ways that reflect the strength of integrity. This effort demands that we act to see that the people can feed themselves, house themselves, clothe themselves, and control their children's education. Growing food, building housing, helping a neighbor, organizing a food co-op, learning to get along without a corporate grocery store—these are traditionalist activities every bit as much as dancing at the Snake Dance or learning to conduct a (Prairie) Chicken Dance.

Traditionalism continues to be a growing force within the Indian communities. It has matured considerably since 1968. Its adherents today organize at a community level to protect their environment, to educate their children, to promote in some way their cultural identity, to protect their land and water rights. More and more people are learning to develop cooperative modes of productive activity. Little by little, the people in the movement are beginning to become productive.

The self-development of peoples is a powerful set of politics. It is the wave of the future for Indian people, not the ghost of the past. It provides the politics from which will grow the efforts to develop the people's culture, to rejoin the people to the spiritual ways, to reenact the respect for the sacred web of life that will provide for the survival of the future generations. Through the unity of hearts and action the people will be empowered.

Traditionalism:
An Organizing Tool for Community Survival

Traditionalism is a form of social organization based on principles developed by Native peoples centuries ago. Its goal is the redevelopment of community life and the empowerment of land-based peoples in ways that promote the survival of cultures and provide a practice of social justice.

One of the reasons that the principles of traditionalism are so difficult to grasp is that the process is best developed when it is culturally specific. That means that there will be differences in the specific ways in which an Inuit community would be organized and the way a Lakota community is organized. The methodology, however, would be essentially the same for both, and it is the methodology that is being discussed here.

Native communities are under tremendous pressure. Some of the pressure originates from policies and plans implemented during the past two hundred years, policies and plans that were intended to terminate the tribe by destroying all Native cultural traditions and usages. But such blatant programs of governments are not the only sources of pressure. The history of the world since the Industrial Revolution has also been a powerful force that works to destroy rural community life, and that force is impacting Native peoples throughout the world in some very negative ways. Traditionalism is a way of reorganizing the community in ways to resist those pressures and, through reempowering the people, to ensure the survival of the communities, cultures, and peoples of the Natural World.

This kind of reorganization is not an easy task. Most adults have been socialized to see the ancient ways of our peoples as folklore. They have great difficulty relating to the principles of those ways as paths to a better and more productive society, and this is why they are unable to readily apply the principles of traditionalism. A reeducation process needs to take place while a practice is developed, and those who undertake the task should understand that there is resistance every step of the way, even within the communities that express traditional values and, sometimes, practice traditional ways.

In most places, practically all of the traditional economy is either destroyed or is in the process of being destroyed. Where it exists, the traditional economy is not viable enough to support the numbers of people who would depend on it, and where it does not exist, the wage economy has so completely replaced it that only its memory dimly remains.

The traditional communities need to find ways to revitalize. The most important aspect of that needed revitalization is economic revitalization, and the needed economic revitalization is the community's economy, not the wealth of the individual.

In the West, economies are based on the ability of individuals and associations of individuals to accumulate wealth. With this accumulated wealth it is expected that they will hold land and buildings, own tools, and that they will organize some forms of production. Other people will be laborers within that system and there will emerge "bosses." That hasn't happened to a great degree in the Native communities of North America as yet, but the process is under way. It is a process that pits people against one another in a competitive way. It creates the promotion of landlords who rent living space to their neighbors, or merchants who sell food to their neighbors, of other merchants who sell other necessities of life to their neighbors, and of a class or group of people who have interests in keeping others dependent for jobs, materials, housing, etc.

Hardly anyone will argue against the idea that it is in the interests of a community that all its members should have adequate housing, adequate food to eat, adequate opportunities for training so that they can support themselves. The Western mode of production, however, has some giant drawbacks in that the purpose of economic activity is not for production and the well-being of the society but rather for the profit of those who own the means of production, be those means factories or land. It is not difficult to see that the interests of merchants are contradictory to the interests of the community.

On the other end of the political economic spectrum we are offered a system called socialism. In practice, socialism has generally meant collective ownership by the state. The rhetoric of socialism suggests that the purpose of this form of organization is to promote the social condition under which everyone has equal access to the products of the society. In actual practice, however, since the state owns the means of production, and since the state is operated by political parties, those parties become a kind of ruling class with specific interests relative to the allocations of power within the society. The workers are not the owners of the means of production except in very abstract ways, and everybody understands that the potential for the development of privilege is not only abstract but real. The most practical alternative to that reality involves rule by a charismatic leader or a strongman, a form of dictatorship that has rarely been enlightened and mostly extremely oppressive. Such is not a practical possibility in most of the Native world.

There are many principles of traditionalist organization, but those principles are not widely understood. The first principle is that nobody owns anything—not the state, not the individual. Given the history of the past few centuries, that is an extremely hard principle to grasp, but it is an essential one. Before we go much further, it would be good if we could try to remind ourselves every little while that under this system nobody owns anything.

The objective of traditionalism is to organize distinct societies in ways of life that have a potential to survive. In the United States alone there are hundreds and hundreds of distinct Native communities, each with their own language, their own specific history, and their own identity as to where they live and who they are. Those societies face extinction not because their ways are out of step with the times but because they are under real economic and ideological pressures that are external in nature.

The pressures on the Native communities are many and varied but these pressures do have some common manifestations. In most places, the survival of distinct communities is threatened because young people are no longer speaking the language of their parents and are forced to leave home to take employment in distant cities. The reason they are forced to leave home is that there is not enough economic base at home to support them. In order to get jobs in the American society, they must learn the skills of that society, and the process by which they learn those skills is called education.

Many Native people blame education for the destruction of their communities. It is true that American schools do teach the children English and they do teach values that are of more use to the factory system of labor than they are to the development of a traditional or community economy, but one must note that the schools also teach the adults some lessons that people often don't know they are learning.

The American school system is based on two realities. The first is that the curriculum—what is taught to the student—is controlled by the state. In that sense, it is possible to say that the state "owns" the education curriculum in a socialist fashion. The second reality is that the decisions on the local level are often made by elected school board officials who often represent the interests of the property owners of the community. The process of decision making by the school board reflects these property relationships and provides the structure by which the power of this class of people is imposed on the community. Under these systems, the concept of the community's well-being is very specific in practice. The children are taught a curriculum that will provide skills to the larger society and prepare them for entry into a university or a trade, where they will learn skills that are needed by the industries whose representative sit on the curriculum planning boards of the state. The specific day-to-day learning experience is monitored by the local property owners.

It should be no surprise to anyone that the children are thus socialized to seek careers in the larger society, a process that takes them to employment situations hundreds, perhaps thousands, of miles from home. Given the representation of the local property owners, it should be of no surprise to anyone that the schools socialize children to the status quo and are extremely resistant to any kind of change.

A community organization that would attempt to preserve the community must be conscious of that process. The school systems do not promote community development. They motivate the children toward jobs in the industrial complex, jobs that take them far away from home. They socialize the children into competitive lifeways that resist and frustrate efforts at family cooperation that might form the foundation of community life.

Once the children have graduated from school, they are then faced with entry into the world of wage labor. In America, wage labor essentially means that people are paid to follow orders and they are paid with the expectation that their labor will produce a profit for the owners of the company. It is a form of social organization under which respect for human beings is extremely hard to cultivate. The laborer is essentially a person who may be treated as a slave for the hours during which he works. It is true that in some jobs he is an extremely well-paid slave, but the wages of labor are that the worker is a second-class person or a nonperson under this system.

People have a lot of trouble trying to see alternatives to these systems. For most people, the word *cooperation* is just that—a word.

Two things were said at the beginning of this essay to which we must now return. The first was that under traditionalism (the alternative, in this proposition) nobody owns anything. The second is that under traditionalism the way in which things are done should be culturally specific.

A traditionalist practice is a community development program. Long before Columbus sailed, Native communities enjoyed viable economies. A lot of things have happened since, and many Native communities don't have viable economies today. A community development program that is real will be designed to rebuild the potential for that to happen. Since there aren't enough buffalo or land for buffalo, we can't rebuild an economy based on hunting buffalo, but in many cases the two greatest assets remain—the people and the culture. To maintain these communities, it will be necessary that economic activity that could be viable be identified and that the people be organized around those activities. The objective, one must remember, is to provide the people with a viable and equitable way of life.

Let us say, for example, that we have identified the assets of a hypothetical community. This imaginary community has a small land base and a relatively small population base. The needs of this community, if it is to continue to survive as a community, are food, clothing, shelter, and some revenue to keep the people comfortable. The community land base consists of five hundred acres of arable land and there is an adult population of twelve hundred people. Of the twelve hundred, about twenty people are interested in participating in a community development program. The tribal government is in the hands of administrators who are not interested in the program, and all of the land is under a form of private control.

It has been determined in this hypothetical case that there is a need among these twenty adults for four houses and that there is some willingness among these people to develop a survival school.

The first thing we need to do is to start small and to take practical steps that we can take at the time. On most Native lands there are idle people who are hungry sitting on idle agricultural lands.

The community developer would see this and begin trying to find a way to help this community produce food for itself, but the question we are dealing with here is—how is this community going to organize to take this step?

The first thing we could look at is the fact that the socialization process has accustomed many of us to accept the idea of bosses but not the idea of leaders. Every project has to have some kind of leaders, and those leaders must have authority. Assuming that we are talking here about an agricultural project, we could look at traditional ways of organizing agricultural production for some ideas on how to proceed. Because this is an Iroquois publication, and because the Iroquois once possessed a genius at this sort of thing, let us look to them for our culturally specific example. (You will remember that it was stated that we would need to be culturally specific. This is not to suggest that people should follow the Iroquois example, but rather to suggest a way of finding an example.)

The Haudenosaunee (as the Iroquois are properly called) elected a woman chief to direct the work of the communal fields. She was given the title *entigowane* and she had the power to delegate authority to others. Once elected, she was to remain the boss for one year, which corresponds to the growing season. The next year, she could be reelected or she could be replaced, but the point is *she was elected by the workers.*

Under this system, nobody owned the land, but the workers did "own" the harvest in the sense that they reaped what they sowed. She was not paid for her job as administrator of the garden. Each person was delegated a work area, and each person literally received the fruits of his or her own labor at the harvest. Worker participation was voluntary but it was communally organized. Once a person volunteered, that person was expected to do his or her share, including taking the directions from the woman chief.

The whole organization of the society was much more complex than time or space permits in this essay, but the point can be made that several principles were enacted in those ancient times that we could learn from today. If a need exists for homes, mutual aid society can be organized to build the houses. Assuming that we can take that step, the next question is, how can we own housing.

In ancient times, people did not own houses in the sense that we know that word today. If there was a need for a house, the community provided the land and much of the labor. The person who needed the house assembled the materials, again often with the help of the mutual aid society. It was inconceivable in those times that someone would build a house in order to rent it to someone. That idea is one that destroys the mutual aid concept, thus destroying the community's practice of distribution of the fruits of labor and the cooperative principle upon which the community life was based. The modern form of such landholding principles is approximated in the movement to form community land trusts.

The problem of land ownership or property relations is that they are not only compulsory but they are essentially unfair and they are not productive. In the work place, the idea is that the worker works for the boss because he has little alternative except to work for another boss. That's a good system for the bosses, but it does little to provide for a basis for community life. Community life essentially means that there is cooperative effort, but it does not mean that there is no organization. In a community of Haudenosaunee, work in the garden is undertaken for the benefit of large extended families, and it provided substance for both.

If we were to organize a modern food-growing effort, we would probably find that we are faced with several problems. If we try to raise food using commercial methods, we could very well find that it costs more for machinery and land and seeds and fertilizer than the food we harvest is worth in the market. The alternatives to this problem would require us to try different modes of production and to organize our work under a different set of objectives, because it is unquestionably possible for a family or a group of families to raise their own food, or large portions of it, without heavy expenditures in land or fertilizer or machinery. In that way, organizing a food-raising effort, even if it is only supplementary at first, is one way of benefiting the community.*

It is possible, using what are called heritage plant varieties, to produce a dietary that would keep people healthy while drastically reducing their grocery bills. It would be an activity undertaken by a group of people that, when done as a community, could promote something called (in Christian circles) fellowship while helping

---

*Oneida, Seneca, Pueblo, Lakota, and many other Native reservation communities in subsequent decades organized food self-sufficiency efforts.—Ed.

people help themselves meet a real need. At the same time, it offers excellent opportunities for people to learn about agriculture, to be with their children, and to speak the language of their ancestors. Among agricultural peoples such as the Iroquois, it would add real meaning to the concept of the relationships between people and the vegetable kingdom and would help to motivate people to a real participation in their culture. That is the basis of community life.

But this can be the basis of community life only if people can access and share land, which is to say that nobody can act as though they have the right to deprive other people of access to land. That is what ownership implies—the right to deprive people of access to something, like land. At the same time, as actually prescribed in our ancient Great Law of Peace, it is also true that those who plant a garden have the right to the fruits of that garden—a right superior to the rights of the state or anyone else, including interlopers. Those who plant a garden own it in the sense that those who do not plant it have no rights to the fruits of that garden. Communal traditionalism means that in work organization, you work for yourself—no one works for you, and you work for no one. Because of the cooperative nature of social relations in this system, the interests of the community become indistinguishable from the interests of the individual. Thus participation in the mutual aid society is a way of socializing work so that labor in practice benefits the whole community.

At the same time, cooperative organization cannot be accomplished in an individualist atmosphere, and some jobs simply cannot be done by an individual. That is why the ancient Haudenosaunee communities appointed a leader in the gardens and why that leader had authority to make decisions about what went where and who did what and when. The workers, however, were protected from outside interests and outside pressures. There was no landowner demanding that they produce cotton export when the need was for corn to eat, in the way that state curriculum boards demand that a community that makes its living producing corn must send its sons and daughters to a school that seeks to produce people who can be trained for computer programming. The intent is not to deny adaptations to social change, but to find our way to being more mutually supportive communities and produce economic well-being while rebuilding our cultures.

The first line of criticism of this kind of thinking is that the Native people would be denying their children and their people access to a "better way of life." It is as though small communities are not allowed to have a strong sense of self-interest or a desire to act on a need for cultural survival. The traditionalist seeks to help his cultural community to survive by strengthening the community's economic and social base. It is the traditionalists' objective that the families become strong, that the children grow up in a cooperative way, valuing their culture and their way of life, and that the people take every possible step in empowering themselves as a group.

The example of the gardening project is used because of its historic precedence, not because it is proposed that every community needs to base its activities on gardens. There are many economic activities that Native people could develop, especially in the areas of cottage industries. The point is that the culture offers many organization points that are potentially more workable than the wage-labor system. It would be ideal if communities began to strive for independence from the American or Canadian market economies because therein lies the true potential for cultural survival. Self-sufficiency in everything—from clothing to housing to food production—would mean that people would be dependent on each other and not on somebody who seeks to make a profit from their labors. And it would mean that a Native community would continue to exist as a distinct community for generations to come.

The way to this possibility would require that we look to the cultures to find the human values of relationships for guidance in our work. We might organize businesses that are in fact worker cooperatives. We might move away from the European concept of ownership and develop (or redevelop) our own concepts about how to hold property. Policy decisions would be shared among the workers, and the benefits of labor would accrue to the workers. The ideal would be when the community as a whole would again begin to take some responsibility for the well-being of its neighbors in the sense that if someone needs a house, his neighbors will help to build him a house, and in return he will help a neighbor build a house.

What people are having the most trouble seeing is that they occasionally copy the exact forms they are trying to escape when they set up organizations. There is a tendency to want to talk about collective ownership as though that concept is entirely contradictory to tradition. Our social training now fuels a tendency to seek strict employee/employer relationships that generate the sense that workers should have nothing to say about the conditions or process of their work.

If we are going to set up schools—and there is much debate on the whole idea of schools—then those schools should not work like the bourgeois schools. They should not teach a curriculum designed by those in power to help the industrial machinery of America but should be teaching a curriculum designed to develop the political and social economies of the specific community they serve. They should not reflect racist ideologies, or "reverse" racist ideologies, and they should not reflect the needs of the reservation landowners as landowners. They must reflect always the needs of the community, and they must be responsive to the needs of the people who have volunteered their time and energy to the effort— the teachers, administrators, and students of the school.

These thoughs are meant to stimulate the potential for community rebuilding among traditional Native peoples. These are examples that almost everyone can identify with, but they are not intended to be specific examples. The same principles can apply to a community garden market or to a community health service or to anything else, even to a cooperative cottage industry. Most of all, we need the creativity of the young people and the coming generation.

The traditional way, when viewed as a methodology, could be the Native peoples' greatest asset. In fact, it could turn out to be the only way that communities of Native people can organize for their own survival. The alternative is to send your children to schools and to jobs of highest promise, and to say good-bye to the ideas of family and community, because we can't have those things if our children move away. As federal grants and other economic hopes dry up, we must develop our own alternatives, with options more hopeful and attractive to our children.

Marxism: Perspectives from a Native Movement

There are clear differences between what is widely accepted as Marxist ideology and the ideologies that comprise the Native Peoples' movements. While both movements are avowedly anticolonialist, anti-imperialist and anticapitalist, it will be seen that the two traditions have entirely different roots. The Native Peoples' movement expresses an ideology that is, by definition, primarily anticolonialist and anti-imperialist and that emphasizes cultural diversity. Marxist ideology, on the other hand, is primarily anticapitalist, and is unquestionably anti *capitalist* imperialism and anti *capitalist* colonialism. Many will be surprised that these two ideologies have very different objectives. In fact, Marxist-Leninist thought and the ideologies of Native Peoples' movements are so different that the question arises whether the two are compatible at all.

For the purpose of discussion, it will be useful to speak only in the most general terms of a Native Peoples' movement because there is not a tradition of a published ideology comparable to the classic works of Marxism. At the same time, there are many Marxist tendencies and almost any general statement about Marxism is almost certain to misinterpret some tendency of Marxist thought. Although there are fundamentalists within both groups, it would be unfair to state that either Marxists or Native Peoples' movements are ideologically static. Both are capable of responding to changing realities and each appears able to incorporate the thoughts of the other to some degree.

Native Peoples' movements constitute a class of ideologies that have arisen, in recent centuries, in response to imperialism and colonialism. Although highly complex and variable in nature, these movements tend to find their roots in the history of specific nations and peoples and their struggle to survive in the face of expanding imperialist (and more recently, industrial) cultures. The ideologies of these movements tend to be pronationalist (with a cultural definition of nationalism), anticolonialist, anti-imperialist, anti-industrialist, proregionalist, anticapitalist and, not surprisingly, decentralist. The Native Peoples of the Western Hemisphere are one of the groups of nations and peoples that comprise this class of movements, but there are many other Native groups throughout the world that adhere to similar principles. There are also ideologies within or on the fringes of the Western tradition that propose very similar ideologies, especially the "back to the land" and neo-tribalist groups that promote human-scale societies and regionally appropriate economies.

Marxism is an ideology that arose in response to the Industrial Revolution. It is today a highly developed, extremely sophisticated intellectual and political tradition that, because of its origins in western Europe, is primarily anticapitalist. The tradition known as Marxism consists basically of analyses of capitalism and a vision of a postcapitalist society. Marxism is based on the premise that a ruling class exists within the industrial (and specifically capitalist) societies and that ruling-class interests exploit the labor societies and that ruling-class interests exploit the labor of the working classes. According to the classical Marxist prophesy (which is somewhat more subjective matter than Marxist analysis), this imbalance of power and exploitation will cause the workers to eventually be oppressed to the point that they will rise up and overthrow their exploiters, the ruling class.

The Native Peoples' movement, at least some sectors of it, has prophesies also. According to the Native prophesies (which are also different from the Native Peoples' analyses), the whole of industrial society is exploiting the physical world to the point that someday the Natural World will be unable to continue to provide the necessary materials for industrial society and the latter will experience some kind of collapse, often initiated by some form of natural disaster.

Both movements predict crises in the capitalist modes of production and economy. Marxism promotes that this crisis will be precipitated by the workers, and the Native prophets state that man-made alterations of the environment will trigger events that take the form of natural disasters (droughts, changing climates, crop failures, etc.) or wars that will destroy the base of industrial society and possibly destroy the basis of human inhabitation of the planet or large parts of the planet.

The Native movements, which see industrial society pitted against Nature, find Nature to be a source of both psychological and economic sustenance. Although Native Peoples employ specific and sometimes fairly complex technologies to maintain their societies in parts of the world that require such technologies, these movements are considered antitechnology because when they speak of technology they are specifically referring to the European development of industrial technology, which they oppose.

Marxism is an ideology that developed as a critique to capitalism. Marxist critique is sometimes criticized because it views all political movements and definitions within the framework of the struggle between Marxist and capitalist ideologies, as though no other ideologies exist or could exist. Marxist writers very often write as though there exist in the world only capitalism and Marxism, and they often describe political thoughts or analyses that are not their own as having either capitalist (or bourgeois) roots or being incorrect (counterrevolutionary) Marxism.

Despite this sense of the world in terms of black and white, Marxism and capitalism, the two ideologies have some striking things in common. Like capitalist ideologists, Marxists generally see nature as an object to be manipulated and exploited. Marxism has developed the almost automatic response that any subjective view of Nature must be a product of bourgeois romanticism. (Capitalists, incidentally, share an aversion for romantic idealists, especially on environmental issues.)

Marxism generally tends to view industrial technology as being almost universally benevolent, and their definition for *progress* sounds alarmingly similar to the definition that capitalist technocrats have for that word. The Marxist tradition, which has developed a simply marvelous methodology for the analysis of capitalism, has simply never been able to apply the same kind of methodology to industrial technologies.

Marxist thought also sees religion as a threat, a diversion from the work of organizing the proletariat against the ruling class, the oft-mentioned "opiate of the proletariat." There are, of course, leftist and Marxist tendencies that do not accept this definition of religion, but the general flow of Marxist ideology holds that religion or spirituality of any kind serves the interests of the ruling capitalist classes.

The Native movements, on the other hand, view spiritualism (which the Marxists would identify as religion) in an entirely different light. Some Native Peoples speak of "liberation theologies," and they base their spiritualism on a reverence for Nature. Native movements have not been averse to the use of scientific evidence to move their arguments forward, a development that fundamentalist Marxists would find a contradiction. Marxism finds religion a contradiction to science. The Native Peoples' movements, especially during the twentieth century, have looked to scientific evidence as a source of proof of their views that industrial technologies are a danger to the Natural World and to peoples who would depend on the Natural World for their existence and survival. Native Peoples also point to their perception that although industrial peoples may not have developed an awareness of reality, they too are dependent upon the Natural World for their survival. Spiritualism, then, is an important ingredient to Native Peoples' movements, although it is a Natural World spiritualism that is in many ways a complete contradiction to the spiritualism or religion of the industrialized West and has a completely different history.

The social objectives of these two movements are also substantially different. The Native Peoples often express a strong desire to promote the health and survival of the extended family. They see the social institutions of the industrial societies as a threat to the family, in general, and to the extended family, in particular. To Native Peoples' movements, the extended family offers an alternative to technocratic, hierarchical industrial societies. The Native movements assert that Native Peoples compose small nations and peoples of the world and that such nations and peoples have rights to continue to exist, to be self-governing, and to determine their own destinies. Since this ideology promotes local autonomy and the development of the integrity of local communities, and since the idealized Marxist industrial society (called socialism) requires that its members' needs be met by a huge and centralized nation-state apparatus, the two movements differ greatly in this area. In fact, even in those countries where Marxist ideology is characterized by a tendency with a reverence for the family, there exists a contradiction that is glaring, at least in ideological terms.

There are other areas in which Marxist ideology and practice are clearly contradictory to the objectives of Native Peoples' movements. It seems unlikely that a huge socialist industrial country would be supportive of the claims of small nations and peoples to local autonomy and cultural identity. The history of the Soviet Union under socialism is not a model that champions the rights of its "national minorities." In fact, it is open to question whether it is possible for an industrial society, under either capitalism or socialism, to be a model that champions the rights of its national minorities. In fact, it is open to question whether it is possible for an industrial society, under either capitalism or socialism, to avoid being a colonialist power. Suppose that a Marxist country found out that it was cheaper to import natural raw materials from some preindustrial society that had been colonized. History has shown us that countries like the Soviet Union have chosen to go to the world market to purchase raw materials (such as rubber) from capitalist suppliers who acquired those materials from the lands and labors of Native Peoples. In that sense, Marxist countries are subject to participating in colonialism because the nature of industrial societies is that industries need raw materials that are to be found in the lands of preindustrial (or postindustrial?) societies. Industrial societies depend on the mass market and are, by definition, colonialist in nature. Capitalist and socialist ideologies share the same view on this subject. Given uranium deposits on the lands of Native Peoples, there is nothing in Marxist ideology that would prevent the exploitation of that resource, even if the result is the predictable destruction of whole cultures.

A student of Marxist ideology could easily conclude that the planet Earth is endowed with practically infinite material wealth, which, given proper social organization, could benefit all the masses of the Earth in the form of material enrichment. Within that ideology is the assumption that all the peoples of the world could, given the fall of capitalism, become industrialized. The peoples of Burma and Thailand could become industrialized, the peoples of the Sahara and the Gobi, the peoples of the rain forests of South America—all could be integrated into a world society of industrial workers. The product of all that industrialization would be a controlled economy, run for the benefit of the proletariat, that would see to everyone's material needs for an indefinite amount of time.

The oil that would fuel the cars of industrialized Nepal and Madagascar would be found and developed. Nuclear power could be expanded indefinitely and, under socialism, that technology would automatically be improved and made safe. Marxist ideology is, to be kind, pretty idealist.

An ideology that envisions an industrial society, whether run by workers (if that were possible) or by a capitalist (or socialist) ruling

class, is bound to conflict with an ideology that favors local autonomy and locally appropriate economies (and thus technologies).

The reasons for this are to be found within the basic structure
of Marxist thought. According to the tenets of Marxism, capitalist
class interest will create such oppressions that the proletariat will
be forced to violent revolution to overthrow the ruling class. Following the revolution (which, by the way, has yet to happen in any
industrialized country and which happened in the Soviet Union
prior to Russia's period of industrial development), avant-garde elements of the revolutionary intelligentsia will take control and organize the country to bring socialism to reality. The emphasis here is
heavy on the concept of organization and hierarchy. This organization is to be undertaken by an intellectual bourgeoisie that, in fact,
has evolved into a privileged managerial class that serves functions
very much like those served by the ruling class under capitalism.
The proletariat will benefit from this benevolent hierarchy because
there will be a more equal distribution of goods and services, and
because there will be full employment in a workers' paradise. This
emphasis on hierarchical organization and the conscious creation
of a privileged managerial class has caused critics of Marxism to
assert that Marxism is, after all, a bourgeois ideology.

When Marxist theory was first formulated, the industrial age
was fairly young, and people had not yet been faced with the hor-
rible excesses of industrialization, nor did they have a full appreciation of the pitfalls of bureaucratic hierarchies. There were, in
those now-forgotten times, no reports of such phenomena as the
Love Canal, no worries about oil or wood shortages or any kind
of materials shortages. The idea that there might one day be major
accidents involving nuclear waste dumps, accidents such as are
reported to have occurred in the Soviet Union, had not yet surfaced. Marxism was born in a day before these things were known.
It was a time when industry could be idealized and industrial societies could be idealized, and when genetic mutation and nuclear
pollution were the subjects of science fiction and not the day's
newspaper headlines.

Modern Marxism is saddled with assumptions that were appropriate to the mid-nineteenth century. Marxist analysts generally
ignore or deny that there are any material shortages in the world
or that there will be such shortages. They assert, in their role as

prophets, that technologies will be developed that will solve any of the industrial world's problems—a prophecy much in agreement with prophesies of their capitalist counterparts. Marxist ideology is clearly committed to promote the opinion that whatever benefits the needs of the industrial proletariat, be it oil drilling in the Artic or uranium mining on the tundra, is justified. If any local peoples happen to be living where the minerals are, their existence must be sacrificed to the needs of the proletariat. That justification is, of course, a lie. The real reason that peoples are sacrificed under socialism is that Marxism creates a ruling (call it a managerial) class that has the same interests in this development as the ruling class in capitalist society.

Marxist ideology is historically a bourgeois ideology in the sense that practically all of its inventors and theoreticians were members of the bourgeois class. It seems without question that most of its organizational fetish is a product of that bourgeois influences—the bourgeoisie, however radical, has a subconscious fear of the masses. Thus the new bourgeoisie is given a role in Marxist ideology—they are to be the intellectual elite, the party members, the "dictatorship of [(over)] the proletariat," the nonworkers in a workers' paradise.

The Native Peoples' movements generally seek egalitarian social structure in a postindustrial society, and there is a considerable amount of assertion that class structure of any kind is to be avoided.

The basic theoretical conflicts between Native Peoples' movements and Marxist ideology lie in the disagreements between the prophets of the movements. The prophets of the Native movement seem to be saying that capitalism and all of industrial society must eventually come into crisis because the material base of their society is finite and has physical limits. When those material limits are reached and exceeded, the industrial society will come into crisis.

The differences between these two movements can be seen as differences between a movement that originates from within industrial society and one that originates outside of that society. At least some of the differences reflect the different realities that face Native Peoples and those realities that are faced by industrialized peoples.

Native prophets state that what will happen is that industrial societies will overextend themselves in the physical world. There are a number of tendencies to these prophesies, but it seems generally to be true that Native prophets see the collapse of industrial society as a product of the exhaustion of the Natural World, although they are not usually absolutely specific about whether that means that it will run out of energy or raw materials or it will pollute itself to death. It is probably safe to state that most of the Native prophets and prophecies do not find it impossible that industrial society will do both. Wars are sometimes predicted.

It is interesting to speculate that the Native prophesies could conceivably come to pass even after the Marxist prophecies had come to pass. That is, it could happen that the workers' paradise could experience crisis because of a coal or iron ore shortage, or widespread poisons that result from the use of chemicals in technology could cause massive social and economic disruption. Wars are always possible, and the wars of the atomic age seem likely to be able to bomb the human race "back to the Stone Age," or into infinity.

Marxist prophecy makes two general predictions. The first (which now reads like early Christian expectations of the second coming of Christ, which they expected within the first two centuries AD) is that the oppressed proletariat will rise up and overthrow the ruling capitalist class. The second is that some form of mismanagement or false management of the world capitalist economy will lead to a crisis that will cause the world market economy to collapse. This area of prophesy has many variations (and the market economy collapse that focuses on the expectation of currency failures is very recent and not correctly Marxist in origin), but all conclude that the world economic crisis, which will cause capitalism to go into serious crisis, will trigger revolutions around the world.

Marxism offers a future world of an industrial paradise where the workers' needs are taken care of by the state and where material want has been eliminated. The Native movement's prophets offer a future world where humans are interdependent with the forces of Nature, where there is little state power but great local autonomy, and where the workers (although they would not refer to the people as workers) are the consumers of the products of their own labors. Some Native prophets offer a future that is considerably more bleak—a world in which Nature has been all but destroyed and where people exist on the submarginal remains of the world's ecosystems.

Aside from the assertion that Marxism is ultimately a bourgeois ideology, the single most damning accusation brought by Native Peoples and other critics is that Marxism is simply a distillation of capitalist industrialist Western society. Some Native political philosophers believe that Marxism is exactly what so many Marxists promote it to be, the most efficient form of social organization for industrialized man. Some of the Native Peoples see the workings of Marxist ideology as leading to a superindustrialized world in which the worst effects of industrial capitalism, which they see already destroying the world, are made to move even faster and more efficiently.

There are some strong arguments in the defense of Marxism, and some weak ones. The argument that Marxism is the only kind of organized resistance to capitalism that has ever worked does not appear to stand the test of history. Most successful revolutions in this century have been nationalist in nature and not class struggles of the type envisioned by Marxist ideology. It is probably more correct, however, that in some of the industrialized countries, especially in western Europe, Marxist critiques of capitalism and the organization of the workers are necessary steps in the development of movements that may free peoples. It is also true that Marxism has many faces and that the Native Peoples' movement can find many allies among workers' groups and organizations. The two movements have greatly different ideologies, histories, and different goals and objectives, but there are many Marxist tendencies that are truly anticolonial in theory. There are also some Marxist tendencies, or at least tendencies that call themselves Marxist, that reject the hierarchical structure that has characterized Marxist history. The Native Peoples' movements are not and should not be engaged in an ideological war with all of these Marxist tendencies.

The movements of Native Peoples and Marxism are two separate and distinct ideologies. In many aspects, Marxism and these movements conflict in ideology. The Native Peoples' movement will, hopefully, develop a well-articulated and published ideology at some point during the ensuing decades, and there could well develop an intellectual tradition that could be studied and shared among many peoples. Marxism has never been critiqued from a perspective that is truly external to the objectives of Western ideologies. The first responses of Marxists has been to fall back on old and tried answers that were applicable in response to capitalist criticisms but that misinterpret the source of criticisms from what the Marxist language calls the third world. The debate, one might say, has barely begun. The struggle, however, continues.

There are also some strong arguments in criticism of the Native Peoples' movements. Foremost among these arguments is the observation that there presently exists no published tradition that really represents this ideology. This lack of a published ideology makes it very difficult for the movement to acquire adherents, since there seem to be no recognized philosophers whose philosophies can be used as a teaching and study tool. In fact, this problem is so significant that even to speak of a Native Peoples' movement and its principles requires that one invent the term for the purpose. This lack of a recognized published ideology leaves the Native Peoples open to unfair criticisms that are not based on any real intellectual history. For example, critics of the movement state that Native Peoples tend to idealize the past and that they are not sensitive to current realities. Some of those criticisms are indicative of the critics, especially those who see Native Peoples as entirely historical beings. There is some resistance by contemporary European writers to accept the concept and reality that Native Peoples and political philosophers exist in the twentieth century, a bias that is shared by both the conservatives and the modern Left. There is also a tendency on the part of many critics to assume that a Native Peoples' movement must be romanticist in nature without any real effort to analyze and compare these movements. There may be tendencies within Native movements that have some romanticist tendencies, but writers within the movement tend to be critical of romanticism.

There is also the tendency on the part of modern critics to see Native movements as antiscientific and anti-intellectual. Thus, Native movements are stereotyped in ways that would be immediately challenged were they applied to other movements, but go unchallenged by a Native community that has no identifiable body of intellectual thought. It is a weakness that Native Peoples' movements need to address.

Finally, too often Native Peoples' movements try too hard to disassociate themselves from all other forms of political ideology.

There is an effort on the part of some Native Peoples to try to be absolutely unique, and to eschew any connection whatever with any other analysis or tool of analysis other than that developed by themselves. There appear to be substantial areas of Marxist thought in the critique of capitalism that should be useful to the Native movement, and there is a kind of progressive humanism that surfaces in the writings of many current writers on the history and development of technology and political economy that can serve to move Native interests forward. There is nothing contradictory about Native People seeking and finding allies within the camps of the ideologies of other peoples, and there is little doubt that social change, were such to take place in the West, would produce ideologies and movement that could complement the objectives of Native Peoples. There is nothing in the annals of history to prove that Marxists cannot acquire some kind of spiritual awareness (even if it is not religion) and that Native Peoples cannot develop or adopt forms of acceptable technologies that meet their needs in the context of their current realities. In fact, these kinds of things must happen.

Racism: An American Ideology

The "discovery" of the Western Hemisphere by European nations seeking avenues of trade sparked a truly revolutionary series of events. One of the initial results was the rise of racism, an ideology that has formed the foundation for modern colonialism and the ruthless exploitation of the Natural World in the names of progress and civilization. The processes of exploitation and genocide, with their concurrent ideologies of racism and progressivism, are not simply historical happenings from the distant past. Those processes are alive and well in the Western Hemisphere today and form the paradigm for all relationships between Native peoples and the Western World.

Racism is an ideology that has its origins, theoretically, in the somewhat shaky premise that some people (specifically civilized people) are biologically superior to other, less civilized peoples. The introduction of an ideology based on biology is a peculiarly modern phenomenon, traceable to the period following the European penetration of the Americas. There had been many instances of cultural antagonism, and caste systems were widely practiced in the ancient world. But nothing was developed that approached the systematic genocide and destruction of whole peoples that followed the development of racism.

So pervasive is that ideology today, so widely are its basic premises simply accepted in the Western world, that the ideology is rarely recognized as an ideology. Its basic premises are restated and reinforced daily in the newspapers of the Western world. Colleges and universities rarely offer courses on the subject. And yet, as an ideology, it has more followers than any religion. Racism is the most powerful river of thought in the West. It is an ideology whose opponents are treated as heretics, persecuted, tortured, and murdered. Racism and the political ideology that it gives sanction—colonialism—are the two most powerful movements of the modern world.

The Origins of Racist Thought

Christopher Columbus was a Genovese merchant-adventurer, sailing under the Spanish flag in search of a shorter passage to the markets of the Orient, specifically Japan. Like many who would follow him, he saw his mission as something of a religious quest. Other European explorers had landed on the shores of the Americas, but generally in the Northern Hemisphere, in areas where the climate was too hostile for other than a short stay. Columbus's voyage was different in several respects from earlier voyages. Navigation technology, although crude, was sufficiently evolved to permit repeat voyages, and Columbus landed in the Caribbean, an area that offered pleasant weather and friendly native inhabitants.

Even his name was prophetic to the world he encountered— *Christopher Columbus* translates to "Christ-bearer Colonizer." During the early contacts, he noted that the island people, though primitive, seemed to be healthy and happy. His log indicated that they might be a good source of slaves, and he kidnapped and took some of the people back to Spain.

Columbus's announcement of the discovery of new lands across the Atlantic set into motion literally hundreds of expeditions in the decades following 1492. Soon, Spanish ships bearing men of arms became a common sight in the Caribbean areas, and Spanish conquistadores rapidly penetrated remote areas of Central and South America seeking potential riches, establishing the feudal encomienda, and spreading the "word of God" among the Native peoples.

The Spanish conquest is probably the goriest and most brutal chapter in all of Western history, although it is a chapter that is arguably not yet finished. It is probable that millions of Native people were killed as Spanish armies entered the land. The streets of Mexico were described as flowing rivers of blood. The Spanish were so cruel that the Native people did not believe that they were even human—such beasts, they thought, must be spawned from the sea.

The Taino and Carib peoples, among the most naturalistic in Central America, were also among the first victims of the conquest. History records that Spanish armies entered their villages, armed and carrying a written proclamation. In the village square, a cleric then read to the Native people a demand, often in Latin, that all the people come forth and present themselves and all their worldly possessions to the tribute and service of the king of Spain. Those failing to do so within a period of about ten minutes were to be put to the sword. The reading of the proclamation provided sufficient rationalization in the form of a "fair and just" warning to justify the slaughter of men, women, and children that customarily followed. In that way, many areas were almost or totally depopulated.

The butchery and treachery of that period stirred the conscience, apparently, of even some of the Spanish. One, Bartolomé de Las Casas, a cleric, began writing treatises denouncing the cruelty of the Spanish toward the Native people. His essays were published in European countries (such as England and France), which were already antagonistic to Spain, and had the apparent effect of exerting some pressure on the Spanish Crown to try to absolve the national image. The Crown decided that the question of the treatment of the Native peoples should be the subject of a kind of administrative investigation, which took form in a sort of trial that became known as the Valladolid debates, argued before the Council of the Indies.

Because of his work defending the Indians, Las Casas came to be called the Patron Saint of the Indians. Las Casas was something of an early humanitarian. By 1540, he had spent most of his life among Indians and had seen their accomplishments, especially in Mexico. But he was not a man without ulterior motives. A priest, he would argue that the Indians were human beings who possessed reason and souls, and this identified them as of a higher order than simple beasts of burden and that they could and should be brought under the reign of the church.

Much of Las Casas's defense of Indians centered on the argument that critics of Indians who said they were incapable of becoming civilized were simply wrong, that the Indians had, in fact, developed civilizations that were admirable.

The conquistadores, who naturally opposed the meddling of the church in their relationships with their slaves, found an advocate in Juan Ginés de Sepúlveda, a scholar who had studied at the University of Salamanca. Sepúlveda is identified as the father of modern racism. In 1540, he was considered one of the most knowledgeable of Spanish authorities on the teachings of Aristotle. (At the time, feudal Europe recognized two basic sources of knowledge—Aristotle and the Bible.) Sepúlveda had never been to America, and it is probable that he never even saw an Indian, but he was amply capable of giving expression to the most widely held ideologies of the Western world. He is one of the most underestimated figures in the history of Western thought.

Sepúlveda argued that the Native people were not really human beings at all. As proof, he cited the fact that such people were totally unlettered, lacking in the civilized arts. They do not, he said, have the "true religion," and are not intellectually capable of a true understanding of that religion. He went on to state that the Native populations are, in reality, brutes, that they are subhuman, incapable of the refinements of civilization. He pointed to the fact that they could speak neither Spanish nor Latin, that their customs were strange, that they possessed not even the rudimentary arts of animal domestication.

His argument deepened when he turned to Aristotle as an authority. Aristotle had developed a theory of universal existence that postulated that the universe contained in some degree or other all that is possible to exist. There is pure light, pure darkness, and in between there exists every possible degree of illumination.

That line of thinking gave rise to thoughts about the nature of man. Since there exists in the world, on the one hand, brutes (described as animals without intelligence or apparent purpose, a distinctly European definition of animals), and on the other hand, civilized, refined, rational man, must not there also exist in the universe gradations of man on a vertical scale, ranging from civilized man at the top to brutish man at the bottom?

Aristotle's philosophy may have originated from a quite different purpose, but Sepúlveda seized on it as proof of the inhumanity, or at least subhumanity, of the American Indian race. At last, said Sepúlveda, we have found the brutish man in Aristotle's teachings. Are not the Indians merely animals in human form? Lacking in religion and culture as they are, are they not merely Aristotle's man-brutes, inferior beings born to serve their natural masters, the Christian Spanish? Indeed, is not their inferiority a plan of Nature? Of god?

As evidence, he cited the widely held opinions of the Spanish. Are not the Indians dirty? Do they not worship idols and strange gods? He gave something that looked like academic substance to the generally accepted attitudes of the Spanish of his day. He placed the prejudices of the Spanish into the arena of the biological and theoretical argument based on the plan of Nature, an argument that is still being waged. The Indians, by appearance, are dark. There never was a handsome Indian. They are not intelligent. They are subhuman. Their only purpose in the universe is to the service of civilized man. In their turn, the other European nations would reach the same kinds of conclusions relative to the non-European peoples of the world. Sepúlveda is significant because he was one of the first to express the thoughts, he expressed them clearly, and he left a record for all to see.

Sepúlveda went on to say that the Indians are found in such a miserable state of material and spiritual existence that it is the right, nay, the obligation, of the Spanish to bring them the light and benefits of civilization. So powerful is this need, so vile their primitive existence, that civilized man has a duty to take whatever measures necessary to eradicate these conditions of darkness. Indeed, even death is a blessed escape to these miserable creatures, an escape from their lives of service to deviltry.

Enslavement was justified, under these arguments, because it accompanied the blessings of civilization. True, the Indians were forced to relinquish their lands, their cultures, their worldly goods, even their lives. But did not the survivors receive in return the knowledge of the wheel and the donkey? Were they not given the blessings of the true religion? Surely the Indians received the best of the trade. Even those who were killed had been rightly treated, for they had been released from service to the Devil. The Spanish, in their kindness, were purifying the Indian with fire and sword, whip and chain. And in return, justly, the Spanish received the Indians' land, their labor, and their worldly possessions. Under this argument, the Indian sacrifices seemed like a fair exchange. In the long run, the Indians would be "better off," their situation "improved."

Las Casas replied with the left-hand version of the same argument. He agreed, basically, that the Indians must be brought to the proper religion and to the service of the king of Spain. His major difference with Sepúlveda was that he believed that this could and morally should be brought about through persuasion and not by the use of force. Las Casas can best be described as a kind of early liberal racist. He believed in generally the same ends as Sepúlveda, but he argued for different means.

Las Casas stated that the Indian people were in fact intelligent people who were capable of receiving the true religion. He pointed to the fact that Indian families have admirable relationships with their children, that prior to the conquest the Indians of Mexico even had colleges and universities. He argued that many had been successfully instructed in the religion and arts of civilization.

He believed that the Indians could be brought to civilization and Christianity through fair treatment and good example. Once they accepted the true religion, he argued, it would be an easy step to bring them willingly to the service of the Crown. He argued, above all, that the Indians were humans, that they possessed souls, and that they belonged under the domination of the church. Under Christianity, the Indians would be "better off," their situation "improved."

The two elements of these social ideologies focused on methods of achieving the same ends. Sepúlveda, the conservative, argued that force was an acceptable, in fact, necessary means. Las Casas favored persuasion. History was to prove that cultural and physical genocide were achieved under both processes.

The Essential Conflict

It is no accident that racism has such powerful cultural ingredients as surfaced in the Valladolid debates. In fact, the long history of racism has indicated that the basic ideology will stand even when the biological premises have been largely removed or at least relegated to new terms. Genocidal policies need not be based on biological ideologies—they can be blatantly pragmatic. In the twentieth century, it is sufficient to state that the needs of civilization or progress "for the national good" provides justification for the taking of a people's resources (land, minerals, water) without ever mentioning that those people are of a separate race. Cultural genocide has become a regrettable but necessary evil, a simple consequence of progress.

The "discovery" of the Americas brought Western civilization into contact and conflict with the Natural World peoples all over the globe. The true nature of the conflict that resulted can be seen through an analysis of Western culture.

The West is a true civilization. It is a culture that organizes its societies into population centers that are not materially self-sufficient. Cities are population concentrations that depend on outside sources for their existence. They must import their food, fuel, materials, even laborers, from other places. This requires, basically, the subjugation and extraction from the Natural World of food, fuel, water, power, and all the things civilizations need in order to survive.

It seems not only logical but actually necessary that Western civilization would develop racist ideologies. Racism basically rationalizes and justifies the subjugation necessary to facilitate the extraction of materials and labor from the Natural World. The actual implementation of that process has been known, variously, as colonialism and imperialism.

The Colonial Imperative

Modern Paraguay and Brazil, among other countries, provide excellent examples that racism and genocide in their crudest forms still exist in the 1970s. In Paraguay, the hunting and killing of Indians is not considered murder because Indians are not truly considered to be human beings. In Brazil, the destruction of Native peoples is for all practical purposes a national policy rationalized in the name of development and progress.

The people of the Natural World continue to be under the most devastating attack by civilized peoples.

Natural World peoples are systematically hunted and killed virtually everywhere they still exist, but especially in regions that contain natural resources. Those who survive the initial period of "just warfare" are often removed to new locations, sometimes called reservations. Sometimes they are allowed to remain in their ancestral homelands. But always they are denied their rights to the land. Aboriginal titles to land are not recognized, or are only partly recognized, because Natural World peoples are not considered legally human, and their nations are not considered to be legal nations in the legal systems of the West. Racism is rampant in the legal systems of imperialist countries, especially in the areas of the denial of the existence of traditional or Natural World forms of government and land titles.

Civilized countries demand that colonized peoples be "domesticated" in the same sense that chattel are domesticated. Policies are implemented that are intended to specialize their behavior in the interests of their colonizers. Natural World people are almost never left alone to live within the definitions of their own culture.

They are specialized ("educated" is the common usage), trained to the needs of civilization, forced into roles that make them a part of the extractive process that sends labor and materials to the cities of their oppressors.

The process of colonization is so widely practiced that it has become almost invisible in the twentieth century. "Civilizing the Indian" has become the standard carried by the modern liberal racist. It is argued on the premise that through civilization the Indian will be better off. Civilization is for the Indian's own good, even if it kills him.

Modern colonialism requires that the Native people participate in their own exploitation. In North America, many of the vestiges of Native freedom, in the form of Native government and economy, have been forcibly eradicated. In place of the traditional or Natural World forms of government and society are Native administrators of colonial policies, people who have been "educated," trained in the skills of the oppression of their own people. There are few places that are exceptions to this rule. Most recognized Native governments in the United States and Canada are not Native governments at all. They are, instead, modern colonial governments with racial Indian (but culturally Western) administrations whose function is to carry out genocidal policies. Racism and colonialism are twins in the process of genocide. And both are alive and well in the Western Hemisphere.

Thoughts from an Autochthonous Center: Postmodernism and Cultural Studies

Yvonne Dion-Buffalo and John C. Mohawk

For approximately five hundred years, European civilizations subjugated or destroyed peoples around the world. By the 1890s, about 85 percent of the landmass of the Earth was either a colony or a former colony of Europe. During this long period of conquest, Europeans developed an intensive and impressive body of ideologies to explain their success as the inevitable result of the inherent superiority of their culture and at points even their biology, although the expansion was actually the result of military success. The psychological and social foundation of this period of conquest and colonization is found in the ability to coerce the peoples of the world to accept the rules by which European politics and ideologies claimed the power to determine what is legitimate about the human experience.[1]

Other cultures have expanded and conquered, but none has expanded so far and so powerfully. At each stage of the expansion, European culture adopted new and more effective utopian ideologies that have proven powerful forces in motivating people either to support aggressive expansion and exploitation of others or to stand docilely in the face of such aggressions.[2] The original utopia, the Garden of Eden, served as a model for the coercive powers of the state.[3]

During the fifteenth and sixteenth centuries, Europeans justified the plunder of the Caribbean and Central America on the premise that Christianity was the "true" religion and that they were doing subjugated peoples a service by forcing them to it. At one point, the Spanish decided that because they were the purveyors of God's message to "new" worlds, they should be exempt from physical labor and other people should do all the menial work.[4] This kind of thinking became the foundation of racism in the modern world. People who can convince themselves they have solutions to all of humankind's problems tend to arm themselves with permission to do whatever is necessary to effect what they consider the desired ends and are almost always the privileged beneficiaries of those ends.[5]

European utopian visions have been used to rationalize a range of criminal behaviors, including the enslavement of millions of Africans and the annihilation of entire American Indian peoples as the (sometimes) regrettable, but necessary, consequence of the construction of some kind of future state of human perfection. Sometimes these visions suggested that the state of perfection would be realized on earth, sometimes in heaven, but always Europeans imagined themselves as its agents. This led to a sense of America as a "high civilization" that would motivate the world's peoples to democracy, and always there were historians who wrote history to conform to such ideologies.[6]

During the nineteenth century and the early decades of this century, there was an intellectual movement to identify and make the world safe for an idealized biological human being. Scientific racism paved the way for an attempt to eradicate from the face of the earth certain types of humans who were deemed biologically inferior. These movements, and a great many others, created the context for what has been called the modern era. Since around the middle of the twentieth century, however, European expansion has stalled, and its influence has declined.

European flags fly over fewer and fewer colonial capitals. Indeed, where Europeans once invaded the lands of brown and black peoples, today brown and black peoples emigrate in large numbers to European-dominated lands. African, North African, and Middle Eastern populations are established and growing in western Europe. Asian, African, and Latin American populations are growing faster than European populations in North America. The unchecked expansion of Europe and European populations that was the defining condition of the modern era has ended. The world has now moved to an irreversible condition of postmodernity.

None of the movements that characterized the five hundred years of European expansion have disappeared, but recent decades have seen countermovements that have caused Europe's utopian ideologies to be exposed, deconstructed, and in the intellectual life of the West, discredited. Postmodernism, a movement that announces the abandonment of Western utopian ideologies, should be seen as a consequence of the halt of five hundred years of European expansion. It is an interesting phase of development of Western ideology that signifies not so much the end of history, or even the end of Eurocentric history, as the intellectual collapse of European ideologies constructed around utopian visions.

Postmodernism and cultural studies seek to develop theory concerning the changing conditions, consciousness, and opportunities and the legacies that domination and exploitation have wrought. Kuan-Ksing Chen has stated that both discourses seek to "bring the repressed voices of history back into the historical agenda."[7] Both share

> on the level of cultural politics…the attempt to decenter or decentralize power and recenter "culture." But this does not mean that politics has gone. Quite contrary, in both positions, culture is pervasively politicized on every front and every ground, hence a cultural politics. Both discourses conceive of cultural practices as collective; cultural politics is empowering and endangering, oppositional and hegemonic; culture is neither the "authentic" practice of the "people" nor simply a means of "manipulation" by capitalism, but the state of active local struggle, everyday and anywhere.[8]

For the purposes of this discussion, it may be useful to conceptualize postmodernism and cultural studies as distinct discourses with similar goals. Postmodernism, in this context, might be seen as the development of the theory of how the dominant culture dominates and might include literature that seeks to demystify and deconstruct those channels of domination. Cultural studies might be seen as the discourse about what must be conceived or constructed to replace and accelerate the demystification of the dominant ideologies.[9] The "limits to what we are able to utter and conceive" are cultural in nature. The lived experiences of people in a culture are different from those of people occupying a distinctly different culture, and the more distant the cultures, the more different the limits.

More and more peoples are responding to the reality of domination in ways that can be echoed throughout the world. More and more indigenous and formerly colonized people are realizing that even after their colonizer has returned home, hegemony remains

> through the body of British texts which all too frequently still act as touchstones of taste and value, and through RS-English (Received Standard English), which asserts the English of southeast England as a universal norm, the weight of antiquity

continues to dominate cultural production in much of the post-colonial world. This canonical hegemony has been maintained through canonical assumptions about literary activity.[10]

Canonical hegemony has been maintained through a wide range of other disciplines as well. Very little of the Eurocentered canon can be considered nonhegemonic, value-free knowledge. Economics cannot make such a claim, and certainly not science and technology, not history, and not literature. Within the framework of emerging definitions can be found strategies for escape from the cultural domination of the West, and in the emerging literatures and strategies that deny Eurocentered hegemony can be found strategies useful for people in the dominant centers.

Philosopher Terry Eagleton has stated that it is possible to view dominant ideologies as factors that support the interests of the rulers and that such ideologies

> Help to *unify* a social formation in ways convenient for its rulers;
> that it is not simply a matter of imposing ideas from above but
> of securing the complicity of subordinated classes and groups.[11]

The idea that the process by which individuals in societies are socialized to norms and that the definition of *normal* is a political question was developed by postmodernist philosopher Michel Foucault. Eagleton finds that

> on the view of Michel Foucault and his acolytes, power is not
> something confined to armies and parliaments: it is, rather, a
> pervasive intangible network of force which weaves itself into
> our slightest gestures and most intimate utterances.[12]

Lorraine Code, speaking from the perspective of the development of feminist theory, urged that this kind of thinking is unproductive:

> There is no point in embarking on such an assessment unless one
> can assume that people can intervene in their lives and take charge
> of the processes that shape them. Indeed, the idea of autonomous
> agency is appealing precisely because it promises maximum

intervention and control. In its liberal articulations it appears even to eschew biological determinism and to offer individuals the freedom to make of themselves what they will. But Marxists and postmodernists insist, however, that these are false promises, that choices are themselves constructed by sociocultural-economic circumstances in which people are intrinsically enmeshed.[13]

According to Eagleton, Raymond Williams, one of the founders of cultural studies, strongly dissents from Foucault's theory:

Every social formation is a complex amalgam of what Williams terms "dominant," "residual" and "emergent" forms of consciousness and no hegemony can thus ever be absolute. No sharper contrast could be found than with the later work of Michel Foucault, for whom regimes of power constitute us to our very roots, producing just those forms of subjectivity upon which they can most efficiently go to work.[14]

Williams takes the view that resistance is always present, that the ideological constructs that serve to quiet the masses while the privileged few loot the planet are always under pressure and that the rulers are always "running scared." Eagleton states that

Williams acknowledges the *dynamic* character of hegemony, as against the potentially static connotations of "ideology:" hegemony is never a once-and-for-all achievement, but "has continually to be renewed, recreated, defended, and modified."[15]

Both views, that of Williams and Foucault, are informative. Foucault's views are exposed to the criticism that they are not productive, but Edward Said was able to use Foucault as a model in his *Orientalism*, in which he deconstructs a British academic discipline. In the social environment described by Foucault, it is difficult to take advantage of the dynamics described by Williams toward the ends desired by Code because social change within the confines of Western thought and experience is a problematic. A problematic is "a particular organization of categories which at any given historical moment constitutes the limits of what we are able to utter and conceive."[16]

Ideology and culture, in some contexts, have similar definitions. It is difficult to imagine a culture that has no ideology. A
practical alternative to the kind of one-answer utopian ideology of
the period of European expansionism is a pluralism that acknowledges many different versions of reality that are legitimate across a
wide range of contexts. Pluralism proposes that a society incorpo-
rates or at least is open to sets of ideas associated with more than
one culture. Pluralism makes sense of the world through interrogation and rejection of the idea that a singular discourse can have
a monopoly on answers to what creates the conditions for the perfection of humankind, or that such conditions are even possible.
This is accurate even though pluralism promotes discussion of its
own definition, its rules, and its exceptions to its rules. It accepts
not only that people experience the world in the context of a diversity of versions of existence, but that both social and extrasocial
realities arise from random convergences.

Postmodernism and cultural studies emerge in the context of
centuries of practice of domination/subjugation, of high culture/
low culture, of war of the rich against the poor, white against black
and brown, of top-down histories, and so forth. Both are posi-
tioned in opposition to domination and, therefore, both seek to
support the reversal of conditions of oppression. In essence, this
requires the encouragement of channels of communication and
invigoration of the powerless and at minimum requires a politics
that proclaims the right of everyone on earth to enough food to
eat, enough clean water to drink, freedom from political repression, torture, and dictatorship. To encourage diversity of discourse,
postmodern cultural studies must hear the ideas of communities
of people distinct from themselves and, therefore, must promote
the acceptance of divergent voices.

This requirement raises an interesting dilemma. The very
complexity of human societies places limits on how much a person
from one society can know about the inner realities of people of a
different culture. The more the two cultures differ, the greater the
limitations. If we assume that the practitioners of cultural studies are serious about reempowering the powerless, that they are
not simply seeking informants from diverse cultures to expand
the self-identity of a cultural revolution or a new age, we must
then expect that the new rules about legitimacy will respect the

limitations of such ambitions. At the same time, some of the views of the culturally distant may help review some of the dominant-centered ideology of the West. Vandana Shiva, a woman scientist from India, finds science to be a Eurocentered ideology:

> The parochial roots of science in patriarchy and in a particular class and subculture have been concealed behind the claim to universality, and can be seen only through other traditions—of women and non-western peoples. It is these subjugated traditions that are revealing how modern science is gendered, how it is specific to the needs and impulses of the dominant western culture and how ecological destruction and nature's exploitation are inherent to its logic. It is becoming increasingly clear that scientific neutrality has been a reflection of ideology, not history, and science is similar to all other socially constructed categories.[17]

All over the world, European powers brought the children of their colonies to the Western education process where the propaganda of Western legitimacy was installed in the minds and cultures of these budding local elites. When the Europeans finally folded up their flags and went home, they left behind cadres of elites socialized to the European discourses of power and these elites continue to act in the interests of the colonizers at the expense of their own poor.

Notes

1. In this instance it is convenient to adapt Terry Eagleton's definition of legitimization from the point of view of the colonizing center: "promoting beliefs and values congenial to it; naturalizing and universalizing such beliefs so as to render them self-evident and apparently inevitable; denigrating ideas which might challenge it; excluding rival forms of thought...and obscuring social reality in ways convenient to itself." Terry Eagleton, *Ideology: An Introduction* (New York: Verso, 1991), 5–6.

2. Utopia—a place with ideal laws and social conditions constructed by the *imagination*; imaginary and indefinitely remote. Utopian—an impractical plan for social improvement toward an impossible social order. In the context of the European domination of the world, the European utopianists did not *know* or did not *admit* their ideas were utopian, i.e., imaginary.

3. "In the Middle Ages it was a standard premise of Christian political thought that the Fall had necessitated the coercive apparatus of the state as a

corrective for the evil impulses of fallen man: politics was the second curse of Adam." Barbara Goodwin and Keith Taylor, *The Politics of Utopia: A Study of Theory and Practice* (London: Hutchinson, 1982), 23.

4. "The idea that someone else should do the hard manual work of the world appealed strongly to sixteenth-century Spaniards, who inherited a taste for martial glory and religious conquest and a distaste for physical labor from their medieval forefathers who had struggled for centuries to free Spain from the Moslems. And when this doctrine was linked to the concept that the inferior beings were also being benefited through the labor they were performing for their superiors, the proposition became invincibly attractive to the governing class." Lewis Hanke, *Aristotle and the American Indians: A Study of Race Prejudice in the Modern World* (Bloomington: Indiana Univ. Press, 1970, c.1959), 13.

5. For an interesting and insightful discussion about the West, utopian ideologies, and the abandonment of those ideologies, see, generally, Isaiah Berlin, *The Crooked Timber of Humanity: Chapters in the History of Ideas* (London: John Murray, 1990).

6. Modern historiography has made great strides in exposing the ideologies that drove history writing. See also Edward H. Dance, *History of the Betrayer: A Study in Bias* (London: Hutchinson, 1960), 60.

7. Kuan-Hsing Chen, "Post-Marxism: Between/Beyond Critical Postmodernism and Cultural Studies," *Media, Culture & Society* 13, no. 1 (January 1991): 37.

8. Chen, 38.

9. Other discourses are working along similar lines. Critical theory, for example, studies the context of human behavior and is represented in the works of Horkheimer, Habermas, Adorno, Marcuse, and others. "Critical theory... has a fundamental practical interest that guides it—a practical interest in improving human existence, in striving for enlightenment and liberation, in achieving personal, social and political change...its purpose...is to connect theory with praxis; and with a critical consciousness of the ideologies, structures and institutions which are oppressive to individuals and groups." Cheryl Lynne Malmo, "Women's Experiences as Women: Meaning and Context," unpublished PhD thesis (Edmonton: Univ. of Alberta, 1963), 18.

10. Bill Ashcroft, Gareth Griffiths, Helen Tiffin, eds., *The Empire Writes Back: Theory and Practice in Post-Colonial Literatures* (New York: Routledge, 1989), 7.

11. Eagleton, 30.

12. Eagleton, 7.

13. Lorraine Code, *What Can She Know? Feminist Theory and the Construction of Knowledge* (Ithaca, New York: Cornell Univ. Press, 1991), 179.

14. Eagleton, 47.

15. Eagleton, 112.

16. Eagleton, 137.

17. Vandana Shiva, *Staying Alive: Women, Ecology and Development* (London: Zed Books, 1990, c.1989), 21.

Thoughts of Peace: The Great Law

The Five Nations have such absolute Notions of Liberty that they allow no Kind of Superiority of one over another, and banish all Servitude from their Territories.

—Historian Cadwallader Colden, 1727

Haudenosaunee oral history related that long before the Europeans arrived, Native peoples of the northeast woodlands had reached a crisis. It is said that during this time, a man or woman might be killed or injured by his or her enemies for any slight offense, and that blood feuds between clans and villages ravaged the people until no one was safe. It was during this time that a male child was born to a woman of the Wyandot people living on the north side of Lake Ontario near the Bay of Quinte. It would become the custom of the People of the Longhouse that this person's name would never be spoken except during the recounting of this oral history in the oral fashion (some say it during the Condolence Ceremony). At other times, he is addressed simply as the Peacemaker.

The Peacemaker became one of the great political philosophers and organizers in human history. It is impossible in this short essay to discuss more than a brief outline of his ideas and accomplishments, but it should become obvious that his vision for humankind was indeed extraordinary.

He concluded early in life that the system of blood feuds, as practiced by the people inhabiting the forest at that time, needed to be abolished. His ideas were rejected by the Wyandot and other Huron peoples; and, while a young man, he journeyed to the land of the People of the Flint, located on the southeast shore of Lake Ontario and extending to the areas today called the Mohawk Valley. The People of the Flint, or Kanien'kehá:ka, are known to English-speaking peoples as the Mohawks.

Upon arrival in the Mohawk Country, he began seeking out those individuals who had the reputation as being the fiercest and most fearsome destroyers of human beings. He sought them out one at a time—murders and hunters of humans, even cannibals—and he brought to each one his message.

One by one he straightened out their minds as each grasped

the principles that he set forth. Nine men of the Mohawks—the nine most feared men in all Mohawk Country—grasped hold of his words and became his disciples.

The first principle that the Peacemaker set forth was indisputable to those who heard his words. He said that it has come to pass that in this land human beings are seen to abuse one another. He pointed to the world in which people live and said that people should consider that some force or some thing must have created this world—the Giver of Life—that had not intended that human beings would abuse one another. Human beings whose minds are healthy always desire peace, and humans have minds that enable them to achieve peaceful resolutions of their conflicts.

From that initial explanation—that the Giver of Life (later addressed as the Great Creator) did not intend that human beings abuse one another—he proposed that human societies must form governments that will serve to prevent the abuse of human beings by other human beings and that will ensure peace among nations and peoples. Government would be established for the purpose of abolishing war and robbery among brothers and to establish peace and quietness. He drew the Mohawks together under those principles and then went to the Oneidas, Onondagas, Cayugas, and Senecas with the same teachings. What is unique about his work is that he not only set forth the argument that government is desirable, he also set forth the principle that government is specifically organized to prevent the abuse of human beings by cultivating a spiritually healthy society and the establishment of peace.

Other political philosophers and organizers have come to the conclusion that governments can be formed for the purpose of establishing tranquility, but the Peacemaker went considerably further than that. He argued not for the establishment of law and order, but for the full establishment of peace. Peace was to be defined not as the simple absence of war or strife, but as the active striving of humans for the purpose of establishing universal justice. Peace was defined as the product of a society that strives to establish concepts that correlate to the English words power, reason, and righteousness.

Righteousness refers to something akin to the shared ideology of the people using their purest and most unselfish minds. It occurs when the people put their minds and emotions in harmony with the flow of the universe and the intentions of the Good Mind or the Great Creator. The principles of righteousness demand that all thoughts of prejudice, privilege, or superiority be swept away and that recognition be given to the reality that the creation is indeed for the benefit of all equally—even the birds, animals, trees, and insects, as well as the humans. The world does not belong to humans—it is the rightful property of the Great Creator. The gifts and benefits of the world, therefore, belong to all equally. The things that humans need for survival—food, clothing, shelter, protection—are things to which all are entitled because they are gifts of the Great Creator. Nothing belongs to human beings, not even their labor or their skills, for ambition and ability are also the gifts of the Great Creator.

Therefore all people have a right to the things they need for survival, even those who do not or cannot work, and no person or people has a right to deprive others of the fruits of those gifts.

Reason is perceived to be the power of the human mind to make righteous decisions about complicated issues. The Peacemaker began his teachings based on the principle that human beings were given the gift of the power of reason in order that they may settle their differences without the use of force. He proposed that in every instance humans should use every effort to counsel about, arbitrate, and negotiate their differences, and that force should be resorted to only as a defense against the certain use of force. All men whose minds are healthy can desire peace, he taught, and there is ability within all human beings, and especially in the young human beings, to grasp and hold strongly to the principles of righteousness. The ability to grasp the principles of righteousness is a spark within the individual that society must fan and nurture so that it may grow. Reason is seen as the skill that humans must be encouraged to acquire in order that the objectives of justice may be attained and no one's rights abused.

Having established the concept of righteousness and reason, the Peacemaker went on to discuss the nature of power. The power to enact a true peace is the product of a unified people on the path of righteousness, and reason is the ability to enact the principles of peace through education, public opinion, political, and when necessary, military unity. The power that the Peacemaker spoke of was intended to enable the followers of the law to call upon warring or quarreling parties to lay down their arms and to begin a peaceful settlement of their disputes. Peace, as the Peacemaker understood it, flourished only in a garden amply fertilized with absolute and pure justice. It was the product of a spiritually conscious society using its abilities of reason that resulted in a healthy society. The power to enact peace (which requires that people cease abusing one another) was conceived to be both spiritual and political.

But it was power in all the senses of the word—the power of persuasion and reason, the power of the inherent goodwill of humans, the power of a dedicated and united people, and, when all else failed, the power of force.

The principles of law set forth by the Peacemaker sought to establish a peaceful society by eliminating the causes of conflict between individuals and between peoples. It was a law that was conceived prior to the appearance of classes, and it sought to anticipate and eliminate anything that took the appearance of group or class interest, even in the form of clan or tribal interest, especially in the area of property. The law was also based to an impressive degree on a logic that looked to nature for its rules. It is one of the few examples of a Natural Law that is available to modern man. It is a law that clearly precedes royal law, or mercantile law, or bourgeois property-interest law.

The government that is established under the Great Law of Peace provides, in effect, that the leaders or chiefs are the servants of the people. Everyone in the Six Nations, wherever the law prevails, has direct participation in the workings of the government. Direct democracy, when it involves tens of thousands of people, is a very complex business, and there are many rules about how meetings are conducted. But the primary rule about the flow of power and authority is clearly that the power and authority of the people lies with the people and is transmitted by them through the chiefs. The fact that all the people have direct participation in the decision of their governments is the key factor for the success and longevity of the Haudenosaunee.

Internally, the law has to be the power by which the people were united ideologically and administratively under a dispute-settlement process to which all had agreed to submit and to remove those customs of the past that had sparked conflict and fostered disunity. The path to unity was a difficult one indeed. The territory of the People of the Longhouse had been composed of five distinct countries, and each sometimes jealously guarded their hunting lands from intrusion by the others. The Peacemaker abolished the concept of separate territories. The law unified the peoples, saying that they were distinct from one another only because they spoke different languages. He said the territories were common to all and that each individual member of any of the nations had full rights of hunting and occupation of all the lands of all the nations of the People of the Longhouse.

In terms of the internal affairs of the People of the Longhouse, the first and most important principle was that under the law the people of the nations were one people. Since the Haudenosaunee call themselves the People of the Longhouse, the Peacemaker's admonition was that under the law the country of the Haudenosaunee was itself a longhouse, with the sky as its roof and the earth as its floor.

The peoples were assigned to clans by the Peacemaker, and so strong was to be the feeling of unity and oneness between them that the members of the clan of one nation were admonished not to marry members of the same clan of another nation, so closely were they now related. The law bound them together as blood relatives.

In one motion he abolished exclusive national territories and the concept of national minorities. Any member of the Five Nations was to have full rights in the country of any of the Five Nations with only one restriction—he or she did not have the right to hold public office, though that right could be conferred upon them by the host nation if they so wished.

The idea that the nations were united as one meant that the nations who were members of the confederacy had agreed to surrender a part of their sovereignty to the other nations of the confederacy. The Confederacy Council was to be the forum under which foreign nations and peoples could approach the People of the Longhouse. Any decision concerning the disposition of Seneca lands must first pass through the Confederacy Council, where the other nations, who also have rights in Seneca lands, can participate in the decision-making process.

The Peacemaker envisioned that the principles under which the Five Nations were governed could be extended far beyond the borders of the Haudenosaunee to all the peoples of the world. The law of the Peacemaker provides that any nation or people may find protection under the Great Tree of Peace, which symbolized the laws of the confederacy. He expected that the principles of the confederacy would be well received by many nations and that the Haudenosaunee would venture forth with the offer of a union that would be designed to prevent hostilities and lay the basis of peaceful coexistence. With that in mind, the Constitution of the Five Nations provides that any nation may seek its protection through becoming knowledgeable about the laws and agreeing to follow the principles set forth in it. Many Native nations accepted that offer.

The Five Nations agreed among themselves that in the event of an attack they would organize a military force to repel the invader and carry on the war in the invader's country until the war was concluded. The opponent had an absolute right to a cessation of the hostilities at any time by simply calling for a truce. At that point, the process of negotiation went into action. The Constitution of the Five Nations prescribes that in the event another people are conquered, the Five Nations shall not impose upon them the Five Nations' religion nor collect tribute from them, nor subject them to any form of injustice. The Five Nations would not seize their territory. What was demanded was that the offending nation of people put away their weapons of war and that they cease military aggression.

Any individual or group of individuals had the right, according to the constitution, to approach the Five Nations, learn the law, and agree to abide by it. When that happened, they were to be offered the protection of the law and the People of the Longhouse.

The vision of the Peacemaker that all the peoples of the world would live in peace under the protection of a law that required that hostilities be outlawed and disputes offered a settlement process is yet today an exciting prospect. When the idea of a United Nations of the world was proposed toward the end of World War II, researchers were dispatched to find models in history for such an organization. For all practical purposes, the only model they found concerned the Constitution of the Five Nations, whose author had envisioned exactly that.

In a way, the Peacemaker was centuries ahead of his time. He set forth a system of government organization that was a marvelously complex enactment of the concept of participatory (as opposed to representative) democracy.

Under the rules of the law, councils of women appointed men who were to act more as conduits of the will of the people than as independent representatives of the people. The society was founded on concepts of moral justice, not statute law, and the rules of the society were designed to ensure that each member's rights were absolutely protected under the law. Women not only have rights but power as a community of people composing half the population. The power of women has never been fully articulated by Western observers and interpreters of Haudenosaunee culture.

Peoples were recognized to have a right to exist unmolested as peoples in the articles of the constitution. Individuals were recognized as having the full right to protection under the laws of the confederacy—even individuals who were not members of the host nation—as long as they observed the rules of nonaggression and as long as they didn't try to create factionalism among the people. The principle was set forth (and machinery to enact it was created) that provided that all peoples have a right to occupy their lands peacefully and that no one may deny them that right. A society was socialized to the ideology that, if an injustice occurs, it is their moral duty to defend the oppressed against their oppressors. The principle was set forth that no one has a right to deprive another of the fruits of his own labor and that no one has a right to a greater share of the wealth of society than anyone else. The Peacemaker believed that if absolute justice was established in the world, peace would naturally follow.

Some of those ideas have begun to take root in the form of United Nations' statements and declarations made in recent years. The genius of the Peacemaker was that he not only set forth the principles, he also designed the machinery to enforce those principles. He seems to have operated on the assumption that universal justice is the product of a spiritually strong society, and many of the rules that he proposed are designed to create a strong society rather than a strong government. That is one of the ideas that has not been widely accepted in the twentieth century and certainly not in a context that the Peacemaker would have understood.

The Peacemaker set out to give some order to society and to create peace among peoples and nations. The rules that he set down were called by the Mohawks the Great Goodness, and by the Senecas the Great Law. It is also referred to as The Great Law of

Peace. The English called the body of teachings the Constitution of the Five Nations. It has never been written down in English, despite allegations to the contrary by anthropologists. The versions that exist in English are highly inadequate efforts compared to the oral versions of the Great Law. This effort is no better—it does not compare in any way to the complexity, beauty, and eloquence of the law.

Some people who have read the history of the Haudenosaunee will be able to point to episodes in the seventeenth and eighteenth centuries when some of the principles of this law appear to have been ignored. It is true that over nearly two centuries of intermittent warfare—warfare caused by pressures created by the expanding interests of European imperial nations—there was a considerable amount of social change and stress. French imperialist missionaries introduced the idea—an entirely foreign idea—that a divine will might guide the fortunes of people in government and in warfare. That kind of thinking was not to be found in the philosophies of the Peacemaker, but throughout history it has been an idea that has accompanied empire builders everywhere. Many ideas of European origin were adopted by different peoples of the Haudenosaunee at different times, ideas that were in conflict with the principles of the Great Law. In the almost two centuries since the beginning of the so-called reservation period, many more ideas that are in conflict with the principles of the Great Law have been imposed by the colonizers.

Most of what passes as Iroquois history was an effort by English and French historians to discredit the Haudenosaunee and to justify the destruction of the confederacy and the theft of confederacy lands. There were few instances when officials of the confederacy violated the laws of the Great Peace, although individuals in any society do violate its laws. Following the American Revolution, the United States, and especially New York State, did everything in its power to dissolve the confederacy and to deal with the individual nations. Great Britain, Canada, Ontario, and Quebec have done the same thing. Since the invasion of the Europeans, the Haudenosaunee have produced a number of patriots but few great philosophers. The outstanding Haudenosaunee philosopher and teacher of the postcontact period was also a confederacy chief. His name was Handsome Lake, and he led a spiritual revitalization that produced an oral document called The Good Word, a teaching on the same level of significance and power in Haudenosaunee culture as the Great Law. Combined, the two are a powerful teaching. Against incredible odds, the confederacy has survived and has continued to this day. Its chiefs continue to meet periodically at the capital at Onondaga, and they continue to carry the titles bestowed upon them by the Peacemaker long before written history began. The ideas of the confederacy continue to live also, and little by little the world is being exposed to those ideas. As long as those ideas remain alive, the possibility remains that the Peacemaker's vision of a world in peace and harmony may yet be realized.

We Are By Nature Social Animals

It was a gray, overcast day. All morning, the people had been gathered inside the longhouse, absorbed in the "reading" of one of the great oral traditions of the people of Six Nations. While the midday meal was served, people gathered in groups in the mudhouse, inside the longhouse, and outside.

My friend was a speaker and teacher of the old ways. He was a soft-spoken, gentle man who had been a leader of his community for two generations. He had been born before the roads became prominent, when the people still lived, to a considerable extent, in the forest. When he was young, the people spoke of the Old Ways, and he still carried a memory of those ways, and he practiced in his own life that which he remembered.

He had seen many changes in his lifetime. He had seen the coming of the roads and had seen the people leave the countryside for the cities. He had observed the arrival of the internal combustion engine, and the automobile and the airplane. That his life spanned the arrival of most of what we know as the modern world and that he was a teacher still of an ancient and almost forgotten world has always been a point of focus for me—a reminder that much of what we take for granted is so very new, and there are still living people who were born and were even adults prior to the arrival of much that is considered modern. I went over to him.

"Have you been listening to what is said?" he asked.

"I have questions," I said. "Some of the people are saying that we should study the old ways, and live by those ways, but there are still many questions about how things were done."

"What they are talking about today," he said, "these things will help you to remember those ways. But it is hard to follow the right way. It is the hardest thing in the world to do, because you must push away from your mind even bad thoughts about people. There aren't many people who are willing to even try to follow the Way of Life of the Indian people. But our Way of Life is clear enough. It's clear.

"The Indian Way of Life is a way that follows Nature. When you were first born, as a small baby, you didn't know anything. As a baby, your spirit was fresh and pure, and you followed the Natural ways. As you grew up, you began to learn things. In these times, people learn things that take them away from the Natural way of living. It wasn't always that

way. There was a time when our people spent much of their time seeking knowledge of the true path of things. But today we are confused."

"And the teachings," I asked, "is a knowledge of the teachings the Way of Life?"

"No," he said. "The teachings are only a guide. Each person must seek his own way in the natural order of things. We were given a mind that we could understand these things. The ancient teachings tell us of the origin of things and the reason that we are told to do things in a certain way. We must remember how things were in the beginnings— what happened when the first person was found to be lifeless, and what the people learned about the meaning of death. And we remember what the people did when that happened. Our traditions are very ancient. There is much to be learned in those teachings—the Indian people are almost the only ones who still remember these things."

His voice did not carry the haughty, almost arrogant tone that one hears when someone is defending his own thoughts. He spoke with the feel of a true teacher—patient and sympathetic. What he had to say was the honest reflection of a mind that had spent eight decades and more learning and teaching the Natural way.

"What you are hearing today [ceremonial speeches]," he continued, "is our people's memory of the ancient way of life, and the lessons that it has for us now. It talks about the things that have happened that draw us away from the natural order of things, and what we must do to set things right. There are things that are said that are specific to the people of the Six Nations, but the basic message could be applied to all people. Almost all the things of importance are mentioned. We are instructed that we have obligations to our young, to the old people, to one another, to the Creator, to the Sustainers of Life. There are things that we are able to do that are contrary to that way of life, and we are told about these things too. A lot of what is said has to do with the necessity of building families and community."

I wondered about how they set up the families in the old ways. "Today at the longhouse, hearing the words to the Code of Handsome Lake, we are told to marry and have families, build a home, and raise our own food in ways similar to the ways the white people do. Did that change from our ways in the ancient times?"

His wife had joined us. She was a small woman, one also knowledgeable in the traditions of the People. "In the old times," she said, "people were pretty strict. Today, you young people think that because no one guides you in making decisions, that this is better because you think you are free to make decisions for yourself. But you are not free— rather, you are lost. You have so many choices open to you that you have no choices at all. That's the trouble today. People make choices, and they don't even know why they made those choices. Our teachings don't tell us that the old ways should be forgotten. The old ways were good ways. When the teachings try to tell people how to choose a husband or a wife, they are simply trying to tell us ways to do things now that the people no longer follow strictly the old ways. The teachings are guides to people who have become lost."

"But think about the old ways. In the ancient times, the women had power. They were in charge of seeing that the community continued to follow the Natural ways. In former times, the older women arranged marriages. You younger people wouldn't like that idea, but there were reasons that they did things that way. Later, when people started moving out of the longhouses and living in their own homes, the women lost their power. That's when we needed to find new ways to talk about marriage—so that people wouldn't get too separated from the right Way of Life."

"What are the things," I asked, "that people are supposed to think about today when they think about marriage?"

"It's simple enough," the husband replied. "If it appears that two people are able to get along together then they are encouraged to see if they can work together. A man and woman can spend time together just working around the house, or in the gardens, or in the community. They are encouraged to spend quite a bit of time together to see if their interests are strong. If they work well together, then it may be that they will develop into a strong couple. Then it may happen that they will get married. If they do, then it is the responsibility of the community to help them in any way to make things work between them. Something has developed between just them two, and it is the job of the community to help them to keep that thing strong."

I remember coming away from that conversation thinking that the advice was too simple. His wife was right, of course. Having too many choices doesn't necessarily mean that you are free—it can mean that you simply have no values, that you have become disconnected from your humanity.

We live in a time when all values are questioned and ultimately found to be without substance. Native people, especially Native people *who are in touch with their culture, have an additional problem. The cultures stand as kind of touchposts with the origins of humanity, and they are powerful touchposts. Within the culture of the Six Nations, there are ancient and complex ceremonies connected with the process of mating and long teachings about the need to maintain and strengthen the family. Some of those teachings go back thousands of years—it is impossible to guess how ancient they are—and people have carried on those ceremonies over all this time. People probably don't do something like that, as a group, for such very long periods of time, unless there is a good reason. To know the complexity of the world of the People of the Longhouse, and to come to grips with the implicit logic that world contains, is to respect it. It is the logic of the People of the Longhouse— a logic apparently invisible or nearly invisible to scholars—that lends the traditions such integrity. The Six Nations' traditions have a way of beginning with a basic, undeniable truth and expanding that truth into every facet of life. The uninitiated, the acculturated, and the ignorant see only quaint ceremonies and chants, a simplistic philosophy of life, and, at best, curious fables and legends, where there in fact exists a complex social order with a legitimate foundation in the human experience.*

The unavoidable conclusion that one must reach after listening to the oral tradition of the People of the Longhouse for long hours is that it advocates the formation of the nuclear family and promotes something that people used to call fidelity within the marriage relationship. There is a lot more to it of course—it also provides for a spiritual relationship to all aspects of the Natural World that are immense and profound—but attention to the nuclear family as an institution that can support that spiritual life is undeniable.

In the twentieth century, the nuclear family has been largely discredited as a tool that can lead to alternatives to Western life, but the arguments against it arise out of critiques of Western economy and Western patriarchal sexuality. The important concerns involve discovering and rediscovering ways that basic human needs can be met.

What about our humanity? Is there anything that gives it definition? Are there any basic principles or human needs that we can identify that are legitimate and, more or less, universal? Some interesting thoughts arise when one tries to come to some conclusions about what we are and where we came from and what connects us all as a species inhabiting this planet. In the origins of our species there may lie answers to the questions that have escaped us.

First, and very importantly, it must be understood that there are no universal rules about social organization that can be applied to all peoples at all times and all places. Our species evolved over millions and millions of years. At one point, ancestors to each of us were cold-blooded and aquatic; at another point they were probably rodentlike mammals. We have ancestors who subsisted on a diet of insects and other ancestors (at different times, separated by millions of years) who subsisted largely on fruits. At one time, our ancestors probably lived in trees, and at other times they probably were largely hunters of small animals. And we have inherited something from each of those periods of time. Humans can still digest and virtually subsist on fruits. It is probable that we inherited binary vision (which gives us the ability to perceive depth) from the time when our forebears lived in trees and needed to be able to climb or swing from branch to branch. That arboreal period probably also gave us the prehensile thumb, which enabled us to grip the branch more firmly.

At some point long before the dawn of history, ancestors of *Homo sapiens* had already begun to evolve feet like ours today and were beginning to stand erect. They had left the forest and were probably hunters and gatherers. Someplace between the tree and the savanna, human evolution would begin to take some turns experienced by few, if any, other species.

In terms of physical evolution, at least, our species would cease to adapt to its environment. In fact, today, there is virtually no place in the world where our species is capable of survival in its environment based on its physiology. In order for humans to adapt to increasingly hostile environments, humans had to learn the means of survival. The learned means of survival is what we call culture. As the species spread out from hospitable climates to less hospitable ones, the level of skill needed to survive became more complex.

Basically, what this means is that humans, over hundreds of thousands of years, were forced to learn to build shelters, to make clothing, and to find and adapt to new foods in order to inhabit different places on the earth. Other species have adapted to their environment by developing a fur coat or hibernating during the cold months or by annual migrations, but *Homo sapiens* must build his shelter, sew his coat, and develop his own way of surviving the elements.

Although our species did not evolve in the way beaver and geese did, there is nevertheless an enormous amount of physical evolution going on. Over two million years, the species experienced profound growth in the size of the skull. That made necessary an altered pelvic structure in order to enable the female to give birth to the big-headed infant. The female experienced the most profound changes (compared to the male and most other primates). The female developed permanent breasts and a menstrual (as opposed to an estral) cycle, which meant that she was sexually accessible all year instead of only at certain times of the year. As hominid evolution continued, the neoteny of the infant became longer and longer. That means that the time between birth and maturity became longer, until our species has the longest neoteny of any species.

It is important to be very careful about the conclusions that can be drawn from all of this. It is almost certain that long ago, when our ancestors were hunters and gatherers but before they invented complex tools, it was an absolute necessity for survival that human (or prehuman) families be formed. And it is arguable (but not provable) that humans evolved sexually to accomplish just that. Given that hunting cultures several hundred thousand years ago depended on animal protein for survival, that infants needed animal protein when there was little visible source of vegetable protein, that failure of the infant's survival meant extermination of the group, and that males are probably the logical ones to do the hunting more of the time because pregnant females can't and infants can't be left unattended, it would seem to establish that there was a need within this species for a cooperative effort.

There are some other questions that science can probably never answer completely. Why did the female of the species (our species) develop permanent breasts? Permanent breasts appear in virtually no other species in nature and are found only in domesticated animals. And why the evolution of the menstrual cycle? Certainly, for purely reproductive purposes, the estral cycle should have served us well.

It has been argued that at least two elements of physiological evolution—the menstrual cycle and the permanent breasts of the female—serve as sexual devices for the domestication of the male. I'm not compelled by that argument. It implies that the adult male had no other reasons for remaining with and hunting for the female and infants other than sexuality, but there is no reason to believe that sexuality and sexuality alone formed the basis for early pair bonding within the human species. There are other factors to be looked at.

The species evolved a larger brain over a long time. The increased brain capacity is assumed in Western fiction to have been the tool that enabled the species to evolve more complex cultures, and, to a point, this is probably true. But much of the evolution of the brain involves the evolution of the frontal lobes, and what we know of the frontal lobes suggests that that area of the brain is more useful for dreaming than it is for manipulating tools. Assuming that evolution tends toward more survival-oriented physiologies, why would so much evolutionary energy be taken up in the development of an area of gray matter that serves little or no mechanical purpose?

To complicate the matter even more, primates exhibit extraordinary needs for intimate behavior. All that we know about primate behavior indicates that primates need to touch and be touched more than other kinds of animals. In fact, intimacy-deprived primates (from chimpanzees to humans) exhibit all kinds of strange behavior. An infant who is totally deprived of any human touch may even die, even though all of its other physical needs (warmth, food, water, etc.) are met. And modern psychologists are beginning to recognize (how long it takes!) that intimacy deprivation is a primary, if not *the* primary, source of behavioral problems among human beings. (The other source of behavioral problems is emerging as diet related.)

There are many other things that can be considered that relate to the evolution of our species, and many of those things relate to culture. Females probably initiated most developments in the area of clothing, shelter, herbology, language, and cooking and food culture. It isn't scientifically provable but given that the female was probably left in camp while males went out hunting, it is probable that females had a lot to do with those things. And females probably also were instrumental in the practices of very early agriculture and animal domestication.

Human survival, virtually since the arboreal period (which was a very long time), has depended on the cooperative interactions of adult males and females. Humans require more than simply food, clothing, and shelter—the survival of the species requires infants, and the well-being of adults also is enhanced by the considerable amount of intimate behavior that is or should be associated with the raising of infants.

None of these factors makes an overwhelming argument supporting monogamy as a universally natural way of societal organization. In fact, that argument cannot be supported. All that is certain, from all of human evolution, is that our species has needs for group association and cooperation that go well beyond our material needs and enter upon the realm of the psychospiritual. In reviewing hundreds of Natural World cultures, we find every kind of conceivable form of social organization, from monogamy to polyandry and polygamy. How humans organize successfully to meet their needs as individuals and as groups seems to depend almost entirely on the context of their existence. The needs are universal, but the variations that meet those needs are many, and the appropriateness of each must be viewed in context. Only one common factor has been demonstrated universally throughout successful human cultures: adult males and females always seem to live with their children. Something that can be described as a nuclear family exists and has existed in virtually every successful culture in human history.

Cultures change (at least during the last ten thousand years they have), the environment changes, all kinds of changes take place that affect human groups. But human needs that have remained pretty consistent for hundreds of thousands of years probably don't change as easily or rapidly. Human groups still need infants to survive as groups. Human infants need intimacy to survive, and human beings still need intimacy to remain healthy long after they have ceased being infants. Human beings, in many ways and many contexts, still need other human beings. We can still breathe and eat and sleep and continue to function biologically without other people, but the definition of our humanity without other people isn't the same. We are, by nature, social animals.

We have inherited those needs from the Natural World, and in the Natural World, those needs are/were satisfied. The problem today is that we no longer have unhindered access to the Natural World, and all of those needs are not being met very well. The West creates institutions (welfare agencies, court systems, mental hospitals) to meet those needs. Natural World people know that those needs can only be met by human beings. The problem, then, is to make it possible for people to be (to act like) Natural human beings.

Human needs are not impositions of nature that must be struggled against and conquered. The more we struggle against our human natures, the more we compound our problems. Our needs for intimacy provide our most profound potential for the expression of our humanity. Nature opens for us both the necessity and the potential to be infants and friends, parents and lovers, siblings and grandparents. That we have both potential and needs to live as groups and families is only a curse if you have been alienated from even the idea of our Natural humanity.

The definition of a Natural way of life is extremely complex, especially when addressing the questions of human sexuality and social organization. One can state, for example, that when you are eating food that appears nowhere in nature, you are not eating Natural food. But human behavior is different in that all forms of societal behavior exists in nature and probably also among Natural World peoples.

Natural World cultures are defined as those that have made an adjustment to their environment in such a way that they are in harmony with its native biology. In the country of the Six Nations, when the people had absolute access to an undamaged Natural World, the social organization that worked to this end was the extended matrilocal family. When the people were confined to reservations and small plots of land and were subjected to the enormous pressures of Western society, they found that the Natural ways were still possible through pair bonding and a community effort to support the survival of what remained of the extended family.

The Natural way of life and the teachings of the traditions are not attempts to answer our problems one at a time. The traditions offer difficult and complex solutions. In the Six Nations country, those traditions urge us to live simply, on a few acres of land, grow our own food, maintain stable and faithful relationships to our spouses, educate our children ourselves, use Natural medicines, and follow the spiritual ways so that our communities remain strong and our minds remain strong in the ways of the Creator. They strongly promote that people marry and have families and work to support one another. It's good advice. Just about all of the traditional societies in North America have the same advice to *individuals*: follow the Creator's ways.

The point is underlined when one considers the difficulties of translating the Seneca thought into the English language. The Seneca word that is usually translated as "creator" actually means "that (m.) which finished [making] the human body." The definition can be expanded, but it could be said that, in the Seneca language, the ways of the Creator involve the ways of the evolution of our species. That is what people should learn to respect—the ways of that which created us, the nature of our humanity, the Natural ways.

Western Peoples, Natural Peoples:
Roots of Anxiety

There are two contradictory phenomena in the relationship between Western peoples and Native peoples today. On the one hand, more people than ever are understanding and sympathetic toward Native movements and cultures than has been the case since 1492. And on the other hand, there is the reappearance of a · mass movement in the United States to abuse and oppress Native peoples throughout the world—including North America.

There may be a difference in the current oppression compared with the past—despite the emergence of such things as federal operations Garden Plot and Cable Splicer, there seems to be no coordinated conspiracy. Indeed, there doesn't need to be one. Oppression arises today as a cultural phenomenon of the time automatically and without need of instigators or leaders.

Take Pine Ridge Reservation, in South Dakota, for example: death, beatings, and goon squads are a constant way of life there. Pine Ridge is hard to understand when it is looked at alone. But as part of the larger scene, one that affects nearly every person living in North America every day of their lives, one can understand Pine Ridge. When we face the reality of FBI agent provocateur Douglass Durham and people like Lieutenant Calley, of My Lai massacre fame, when we look at our own communities and the almost unexplainable hostilities and violence present there, we need to ask ourselves for an honest answer to a question.

What is happening to the People?

What could possibly cause behavior among human beings that force and violence can be elevated to a way of life? Why do we experience the abuse of human beings by other human beings, even to the point of mass movements that personify these things, such as the Ku Klux Klan or the Nazi Party, which so recently dominated German political and cultural thought?

What motivates people who, to all outward appearances, are good family people to invade a country of rice farmers who posed absolutely no threat to the United States, and to bomb and kill civilian populations in that distant land in the name, mysteriously, of freedom?

Why do secret societies exist that appear capable of attacking civilian Native populations with force all out of proportion to any danger—physical or economic—that those Native people pose to them?

What kind of people stand by silently and dispassionately while goon squads, US marshals, and the FBI conduct a reign of terror among the men and women and children of the Oglala Nation?

What kind of people are we dealing with who have abandoned all standards of human conduct and fair play and who have imposed a condition of warfare in South Dakota and Arizona, in Nebraska and Alberta—while all the time insisting upon maintaining a facade of justice and democracy?

Sitting Bull once stated, "The love of possessions is a disease with them." Certainly it will be helpful to view the behavior pattern of Western civilization as a disease, but perhaps even Sitting Bull's statement was incomplete in this regard. Mohawk historian Rarihokwats has said that, indeed, the behavior pattern that we are responding to is a disease of the spirit that has many of the characteristics commonly ascribed to rabies. A wild animal with rabies suddenly becomes tame and meek, even friendly, and will approach in such a manner that most people will be totally off guard. Still, it bites or scratches its victims. While the disease is fatal to the carrier, the newly infected victim repeats the process and will go on to bite another and another, and in this way the disease spreads, making carriers of all who are victims, and the victims of all who come in contact with carriers.

From the viewpoint of a Native person, this disease that the Western man, the white man, carried to the rest of the world, is the most destructive disease ever to appear on the face of the Earth. It is a disease that has resulted in the extermination of thousands of species and many Natural World human nations The disease reached fever pitch at times such as the Pequot Wars, at Wounded Knee in 1890, and at My Lai.

Its symptoms are to be found in every household in the Western world.

When a rabies epidemic is rampant, there is only one way to avoid the infection—avoid contact with all animals, including loyal pets. There is a similar analogy with Native contact with Western peoples—since it is impossible to know who has credibility and who does not, some peoples have chosen to avoid dealing with any Western contacts. Many of our peoples take exceeding care who they let into our sacred ceremonies. Only Native Natural peoples may attend. Those who allow Western cultural individuals report that these folks require much purification.

People of non-Western cultures experience great difficulty dealing with European peoples, especially in the areas of credibility. Native people discover quickly that Westernized peoples often do not mean what they say, and they do not say what they mean. Duplicity is found in every culture; in the West, it is expected. In short, they lie a lot.

People living in the Western world have come to accept and to some degree, adapt to that reality. They get receipts for every transaction. They require witnesses—the more the better—when testimony is given. They understand that television commercials regularly misrepresent their products, that politicians make promises they do not intend to keep, that most movies and magazine articles are either fiction or gross exaggerations. People who believe everything are said to be naive.

I am inclined to dwell on this aspect of the culture for a reason. In Western culture, it is very difficult to determine the truth, because it is hard to tell who you can believe. This also means that it is pretty difficult to determine who you can trust, since in the culture almost everyone's capability of stretching the truth is trained and honed.

This is not true of all people in all cultures; in fact, it is an exception among Natural Peoples. One aspect of the Natural World life appears consistent—as a general rule, Natural people do not lie. Theirs is an oral tradition, and lying destroys language and the destruction of language means the destruction of culture, the nation. The Western pattern of lying as a way of life is looked upon with amazement by Natural Peoples. In Guatemalan Maya life, as a Natural person moves away from the Native community, he becomes more *ladino*, meaning "sly, cunning."

Living in a world of lying people one cannot trust gives rise to another phenomenon: anxiety.

Anxiety is a product of Western culture to a degree and intensity that may be unmatched in any culture in the world, now or ever. At least the fact is undisputable that there is a great deal of anxiety in the Western world today. While the theories and effects of anxiety are too complex to deal with here, there is value in recounting a few highlights, for we may gain understanding of why Western people behave as they do toward Native peoples and why they destroy the Natural World. It is important to note, too, that the sense of utter dependency, for food and other essentials, plays a big part in the general anxiety.

Anxiety causes distress, sometimes extreme distress. Anxiety attacks, we are told, are based upon irrational and almost always subconscious fears, and those fears can have many origins. Some theories have indicated that there are at least four basic common responses to anxiety: people seek affection (really, reassurance against their fears); they seek submission (on the basis that submission is a way of avoiding injury); they seek power (including possessions, for people with power cannot be injured); and they seek withdrawal (an avoidance of that which they fear).

And as people respond in these ways within Western culture, with its desperation for raw materials and sense of group vulnerability, they often kill Indians. They destroy the Natural World. These destructions are not the disease, but reactions that, temporarily at least, reduce the distress caused by the anxiety produced by the way in which Western cultures operate—and that operation itself often revolves around ways through which people reduce distress caused by anxiety. It is a devastatingly complete cycle from which hundreds of millions of people seemingly cannot escape.

The West is a competitive world in which people even compete for affection. It is a world in which romance includes standards of appearance, strength, social status. Many people fail—or think they fail—to achieve these standards. Such persons often seek constant reassurance of their worth. Because they also live in a culture in which it is very difficult to trust other people's words, the search for true reassurance becomes compulsive, especially when statements of real affection are met with skepticism since the person really thinks himself or herself unworthy.

How do you find and accept even reassurance in a culture in which people lie all the time?

Submission is another response to anxiety that has some interesting manifestations in this culture. The West is a very authoritarian place. The Christian religion, for example, defines as "good" people who have a "fear of God." People are encouraged to submit to religious authority by creating anxieties that if they do not do so, they will go to hell or at least be considered bad by others. The distress of anxiety can be lessened by accepting authority, be it a book, a set of laws, a government, or a priest. It encourages people to believe and do what they are told without question. If you submit, you will not be injured, people come to believe. And in the West, of course, God is not the only thing to be feared.

The West has produced a culture in which failure to submit to authority is met with force. The history of Europe is one of slaughter of infidels and heretics, and any kind of resistance to either religious or governmental authority has been met with torture and death. A lot of people have come to believe that if you do not submit to authority, you will be destroyed, if not by some divine force, then by some secular force acting in the name of divinity. Today, Christianity and the church largely have been replaced by the government, and the inquisitors often wear FBI fatigues.

The other side of this coin finds people obsessed with power. If you submit, you will not be injured. But if you have power, no one will be able to injure you. To seek power in the West means to seek control, meaning that you can tell others what to do and they have no choice but to do it. People acquire power in the West by acquiring possessions, and the concept and reality of possessions is that other people are excluded from access to that which they possess. You can also destroy what other people have as a means of gaining control—as the buffalo were destroyed by the US government to obtain power over the Plains People. Thus, power and greed are closely related in Western culture.

People in the West become obsessed in their quest for wealth and power to a degree that defies rational explanation. That is, the needs are not real, but psychological. Anything that frustrates needs for power and wealth is met with hostility. Thus, to a Western mind, it is not only necessary to steal Indian land to meet needs for possession, it is also necessary to hate Indians for fighting to protect their land. Some would say that is the legacy of the ruling class but it is present throughout the culture. It forms the basis for the psychology of racism.

The final response to anxiety involves withdrawal. Some people, when confronted with the uncertainties of personal relationships, and who neither submit to authority nor develop compulsive greed for power, simply seek to put distance between themselves and the world. This takes a number of forms, but often results in people withdrawing into themselves and participating as little as possible with other people. There is also blurring the anxiety by retreating behind a curtain of drugs and/or alcohol. Some try to sleep a lot. Others commit suicide—death is the most final and complete withdrawal from anxiety, whatever the cause.

There is a fifth possible response, but one that Western people are encouraged not to use and are merely trained to use. Schools teach people how to more successfully compete for affection. They teach how to reach careers with increased amounts of money and/or control. To a degree, they teach ways of escape and with-drawal—look at the amazing amount of senseless diversions avail-able to students on any campus.

But they don't teach people how to change the situation caus-ing the distress of anxiety. The culture, the system, the way of life are presented as unchangeable, mandated by God, history, and charts of progress. In fact, a whole system of "therapy" by counsel-ors, clergymen, and psychiatrists has been set up to help people to "adjust," while leaving unchanged the root of the anxieties.

Persons who rebel against the anxiety-producing system are called maladjusted, neurotic, hyperactive, criminal, insane, and it is their behavior that is judged to be problematic. Often, the visionary artists and other cultural rebels can see the diseased nature of the society, but to little avail. Perhaps it is the people who have adjusted their attitudes, those who are considered "normal" or "adjusted" according to Western values, who are really in trouble, for surely they are the deviants from the Natural laws that govern the Creation.

In a world faced with crises of pollution, poverty, food short-age, rising fascism, failures of economy, and crumbling institu-tions, the person of Western culture who has a high degree of anxiety is probably reacting in a very healthy fashion. But the only ways such persons have been taught to handle anxiety only con-tribute to the crises, or, at worst, allow the crises to continue.

Persons who have some degree of intelligence and sensitivity will realize they have been had—they have been betrayed by their forebears, by their nation, by their culture, by their education— because they don't know how to change the system. They can't even change their lives, it seems, in many cases.

Such persons may realize that they live in a culture that creates behavior patterns that have been destructive to the Natural World and Natural Peoples. They see that people within their culture brutalize and abuse one another, continuing the practice of abuse until no one exists within the culture who can resist becoming part of the behavior pattern. There are few people in the culture who are not guilty of directing abuse toward other people—there are no living saints in the West.

While there are good reasons why Western people are the way they are, this does not mean they will like themselves. Nor does it mean they will be adopting human standards of behavior. Being driven by needs of reassurance in a world where you can believe almost no one and trust almost no one may be a normal reaction, but it is also a formula that denies a person access to true affection and leads people to continue the circle of untruth and unfaithfulness. Being driven by ambitions for power and possessions in a world in which poverty is synonymous with slavery may be understandable—but it produces destructive, cold-blooded people hostile to everything and everyone failing to serve their needs. Submitting to the authority of people driven by power needs is understandable in a world in which failure to submit results in oppression in the form of brutal force, but it also makes us participants in processes that are destroying people—and, in fact, the whole Creation.

But the disease is not the anxiety—the disease is the culture itself, and the diseased have to look to other cultures to find the cures.

One of the symptoms of the disease is that people who have it usually do not know they have it and will deny that there is anything wrong. The culture aids them in this, by denying the existence of problems, by promoting the sickest specimens into the positions of highest authority, by providing cosmetic touches to blemishes, affording temporary relief of distressing pain.

Another unusual symptom is that people defend the disease and its symptoms.

So if individuals or groups or families are going to rid their systems of the poison of this disease, they need to recognize, somehow, that they are contaminated. They need to see as early in life as possible that people in Western culture are sick. If we understand this is a world in which people are confused, depressed, often unable to direct honest affection, and often unpredictable, we will be more understanding and less likely to suffer disappointments—which lead to our own hostilities, repressed or otherwise, and our responses to them will be both consistent and compassionate.

The Earth continues to have great healing power, and for some, retreat to the forest and an extended fast may well be the best form of treatment. Diet may have some beneficial effects—it is accepted today that food additives have some effect upon hyperactivity among young children, at least. Also, sugar consumption (in soda pop, pies, cakes, etc.) at an astounding 115 pounds per person per year among Western populations—more than 100 pounds above sugar consumption of Natural World people—has undoubtedly had an effect on the nervous system, as it has increased gall disease, diabetes, coronary and ulcer infections, and decayed teeth among Western peoples, especially Native people who take on the Western diet.

This means it would probably be wise to abandon all processed foods and foods containing white sugar and white flour. It is difficult to say how much diet affects people's overall state of mind, but it seems clear that processed foods, which have largely eliminated many natural vitamins from the diet and have introduced substances to which our bodies are unfamiliar, must have negative effects.

True, Western society had problems before it had food additives, but the point here is that a Western diet cannot enhance our physical conditions, and fasting can be a great help in generating spiritual strength and in finding peace of mind. Even if people acted on the fact that to obtain healthy food economically might mean they had to grow it themselves, it would bring tremendous benefits into their lives.

The most appropriate treatment of a disease of this nature would include a number of elements. It would include fasting and an attention to the spiritual, which would avoid the theme of man's domination over the earth and promote some humility in man's relationship to the Natural World. In that respect, the individual would endeavor to reject the material values of the West and work to adapt something akin to Gandhi's philosophy of desirelessness as an ingredient of good physical and spiritual existence. There would be a need to reject processed and contaminated foods for the same reason and to approach food and eating as spiritual experiences.

There is a need to approach Western people as a contaminated people, regardless of color or heritage—Indians are not exempt from the disease. Western people should be faced with an attitude similar to that suggested for alcoholics—these people are ill, but only they can help themselves, and they must recognize their illness before they can treat it. Then they must want treatment and be willing to give up some of the pleasures gained from their disease. Until they do so, they cannot be relied upon to participate in human standards of conduct because their illness produces deviations from those standards.

Since Western culture does not support persons who do not participate in it, the appropriate strategy would require a return to some type of home food production as a form of good medicine. That particular way of life meets the needs of a food economy and of time and insulation necessary for the spiritual development. Of the possible responses to Western culture, the most logical is withdrawal—not withdrawal from life, but withdrawal from that culture. The withdrawal spoken of is withdrawal from Western culture, not from life itself. And it is not withdrawal into emptiness, but into the richness of the Natural World. The move is to simply redirect one's life away from things that are found to be corrosive. But the individual must turn to his way of life exclusive of expectations of community.

Of course, living in a loving, sharing community is the norm for humans—seemingly it is the Original Instruction for human beings from the Creation. But communities are gatherings of individuals engaged in some cooperative purpose. Truly primitive people have not survived contact with Western man. To reestablish community, where human standards of conduct are once again normal standards, where truthfulness and constancy and trust are possible and, in fact, normal, there is a need to promote the purification of the individual toward these goals. That purification must be initiated by the individual—he cannot ask the community to do it for him.

Since the problem involves what we generally describe as materialism, possessiveness, exaggerated needs of reassurance, a feeling of helplessness and hopelessness, it is important that the process of treatment be designed to release people from these needs. The treatment must involve a release from needs to dominate or be dominated, to possess or to have power over, to be reassured when all reassurance must be false.

Many of our Native people, and others as well, believe that a traditional lifestyle is an appropriate strategy to the problems of our people and our times. They wonder what they, living in Los Angeles or Chicago, can do. Knowing there are no self-sufficient communities in the city, they wonder, *Where can we go? How can we leave this corrosive way of life?*

First of all, it must be understood that the traditional lifestyle is following the Original Instructions given to all human beings in the Beginning. It is the seeking of harmony with all living things, a sharing, cooperative, loving lifestyle, etc.—all else are embellishments and regional variations.

The answers to "What can I do?" are ones people generally do not want to hear. One of the symptoms of the Western disease is helplessness. This creates an exaggerated fear that the individual is truly helpless. People withdraw from the idea of moving away from cities to the Natural World because they believe they would starve to death. This is not a rational fear—you simply will not starve to death, but there are many changes that you may find uncomfortable.

Those who are in a major city, have never planted a seed or cut a stick of wood, have never experienced a sweat lodge or gone on a fast should not seek first to learn the traditional ways, which, after all, require community. As an individual, try, as a first step, instead, purification through fasting.

Fasting may seem like a small thing to do, but for those who feel helpless, it is a first and basic step in taking control—again—of your own life. It is a real activity, possible for just about anyone, an exercise in overcoming helplessness and refocusing a sense of reality that will give us the strength and ability to take on the hard tasks.

Take life one day at a time. Go twenty-four hours without alcohol. Without buying something. Without white sugar and additives. If you are healthy and not pregnant or nursing, try—just once—going twenty-four hours without food. Go a day without telling someone what to do. How about trying for two days, now? Go without watching television.

We have been educated to really be helpless. It is not our imagination: without grocery stores, city people would be starving, not fasting. There is a difference—fasting is something you undertake to do, while being hungry or starving is usually an involuntary experience.

The inability of most people to return to a natural lifestyle is more of a matter of psychology than of material conditions. When most people think about being self-sufficient, their thoughts turn to nineteenth-century America, when people lived in large farmhouses, had cattle, horses, many acres of land, fruit trees, and any number of possessions. Without those possessions, many people will say, self-sufficiency is impossible. But a farm of that description would cost many thousands of dollars, and the people who built and occupied those farms were hardly Natural World people—in fact, many of them built their farms on the blood and bones of the Native people.

So we need to ask many questions—what does a true Natural World lifestyle include? What is absent in a Natural World lifestyle? If there is to be real change, the Good Medicine Life, its future participants must come to an understanding of what they are trying to do. To cease the feeling of helplessness, an individual must come to a new understanding of his or her needs. And owning a nineteenth-century farm, which might be worth $100,000, is not needed. If this is what you want, you are still possessed by the disease you seek to escape. And unless you are very wealthy, you are, in fact, helpless.

Families used to be self-sufficient in other ways besides food. They made the tools they used and the clothes they wore. They built the house they lived in and tended to their sick and lame. They taught their children, and they often buried their dead. And as they did these things, they learned to care for each other.

We need to remember that, historically, it has been these same things—anxiety, submission, helplessness—that have caused Native people to lose their natural ways and their independence. And we need to remember too that while we try to achieve cultural survival, the schools, the television, and our assimilated friends continue to draw us deeper and deeper into this false way of being.

As the family shifted from being a place of support, persons lost contact with people one could count on. While Western society still sentimentally talks about its family structure, this is now largely rhetoric for the vast majority of people. As the family ceased to be a unit of production, however, it became a unit of consumption. The family who consumes together stays together, is the motto. All the other basic activities have been taken on by other institutions. Child raising, in particular, has been handed over to the state, whose schools are agents of the consumer ideology.

Changes are going to occur whether we want them to or not. As foretold by our ancestors, the Natural World is going to purify itself. Materialism is already out of the reach of many people, and soon maybe food costs will be out of the reach of most families, indeed, if there is food available to purchase at all, even adulterated chemical food. So the question isn't whether the Western world will continue without us. The real question is—will we know how to live and survive in the Natural World when that is the only world left?

Words of Peace—A Six Nations Tradition

When, a long time ago, the Indian peoples of North America found themselves in a period of extended unrest, including blood feuds and warfare, there arose among them a man one could call a combination of political philosopher and spiritual leader who, though his name is not to be pronounced anymore, has the name of the Peacemaker. The Peacemaker taught the Iroquois Peoples some interesting theories that might be useful to express to people today—especially those individuals and groups who are seeking solutions to the very grave problems posed by the proliferation of nuclear weapons.

The existence of the Peacemaker is a historical as well as a spiritual reality for the Haudenosaunee Peoples, and it is probably, at the same time, the least well-known and the most vibrant quest for peace in the history of humanity.

There have been several different extended periods of peace in world history—including such ones as the Pax Romana and the Pax Azteca. Some are better known than others. In the Northeast region of North America, for several hundred years the thoughts and works of the Peacemaker created the conditions for what can be called the Pax Iroquoia, which spread a system of alliances over nearly a third of the territory that is currently known as the United States of America. This Pax Iroquoia was a unique quest for peace— one that articulated the belief that true peace in the world is not simply the absence of war, but is rather defined in the understanding of the human beings' relationship to the Great Universal Mind.

The Peacemaker spoke of a kind of peace that would be possible in this world as a result of a kind of divine inspiration. He said that there was a spirit that created life in the world and that by the manifestations of the Life one could see that the plan for that Life was perfection itself, that everything that humans needed to exist, and to be happy, and to prosper was placed in the world—plant life, animals, water, air—everything humans needed to survive.

Thus the Peacemaker also expressed our need to understand that the Plan for Life has an origin—an origin that can be called a Universal Intelligence, is a state of perfection, and whose will requires that humans in society manifest a desire for Life—as opposed to simply a desire for a lack of conflict.

The Peacemaker perceived that it was this ability of the human mind to understand the relationship of human society to this Plan for Life, upon which could be built a lasting peace.

The Peacemaker also said that this superior intelligence, which he called The Master of Life and which other people will call God, is perfect—and this perfection calls for humans to live in peace. But this manifestation of the perfect peace and this desire for Life could only come about if human societies could eliminate social injustice in the world. He said that any injustice that existed in the world would be a danger or an insult to this perfect mind, and he urged that human societies establish a peace based on the highest possible principles of justice. He tried to eliminate the concepts of cultural and racial antagonisms and also the conflicts that arose out of the unjust distribution of the natural wealth of the world.

The Peacemaker symbolized these principles of peace with the planting of the Great Tree of Peace, saying that those peoples who had grasped these principles could come and seek shelter under the leaves of this Great Tree by following what he called the Great White Roots of Peace. The Great White Roots of Peace were these pure thoughts that attracted peoples to the shade of this powerful protection, which was to be this great and all-encompassing law of nations—which demanded from all who sat under this shade that they eliminate the custom of having borders, and also the concept of one nation being able to dominate another nation through religion or on the basis of the language that they spoke or any other self-perceived superiority.

All peoples who would come under the protection of the Great Law would be enlightened to the philosophy that humans could resolve all of their difficulties on the basis of discussion and negotiation, that there is no need for warfare, and that all those who embraced the Law would cast their weapons of war into a hole dug under this Great Tree of Peace.

The Peacemaker pointed out that wars are fought over what we recognize today as territorial conflicts, over greed among nations, over cultural antagonisms (racism), and over unfair distribution of wealth. In the Great Law of Peace, which is the underlying basis of the Iroquois Confederacy, he created a system that for many centuries was capable of maintaining peace in this part of the world.

The formulation of this Great Law took place a long time ago, but it appears to us just as applicable today. They understood then too that people had the ability to exterminate life on this planet and that it was precisely the misunderstanding of the humans' relationship to the Master's Plan for Life that would create the destructive condition. It was a very religious way of looking at life, and it was the active engagement of a people trying to strive for a perfect world, a perfect justice, beginning with the idea that it was our Creator's will that all people be treated equally and with the full understanding that the physical universe was also a manifestation of the Creator's will and could not be owned by anyone or claimed as territory. It required that Life itself be central to religion, and the Plan of the Master of Life was looked upon as an intelligence in itself, something to be preserved. This is what the old people taught us.

Clear Thinking: A Positive Solitary View of Nature

I come from a complex tradition that acknowledges a wide range of beliefs. The fundamental thing about being Iroquois is that people will not argue about beliefs or religions. Inside our traditional religion are all kinds of different beliefs, and not everyone shares all those beliefs.

But there is also in our culture a core requirement that ultimately, whatever our beliefs are, we are encouraged to maintain the tradition of *clear thinking*. Clear thinking is the foundation of the Great Law and is an ever-recurring theme in what is known as the *Ganyodaiyo* or Good Message of Handsome Lake. It's also discussed even in parts of our ancient tradition, the story of how the world came to be the way it is. We call it in English the Creation Story.

My version of Native American studies was that we would be the critics of Western culture. We would do what Western culture and anthropologists do to Indians: review it, point out what's wrong with it, explain where it went wrong, tell them it was wrong, and basically have a version and understanding of it. To do that meant that I had to take a close look at the origins and the philosophies around science and the origins and philosophies about philosophy: the whole question of where the culture tells us it is coming from, where it says it is, and where it says it is going.

I am surprised a little, given that history, that we seem to be moving toward a different place. We have people now who are very clearly among the best scientists who are willing to agree that there are limits to the knowledge that science can have about nature. We're reaching a place in which there's ever-wider agreement that poetry gives us as much information about our relationship with the universe as telescopes do and that those two strains can live together and complement one another harmoniously. Those two things can happen, and that's actually not dissimilar to my culture, which asserts that on the one hand there are dreams and visions, and on the other hand there's a responsibility to maintain a clear version of reality, and those two streams of thoughts and reaction have to live cooperatively together.

The idea that the spiritual and the secular can live side by side is extremely important at this time. I also believe that, while we may not agree on everything that we believe in, there are a few things that are emerging that almost everyone can believe in.

The Iroquois culture has a tradition that every time we gather together to have a meeting, we open with what is called a *ga no ya* or opening speech. Some people call it a thanksgiving address. That talk is what everyone who is sane in the world should agree on. It's kind of like Iroquois diplomacy: we start with what we agree on and then we keep going to the things that we cannot agree on. So what is it that we all agree on? The speech starts with an opening that we see one another; we need each other; we need people to be in the world and it's a good thing that there are people in the world; we're grateful and thankful that there are other people in the world and it's good to see them here, so we give a greeting. We acknowledge the greetings and thanksgiving that there are one and another, that we can greet one another. Since that's the way we do things amongst ourselves, we should be able to do that with other beings, and so it goes on and we do greetings to the Earth. Everybody should be able to give greeting to the Mother Earth. She's a person, and—call it poetic—it's a way of us having a relationship with that, so we acknowledge that relationship. It's fundamental: right after people, Earth. Then it goes to grasses, waters, trees, plants, winds, the moon, the stars, the sun, the universe, the whole thing. Everybody in the world ought to be able to agree that we depend on those things. Those things are actually essential to us, and that's the rational mind with a poetic way of expressing a rational mind. Some people look at that and say that's spiritual. Whatever you call it is fine. It's us expressing our positive relationship to all the others, every other that we can think of. We have not separated ourselves from them. They are others and we are part of the others.

We have to do this speech at the beginning and the end of every meeting because people need to be reminded of that. It's a constant reminder.

I think that now we need also to acknowledge science as a form of gathering information, a very important one. In a way, science has claimed to be more than that. There has been a tradition in the West claiming that science had a power greater than a system that gathers information for us. I think that leaves a lot of people feeling negative about science. But I want to be positive about science because we are now beginning to have a moment when it is possible for people across cultures to have a positive view of nature. Nature is what keeps us alive. It is not our enemy. It is what gave us life in the first place.

In my culture they call the givers of life *Jo Ha Cho*. They call the creator of life *Ho Cha Ne Tom*. The creator of life and the givers of life are different. The creator of life is that which existed in the universe, and the *Jo Ha Cho* is what existed here on this planet in this sphere: the physical beings with a spiritual face that create our lives and make us live.

Now we're faced with a reality that people have been playing with the *Jo Ha Cho*. They've been concluding that they can play God, a version of God. They would claim the right to splice genes, to fool with the building blocks of life. I propose to you that they've been doing that for a long time. This isn't new. It's been happening for a long time, ever since the evolution of chemistry, and it is coming into everyday life. Every one of us has things in our bodies that our ancestors never had in their bodies. Everything that is alive on the whole planet has chemicals in its being that didn't used to be in its being.

The second thing is that the things of nature are no longer available to us. From the air we breathe to the water we drink to the food we eat, every one of these has been altered from the way our ancestors experienced those things. The Earth itself, when you pick it up and analyze it, is not the same. Everything has been changed. Yet if nature is sacred, it would be our mind to change it back to make it the way it was when it was supportive of life on the Earth. To make the food the way it was, to make the water the way it was, to make the air the way it was, to make our bodies and everything on the planet the way it was, the way nature made it to be. I can see now that scientists can help us do that. I can see now that there are scientists who think that way too, and in that regard it seems to me that the Natural World people and scientific people—all kinds of other people, even business people—can be on the same side of something.

We all have to have as a goal that we should see nature restored. The word *nature* is a little bit fuzzy here. When I say nature, I mean everything that supports life on the planet is nature. Nature is so complex and its interactions so dynamic that the idea that science could ever understand it all is utterly laughable. We can understand the more simple things that we do to interfere with it: to degrade it, to wreck it. But we can never understand it. It is beyond our comprehension.

The Indian cultures that I know have said that nature is a great mystery. It is so complex, so great, so above us that we should never be so arrogant to think that we can understand even a little bit of it. But we can understand our nature. We can understand the profit motive can be dangerous. We can understand wrong thinking. We can understand the concept of science as a revitalization movement that makes outlandish claims for itself, and of course the real scientists say that's not real science but pseudoscience. I have really come to embrace that idea, that real science doesn't do that. Of course, many of the pseudoscientists are paid to say that. Large corporations that have profits in mind head right for the universities and buy the guys who are supposed to be the experts. Then they have people who claim to be scientists saying, "Tobacco smoke doesn't cause illness. No, there's no problem with changing genes around. There's no problem with atomic bombs. What are you worried about? Okay, so things are dying, but what are you worried about?"

So I want to propose that I can see that we are headed into a new space that puts the Natural World people and the indigenous people who still maintain their mind about nature with very vast allies in the industrialized world. I never thought I would have that thought.

We can look at this as a global consciousness that is rising and, in English, is coming from people to whom nature is like religion. What that means in English is actually not accurate enough. The culture that I come from saw the universe as the fountain of everything including consciousness. In our culture, we're scolded for being so arrogant to think that we're smart. An individual is not smart, according to our culture. An individual is merely lucky to be a part of a system that has intelligence that happens to reside in them. In other words, be humble about this always. The real intelligence isn't the property of an individual corporation—the real intelligence is the property of the universe itself.

Afterword
A Constellation of Memories

As the sorrowful reality of John Sotsitsowah Mohawk's untimely passing unfolds in our ongoing daily lives, our tears wash ashore the multitude of anecdotes, narratives, opportunities—both those seized upon and those left for "later"—and outright magical moments that we must renew in our hearts to memorialize his having been here among us in his many guises.

In my family, John was counted as a brother. In that context, I always called him by his Seneca name, Sotsitsowah, or Corn Tassel. In the small hours of a June 9, 1980, dawn, Sotsitsowah climbed the two-mile logging road that led to Hilltop, our home in the Adirondacks, where in those politically turbulent years *Akwesasne Notes* was edited and produced by John Mohawk and my husband, José Barreiro. I had asked Sotsitsowah to burn tobacco for my home birth there at our primitive cabin in the mountains for our son Anontaks Joaquin. José and I remember that we could hear John coming before we could see him, as he walked toward our home singing welcoming songs for our soon-to-be-born son. These songs were traditionally sung to let a village know that you are coming toward them. They are then answered from within the village to let the visitor know that their announcement has been received and that it is safe to enter the clearing. They are perfect songs for a birth, as they enfold within them the human enunciation of presence, intention, and performance. Quickly assembling a pile of dry kindling into a fire, John further burned tobacco for our protection. Almost to the day a year later, John would use this same set of songs for the home birth of his own son Teiotsiataronwe. In these and in so many other spiritually profound and politically dangerous moments like it, John applied performativity of voice, using the power of breath in language and song to call forth life; to summon the capacity to think, to speak, to move, and yes, to act.

Our brother has found his place now among the *Rati iah kerahnoron*, the Sky Beings, upon whom we continually depend for our lives here on earth. Let us seek and find his friendly embrace in the arms of our Mother Corn for whom he himself had been named, though now that splendid name has been lifted from him and returned to his clan. We look to the Turtles and their continuity to make use of that highly esteemed name again. In the fall of 2005, on our way to one of his many lectures at City University of New York School of Graduate Studies, John told us that he thought that there were only about forty more years left before the hope of the survival of the ways and ceremonies of our ancestors become extinguished.

"Keep it all happening," he instructed us. Eat a bowl of corn soup. Chew on a few kernels of roasted Iroquois white corn. Rise in darkness and sing a song to the early dawn, asking the wind, the source of our breath, to protect the life of the people. Check out www.bioneers.org. Teach a child a traditional story at the proper time of year. Plant a garden. Go to the Longhouse. Support the ceremonies. Live life as though this was your last day on this beautiful earth. Let us step outside of ourselves and donate time and money to the many worthy causes he founded and supported, like the Akwesasne Freedom School and his own White Corn Project at Pinewoods. In small and big ways, let us memorialize him and the teachings he shared.

He told us once, in his modesty, "I am not a star." For me and my family, he has become a constellation, a map in the sky that points the way to our future.

—Katsi Cook Barreiro

Credits

The following are previously published material appearing in this volume.

"The Creator's Way," in *Akwesasne Notes*, Late Summer 1975: 35.

"All Children of Mother Earth…," in *Akwesasne Notes*, Early Summer 1976: 4–5.

"The Public Eye: Hopi-Haudenosaunee; Sharing Prophetic Traditions," in *Native Americas* 16, no. 3 and 4 (December 31, 1999): 90.

"Wild and Slow: Nourished by Tradition," Center for Ecoliteracy, www.ecoliteracy.org/essays/wild-and-slow-nourished-tradition.

"Last Words: The Sacred in Nature; Mythology Can Change Our Minds," in *Native Americas*, June 30, 1995: 64.

"Enduring Seeds," in *Native Americas* 16, no. 1 (March 31, 1999): 63.

"Indians and Sugar: Thoughts on Nutrition, Disease," in *Indian Studies* 11, no. 4 (Winter 1985): 8–12.

"The Darkening Horizons," in *Akwesasne Notes*, July 1977: 4–6.

"Our Strategy for Survival, *Basic Call to Consciousness*, ed. Akwesasne Notes (Summertown, TN: Native Voices, 1978), 119–125.

"Present Potential, Future Reality," in *Akwesasne Notes*, Late Summer 1982: 4–5.

"Indian Economic Development: The US Experience of an Evolving Indian Sovereignty," in *Akwe:kon Journal* 9, no. 2 (Summer 1992): 42–49.

"A Sovereign Manifesto," in *Multinational Monitor* 7, no. 10 (June 1986).

"Regaining Control of Our Lives: The Promise of Appropriate Technology," in *Akwesasne Notes*, Autumn 1978: 4.

"Technology As Enemy: A Short History," in *Akwesasne Notes*, Winter 1979: 19–21.

"Small, Indian, and Beautiful: Development through Appropriate Technology," in *Indian Studies* 1, no. 3 (Fall 1984): 8–9.

"The 'Disappearing Indian': 20th Century Reality Disproves 19th Century Prediction," in *Native Americas* 19, no. 1 (June 30, 2002): 40.

"The Future is the Family," in *Akwesasne Notes*, Late Spring 1977: 4–7.

"Indian Nations, the United States, and Citizenship," Center for World Indigenous Studies, Fourth World Documentation Project (1983), www.cwis.org.

"Reviews: The Spirit of Regeneration," in *Native Americas* 15, no. 4 (December 31, 1998): 62.

"American Indian History: Five Centuries of Conflict and Coexistence," in *Native Americas* 21, no. 2 (June 2004): 64.

"The Confusing Spectre of White Backlash," in *Akwesasne Notes*, December 1977, 22–23.

"The Great Bowhead Controversy: 'We are the People of the Whale,'" in *Akwesasne Notes* 10, no. 1 (Early Spring 1978): 20–21.

"The Longest Walk: Vignettes," in *Akwesasne Notes*, Summer 1978, 6–11.

"The Iroquois Land Claims," in *Native Americas* 17, no. 1 (Spring 2000): 20–23.

"Rights of Indigenous Women are Advancing on Several Fronts," in *Native Americas* 21, no. 1 (Spring 2004): 64.

"Traditionalism. The Wave of the Future," in *Akwesasne Notes*, Late Spring 1982, 4–6.

"Traditionalism: An Organizing Tool for Community Survival," in *Akwesasne Notes*, Early Winter 1982, 21–23.

"Marxism: Perspectives from a Native Movement," in *Akwesasne Notes*, Early Spring 1981.

"Racism: An American Ideology," in *Akwesasne Notes*, September 1977, 6–7.

"Thoughts from an Autochthonous Center: Postmodernism and Cultural Studies," in *Akwe:kon Journal* 9, no. 4 (Winter 1992): 16–21.

"Thoughts of Peace: The Great Law," in *Basic Call to Consciousness*, ed. Akwesasne Notes (Summertown, TN: Native Voices, 1978), 31–40.

"We Are By Nature Social Animals," in *Akwesasne Notes*, Winter 1978, 7–9.

"Western Peoples, Natural Peoples: Roots of Anxiety," in *Akwesasne Notes*, Early Spring 1976, 34–36.

"Words of Peace—A Six Nations Tradition," in *Akwesasne Notes*, Early Summer 1982, 5.

"Clear Thinking: A Positive Solitary View of Nature," in *Original Instructions: Indigenous Teachings for a Sustainable Future*, ed. Melissa K. Nelson (Rochester, VT: Bear & Company, 2008).

Index

A

Aboriginal and Torres Straight Islander Commission, 190

Africa, 32, 118, 130, 133, 233

agriculture: agricultural societies, 95, 123, 125; alternative technologies, 106; American farmers, 198–99; conventional farming, 105; foods of the agricultural revolution, 27–28; history in the Southwest, 19; human manipulation and intervention, 27–28; Native farmers, 28; organic farming, 105; surface waters of North America, 45; water-use technologies, 96

Akwesasne Freedom School, 64, 126–27

Alaska, 161–68

Alaska Eskimo Whaling Commission (AEWC), 162, 163, 165, 166

Alaska Native Claims Settlement Act of 1972, 167, 168

Alaskan Inupiat people (Eskimos), 161–68

Albany, NY, 183, 184

Alberta, 260

Alcatraz Island, 65, 176, 195

Ali, Muhammad, 176

Allegany Indian Reservation, 14

American Indian History: Five Centuries of Conflict and Coexistence (Venables), 144–47

American Indians/indigenous peoples. *See also*

Haudenosaunee: acculturation policies, 61, 71, 85–86, 116; American Indian Movement, 195–202; bingo casinos, 70; ceremonies, 6; Christian missionaries, 71; citizenship, 130–31, 136–39; communities and community life, 68, 69, 203–12; cultural extinction, 73, 197, 199, 203; cultural revitalization of traditionalism, 195–212; culture and economic growth, 71, 79; dependency, 60–61; as distinct peoples, 189, 205; economic development, self-sufficiency, and revitalization, 60–73, 79, 85–90, 105–7, 203–12; education and schools, 111–12, 116, 126, 195, 205–7, 212; federal and state bureaucracy, 65–73, 81–82, 85–86, 89–90; federal funds, 84–85; groups and group rights, 68; identities, 80, 113–17; impediments to self-development, 104–6; Indian forms of government, 60, 71–73; Indian rights, legislation and citizens action groups, 153–58; lack of published ideologies, 222; land and land claims, 69, 76, 138–39, 154, 155–56, 158–59, 182–87; liberation theologies, 215–16; Marxist ideology v. Indian ideology, 213–23; movements for tribal sovereignty, 65–73; myth

of the vanishing race, 111–17; nature and the Natural World, 154–55, 215, 216, 220, 275–77; per capita income, 104–5; prophets and prophecies on capitalism, 214, 219–20; racism, 67, 126, 139, 153, 158, 224–31; relationship with Western peoples, 259–70; resources in Indian territories, 157–58; social change and development, 79–80, 88, 200; societal units, 126; traditions and traditional lifestyles, 257–58, 268; treaties with European invaders, 135; trust responsibility theory, 137–38; unemployment, 60, 77, 84; US treatment of Indian nations during the nineteenth century, 136–37; way of life and the family, 118–23, 125–29, 216, 249–52, 269–70; welfare economy, 81–82; white backlash and anti-Indian movements, 153–60

American Revolution, 136, 182

American school system and curriculums, 206–7, 264

Ananda Marga (organization), 179

Anasazi (Pueblo) Indians, 17

Anatolia and the Fertile Crescent, 96, 98

Andean Project on Peasant Technologies (PRATED), 141–43

anxiety, 261–65
Apache, 70, 197
Apffel-Marglin, Frede-
   rique, 141–42
Arctic North, 167–68
Arctic Slope Regional Cor-
   poration, 168
Aristotle, 226, 227
*Aristotle and the American
   Indian* (Hanke), 134
Arizona, 14, 20, 70, 260
Articles of Confederation,
   136, 183
Asgeirsson, Thordur, 166
Asia, 46, 130, 233
Atlantic Ocean, 48
Augustine of Hippo (Saint
   Augustine), 16
Australia, 118, 130, 161,
   165
Azores Islands, 132, 133

B

Banyacya, Thomas, 14–15,
   19, 91, 112
Barrow Whaling Captains
   Association, 165
Barton, John, 48–50
Bellecourt, Vernon, 171,
   176
Berman, Harold J., 131
Blackfeet Indians of Mon-
   tana, 70
Blackgoat, Roberta, 171–72
black people, 175, 176
Bosque Redondo, 71
bourgeois ideology, 219,
   221
Bradford, William, 145
Brando, Marlon, 176
Brazil, 67, 138, 230
Brower, Arnold, 165
Buddhists, 174, 176
Buffalo Creek Treaty, 185
Bureau of Indian Affairs
   (BIA), 65, 66, 68, 71, 73,
   81, 84–85, 175
Bureau of Land Manage-
   ment (BLM), 65

C

Cahn, Edgar, 67
California and Proposition
   13, 83
Canada, 163, 165, 166,
   167, 247
Canadian Inuit people
   (Eskimos), 35, 37, 190
Canadian Inuvialuits'
   Committee on Original
   Peoples' Entitlement
   (COPE), 166
Canandaigua Treaty, 185
Canary Islands, 132–33
Canny, Nicholas P., 135
canonical hegemony, 235
capitalism, 195, 214, 215,
   217–23
Caribbean, 133, 232
Carib peoples, 225
Carter, President Jimmy,
   43, 163, 172, 173
Cayuga Indians, 114–15,
   186, 241
Central America, 225, 232
*Changes in the Land:
   Indians, Colonists and
   Ecology of New England*
   (Cronon), 135
Cherokee Indians, 36, 70,
   146, 147
*Cherokee Nation v. Geor-
   gia,* 66
Chief Leschi, 147
Chief Seath'tl, 147
Chief Standing Bear, 147
Chippewa Indians, 114
Choctaw Indians, 70, 147
Christianity and the
   church, 99–100, 263
cities, 19, 45, 97, 229–30,
   268–69
civilization, 19, 96–99,
   102, 231
Civil Liberties for South
   Dakota Citizens, 153
Civil War, 185
Cochiti Pueblo Indians,
   70, 71

Code, Lorraine, 235–36
Code of Handsome Lake,
   250
colonialism, 55–59, 86,
   154, 160, 224, 230
colonization: civilized
   countries, 230–31; and
   deprivation, 54; mass
   starvation, 54; social
   organization, 54, 113,
   116, 159
Columbia, 190
Columbia River, 65
Columbus, Christopher,
   113, 133, 224–25
Comprehensive Employ-
   ment and Training Act
   programs, 61, 83
Congress and legislation,
   157–58, 184, 186
Constitution of the Five
   Nations, 245–47
Creation, 7–13
The Creator's way, 3–6
Cree Indians, 201
Creek Indians, 147
Cronon, William, 135
Crosby, Alfred W., 133
cultural studies, 234, 237
cultures: absence of, 86;
   continuum of locally
   based cultures, 56;
   development of, 93–96;
   and economy, 85–86;
   and education, 25–26;
   European, 232; folk
   cultures, 56; human
   cultures and identity,
   116–17; and ideology,
   237; as learned means
   of survival, 253; Natural
   World, 196, 256–57; and
   politics, 234; rekindling
   locally based cultures,
   56; revitalization, 59,
   195; and technology, 88,
   95–101; Western, 98–99,
   229–30, 259–70
Cunningham, Jack, 82

Cunningham Bill, 158

D

Debo, Angie, 137
Deere, Phillip, 197
Deere v. St. Lawrence River
   Power Co., 186
Defenders of Wildlife, 165
Deloria, Vine, Jr., 142
Denmark, 166
Dion-Buffalo, Yvonne, 232
Durham, Douglass, 259
Duwamish Indians, 147

E

Eagleton, Terry, 235, 236
Early Spanish Main, The
   (Sauer), 133
Ecological Imperialism:
   The Biological Expan-
   sion of Europe, 900–1900
   (Crosby), 133
Economic Development
   Administration, 84, 85
economic networking, 89
Egan, William, 162
Egypt, 103
Eldorado Nuclear, 48
Elizabethan Conquest of
   Ireland: A Pattern Estab-
   lished 1565–1576, The
   (Canny), 135
Enduring Seeds (Nabhan),
   27, 28
energy czars, 198
energy lobbyists, 54–55
England, 131–34, 135, 182,
   183, 185, 226
enslavement, 69, 133, 146,
   225, 228
environmentalists, 154,
   158, 162
Etruscans, 103
Eurocentered hegemony,
   235
Europeans and the Euro-
   pean era, 113–14, 130–
   36, 144–45, 225–26,
   232–34

Everett, Edward, 186
Everett Commission, 186

F

Fallen Timbers, 185
Fields, Jerry, 145
First Environment pro-
   gram, 64
Five Nations, 244–45, 247
Florida, 134
food and food production:
   alternative agricultural
   technologies, 106; and
   diseases, 266; export
   crops, 33, 57; food additives and hyperactivity,
   266; food shortages, 57,
   198; organic foods, 105,
   106; processed foods,
   30–38, 266; regional and
   worldwide famines, 51,
   54–55; surplus foods,
   105; technology, 89;
   traditional vs. cultivated,
   21; and the weather, 51
Fort Niagara, 182
Fort Oswego, 182
Fort Stanwix, 182
Foucault, Michel, 235, 236
Four Horsemen of the
   Apocalypse, 100
France, 131, 136, 165, 226
Friends of the Earth, 154
Fukuyama, Francis, 16–17,
   18

G

Gandhi's philosophy, 266
Garrett, Tom, 165
genocide and genocidal
   policies, 188–89, 224,
   229, 230, 231
Germany, 82, 83, 172
Gila Indians of Arizona, 70
Good Message of Hand-
   some Lake, 274
The Good Word (oral
   document), 248
Grant mineral belt, 76

Gray, Reverend Robert,
   145
Great Britain, 247
Great Depression, 60, 82
Great Law of Peace, 115,
   210, 243–44, 247, 272–
   73, 274
Great Society program, 82
Great Tree of Peace, 272
Great White Roots of
   Peace, 272
Greenland, 166
Grillo Fernández, Edu-
   ardo, 142
gross national product, 82
Guanche peoples of the
   Canary Islands, 132–33,
   134
Guatemala, 190, 199, 261
Gulf Oil Company, 76

H

Handsome Lake, 247–48,
   250
Hanke, Lewis, 134
Harlan, Chief Justice John
   Marshall, 111
Haudenosaunee (People of
   the Longhouse): citizenship, 130; cooperative
   organizations, 210; the
   Creator's way, 5; formation of the Confederacy,
   145; Great Law of Peace,
   244–48; internal affairs,
   244–48; land claims and
   fair treatment, 186–87;
   and liberation theol-
   ogy, 58–59; oral history,
   240–41; Peacemaker,
   244–48, 271–73; religion
   and way of life, 118–20;
   Six Nations Iroquois
   Confederacy, 14, 19,
   114–15, 180–81, 182,
   184, 185, 243, 249, 252,
   257–58, 271–73; and
   treaties, 14, 135; and
   Venables's narrative, 147

Havasupai Indians, 154
Havel, Václav, 24
health issues: alcohol, 30, 120; diets and diseases, 20–23, 27–28, 30–38, 266; exercise, 21–22, 34, 120; fasting, 266, 268; industrial pollution, 43–46; nutrition and education, 22, 34; radiation sickness, 48–49; refined white sugar, white flour, and refined carbohydrates, 30–38, 120, 266
Hearne, David, 67
history: American Indian, 144–47; ancient civilization and Rome, 18; conventional histories, 98; cultural revolutions, 53; European, 130–35; human societies, 95; political histories of the world, 53–54; social history and technological changes, 53; Western civilization and technology, 15–17, 92, 100–101
History of the Indians and the United States, A (Debo), 137
Hopi Indians: culture and decline, 17, 18, 113; Grandfather David, 174; and the Navajo Indians, 171; prophecies and philosophies, 14–19, 91–92, 112–13; traditionalism, 201
Hopson, Eben, 162, 164, 167, 168
House Committee on Interior and Insular Affairs, 166–67
human beings: evolution, 93–95, 253–56; and intimacy, 256–57; spiritual relationships, 4–5

human groups, 256
Huron peoples, 240

I
imperialism, 230, 247
India, 33, 36, 138, 141, 179, 238
Indian Citizenship Act of 1924, 139
Indian Claims Commission Act, 186
Indian Reorganization Act (IRA), 67, 157
Indian reservations and territories: alternatives to reservation life, 104; and exploitation of natural resources, 61; land resources, 60, 68, 69, 104; and multinational corporations, 76–77; revolution for control and ownership of, 68
Indonesia, 138
Industrial Revolution: and agriculture, 27–28; and the family, 121–25, 203; and Marxism, 214; and technology, 101–2
industrial societies, 50–51, 214–21
International Labor Organization Convention No. 169, 190
International Whaling Commission (IWC), 161–62, 163, 164, 165, 166, 167, 168
Interstate Congress for Equal Rights and Responsibilities (ICERR), 153
Invasion of America: Indians, Colonialism, and the Cant of Conquest, The (Jennings), 136
Ireland, 134–35
Iroquois Indians. See Haudenosaunee

Isaac Walton League, 154

J
Japan, 82, 83, 174
Jefferson, Thomas, 111
Jennings, Francis, 136
Jimenez Sardon, Greta, 142
Johnson, Sir William, 183

K
Kant, Immanuel, 16
Kuan-Ksing Chen, 234
Ku Klux Klan, 259

L
Lake Ontario, 48
Lakota communities, 197
Las Casas, Bartolomé (Patron Saint of the Indians), 133–34, 144, 226, 228–29
Latin America, 75, 134, 142, 198, 233
Law and Revolution: The Formation of the Western Legal Tradition (Berman), 131
League of Nations, 139
liberation movements, 57
liberation technologies, 56, 57–58
liberation theologies, 57–58
Life Supportive Index (LSI), 102, 103
Life-Supportive Processes of the World, 12
The Longest Walk to Washington, DC, 170–81, 197
Louisiana Purchase, 185
Louisville, KY, 179
Lovejoy, Samuel Holden, 48–50
Lummi Indians, 70

M
Machiavelli, Niccolò, 16

Madeira Island and the Portuguese peoples, 132
Maine land dispute, 156
Malcolm X Park, Washington, DC, 175–80
Manifest Destiny, 111
Mann, Barbara Alice, 145
Marshall, Chief Justice John, 66
Marx, Karl, 102
Marxism, 79, 213–23, 236
Maryland National Guard, 170–71
materialism, 15, 267, 270
Means, Russell, 172–73
Meeds, Lloyd, 157
Meeds Bill, 157–58
Menchú, Rigoberta, 190
Mescalero Apache Indians, 70
Mexican War, 185
Mexico, 20, 33, 103, 225, 229
Middle East, 233
modern society and the modern family, 121–25, 128
modern technology: air pollution and acid rains, 46, 51, 101–2; alternative energy sources, 106; appropriate technology, 89–90, 105–6; capital intensive, 86–87; cheap energy, 44, 45, 54; coal mining, 77, 87, 158; and cultures, 98–99; current crisis, 54; and disease, 45–46; energy consumption and conservation, 54, 55; evolution of, 96–98; for food–storage, 100; fossil–fuel resources and predicted shortages, 43–46, 50–51, 54–55, 100; geothermal energy, 50; and global warming, 18, 19; hardware and software technologies,

87; harnessing of tidal power, 50; and human societies, 95; and Indian/government relations, 76; industrial pollution, 43; intermediate technologies, 88; labor–intensive, 87; lost technologies, 103; mercury-polluted waters, 44–45; nuclear reactor development, meltdowns, and radioactive gasses, 46–50, 55; nuclear reactor development and security required, 48–50; oxygen deficient waters, 45; people-oriented, 62–63; problems with, 97–103; projected energy needs, 47; proposed Navajo agribusiness project, 87; replacement energy production, 43, 46; social impact of new technologies, 88; solar energy, 50–51; synthetic-fiber production, 44; synthetic-plastic, 44; toxic chemicals, 102; uranium mining, 77, 158, 199; use of chlorine, 44; water-use technologies and conservation, 96, 106; wind generators, 50; world food-production crisis, 43
Mohawk, John C., 232
Mohawk Indians, 114–15, 116, 186, 240–41, 246
Mohawk Valley, 182, 183
Mondale, Vice President Walter, 164, 172, 173
Montana, 70, 76, 153
Moore, Rod, 166–67
Mormons, 115
Mother Earth, 7–13
multinational corporations, 55, 56, 76–77, 189

mutual aid societies and concepts, 209, 210
My Lai, 260
Mystic massacre, 145

N
Nabhan, Gary, 27
National Wildlife Federation, 155
Native Seeds/SEARCH's Desert Foods for Diabetes, 20
Native Self-Sufficiency Center (NSSC), 104, 106–7
Natural Law, 243
Natural World: the Creator's way, 9–12; diets, 34, 36; and human beings, 256–57; its possible destruction by industrial technologies, 103, 214–16, 220, 262; and lifestyle, 269–70; and spirituality, 266
Natural World peoples, 230–31, 261
Navaho Indians (Diné), 76, 87, 114, 170–73
Nazi Party, 259
Nebraska, 260
New Deal, 82
New England, 135
New Frontier program, 82
New York State, 14, 47, 182–83, 185–87, 247
New Zealand, 165
Nonintercourse Act, 1790, 156
Northern Cheyenne Reservation, MO, 76
North Slope Burrough, AK, 162, 164, 168
North Vietnamese, 200
Northwest Ordinance, 183
Norway, 165
nuclear families, 126, 252, 256

O

Oakes, Richard, 176
O'Donoghue, Lois, 190
Oglala Indians, 64, 85, 260
Ohio, 182, 184–85, 199
Oklahoma Indians, 130
Omaha,.147
Oneida Indians, 70, 114–
 15, 186, 241
*Oneida Nation v. County of
 Oneida*, 186
Onondaga, NY, 14, 170, 248
Onondaga Indians, 114–
 15, 186, 201, 241
opportunistic expropria-
 tion, 72
oppression, 259
Oraybi, AZ, rock picto-
 graphs, 14–15
Organization of American
 States, 190

P

Pan-Indian politics, 195,
 201
Paraguay, 230
Passamaquoddy Indians,
 156
Pax Azteca, 271
Pax Iroquoia, 271
Pax Romana, 271
Peabody Coal Company, 76
The Peacemaker, 240–48,
 271–73
Penobscot Indians, 156
Pequot Wars, 260
Peru, 103, 141, 142
Pickering, Timothy, 185
Pine Ridge Reservation,
 SD, 64, 153–54, 259
Pit River, 65, 195
pluralism, 72, 237
Pokiak, Randy, 166
political organizations and
 Native rights, 155
politics and economics, 55
Porter, Thomas, 126–27
postmodernism, 233–34,
 236, 237

power, 243–44, 263
Pratt, Captain Richard,
 111–12
priest-classes, 96
progressivism, 224
Provincial Assembly of
 Antioquipa, 190
Prudhoe Bay, 162, 167
Puerto Rico, 139
purification, 19, 266, 267,
 268

Q

Quinault Indians, 70

R

racism, 67, 126, 153, 158,
 224–31, 232
Raddi, Sam, 166
Rarihokwats, 260
Reagan, President Ronald,
 195
real income, 61–62
reason, 242
reindustrialization, 83
Removal Act, 146
Rengifo Vasquez,
 Grimaldo, 142
righteousness, 241–42
Robert E. Moses Power
 Project, 91, 112
Ross, John, 146
Russia, 95, 218
Russian-American Com-
 pany, 147

S

Said, Edward, 236
Sauer, Karl, 133
Seneca Indians, 85, 114–
 15, 145, 186, 241, 244,
 246, 258
Sepúlveda, Juan Ginés de,
 134, 138, 226–28, 229
Seven Years War, 136
Shiva, Vandana, 238
Sierra Club, 154, 163
Silver Covenant Chain, 135
Simon, Mary, 190

Sioux Indians, 114
Sitting Bull, 260
social injustice, 272
socialism, 204–20
social organization, 256–57
South Dakota, 64, 75, 153,
 199, 259, 260
Soviet Union, 33, 165, 172,
 216–17, 218
*Spirit of Regeneration:
 Andean Culture Confront-
 ing Western Notions
 of Development, The*
 (Apffel-Marglin), 141–42
Spiritual Unity Caravans,
 195
sportsmen groups and
 Native rights, 155
sweat lodges, 178
Swinomish Indians, 70

T

Taino peoples, 225
technology. *See* modern
 technology
Tecumseh, 146, 185
Tohono O'odham Commu-
 nity Action, 20
Tokyo, 164, 166
Tonawanda Reservation,
 118
Trade and Intercourse Act,
 1790, 184, 185, 186
trade routes, 96–97
traditional economy, 203–7
Trail of Broken Treaties, 65
transnational corpora-
 tions, 197, 198, 199
Treaty of Paris, 182
Trilateral Commission, 195
Tuscarora Indians, 114–15,
 186
Two Row Treaty, 135

U

United Nations, 19, 59, 246
United Nations Working
 Group on Indigenous
 Populations, 190

United States v. Boylan, 186
Universe, The, 24–26
US civil rights movement, 67
US Commerce Department, 163
US Constitution, 136, 137, 146
US Department of Labor, 85
US Department of the Interior, 162
US economy and industry, 82–85
US Endangered Species Act of 1973, 161
US Marine Fisheries Service, 163
US Marine Mammal Commission, 167
US Marine Mammal Protection Act of 1972, 161
US Senate, 185
US State Department, 162
US v. Cook, 66

V

Valladolid debates, 226, 229
Valladolid Rivera, Julio, 142
Venables, Robert W., 144–47
Voices from the Earth, 179
Volunteers in Service to America, 83

W

wage-labor system, 211
Warm Springs Reservation, OR, 70
War of 1812, 185
Washington, DC, 174–81, 183
Washington, President George, 184, 187
Watt, Harry, 14
Wayne, General "Mad Anthony," 184–85

whales: beluga whales, 166, 167; bowhead, 161–68; commercial whaling, 161–62, 163; conservation groups, 163; lactating female bowheads, 165–66; population of, 161, 163; sperm whales, 164; whalebone carvings, 164
White Mountain Apache Indians, 70
Whitman, Marcus, 147
Williams, Raymond, 236
women, indigenous: as activists, 189–90; disadvantages societies place on their gender, 188–90; education, 188, 189–90; and the Haudenosaunee culture, 246, 251; issues of human rights and reproduction, 189; physiological evolution, 254; and world politics, 190
Worcester v. Georgia, 66
world market economy, 57
world trade balance, 82–83
worldwide market economy, 55–56
Wounded Knee, 65, 260
Wyandot Indians, 240

Y

Yagari, Eulalia, 190
Yakima Nation, 83
Young, Don, 166–67

About the Editor

Presently a senior scholar at the Smithsonian National Museum of the American Indian, José Barreiro is a novelist, essayist, and an activist of nearly four decades on American indigenous hemispheric themes. In 1974, Barreiro was enlisted by John Mohawk to help produce the national Native newspaper *Akwesasne Notes*, published by the traditional Mohawk Nation. For ten years, they served as joint coordinators on numerous indigenous human rights and community building campaigns. As editor in chief of Cornell University's Akwe:kon Press from 1984 to 2002, and later as senior editor of *Indian Country Today*, Barreiro published dozens of Mohawk's essays and columns. Barreiro is a member of the Taino Nation of the Antilles.